Sarah Holland Adams

American Husbandry

Sarah Holland Adams

American Husbandry

ISBN/EAN: 9783742832467

Manufactured in Europe, USA, Canada, Australia, Japa

Cover: Foto ©Thomas Meinert / pixelio.de

Manufactured and distributed by brebook publishing software
(www.brebook.com)

Sarah Holland Adams

American Husbandry

AMERICAN HUSBANDRY.

Containing an ACCOUNT of the

SOIL, CLIMATE,

PRODUCTION and AGRICULTURE,

OF THE

BRITISH COLONIES

IN

NORTH-AMERICA and the WEST-INDIES;

WITH

Observations on the Advantages and Disadvantages of settling
in them, compared with GREAT BRITAIN and IRELAND.

Y AN AMERICAN.

IN TWO VOLUMES.

VOL. I.

LONDON,

Printed for J. BEW, in Pater-noster-Row.

MDCCLXXV.

AMERICAN HUSBANDRY.

CHAP. I.

NOVA SCOTIA.

Soil and climate of Nova Scotia—Agriculture—Fishing—Lumber—State of the Settlers—Islands of Cape Breton and St. John—Observations.

TO judge of the climate of Nova Scotia by the latitude would lead any person into the most egregious mistakes. Between 44 and 50 degrees of latitude in Europe we find some of the finest and most pleasant countries in this quarter of the world; but in Nova Scotia the case is very different. The winter lasts seven months, and is of a severity that is dreadful to new comers, the deepest rivers are frozen over in one night, so as to bear loaded waggons; the snow lies in some places ten feet deep, and upon level tracts it has

Vol. I.   B   been

been known to be fix feet deep: the inhabitants are fhut up in their houfes, and,
except in the towns, lead a miferable life;
are almoft in as torpid and lifelefs ftate as
the vegetables of the country; much of
the fummer is fpent in laying in fuel for
the winter, and brandy and rum are then
the greateft luxuries the people indulge in.
Such a degree of cold as is then felt be-
numbs the very faculties of the mind, and
is nearly deftructive of all induftry. When
this fevere winter goes, at once comes a
fummer (for they have no fpring) of a heat
greater than is ever felt in England. The
fnow is prefently melted, and runs in tor-
rents to the fea; the ground is thawed, the
trees are prefently in leaf, and the little
hufbandry here practifed is then begun.
But what is almoft as bad as the extremes
of heat and cold, are the perpetual fogs,
which render the country equally unwhol-
fome and unpleafant; and, what is peculiarly provoking to the inhabitants, laft
far into fummer. Such is the climate; it
is bad almoft in excefs; but we are not to
imagine that it banifhes hufbandry, which
might be the firft conclufion of fuch as
were unufed to northern latitudes.

The

The foil varies greatly : in many parts it is thin and gravelly on a bed of rock; for many years this was what they endeavoured to cultivate, but ill fuccefs taught the inhabitants a change which has proved very advantageous. They fixed in the falt marfhes on the bay of Fundy, which, although they required a very expenfive drainage, yet, from the fertility of the foil, repaid the farmer much better than other tracts gained with much lefs difficulty. The foil in thefe marfhes is a white or blue clay, mellow when in culture and marly; if the water is well conveyed off, it is capable of producing great crops, being fuitable to the heat of the fummer. But the expence of getting this land is not fmall ; the fea is to be dyked out, thofe dykes are to be kept in repair, and the temporary flafhes conveyed off. Further, only the line next the coaft is of value, as that only has the benefit of harbours for boats and fchooners, and for carrying off lumber for the Weft Indies. Moft of the advantageous tracts were patented feveral years ago; but the lotts change hands often, and at prefent many of them are to be fold cheap enough, though under culture.

An

An idea of their management may be gained from the following particulars: upon the settlers first going they fix upon a piece of marsh, with an adjoining one of wood-land, seldom less in the whole than from five hundred to eight hundred or a thousand acres: if the marsh is already banked, they pay an annual tax for that work ; if not, they must execute it before any profit can be made. They build the house on the edge of the wood-land ; a work that costs nothing in materials from the plenty of wood, which is fine, consisting generally of oak, pine, or black birch': but all the trees are grubbed, which makes the labour heavy.

Three years are nominally given to settle the tracts assigned; but this is not strictly adhered to, but extended by favour to six or seven. After ten years a quit-rent is paid to the king of two shillings for every fifty acres ; also a covenant entered into of planting two acres with hemp of every fifty taken up : the planters are kept to this article, but with very little effect, for the climate is utterly improper for that production.

The marsh land is fine, and wants little more after draining but to set the plough to work for fowing wheat: it is all covered with a fhort but thick and fpongy mofs, which they plough in, and on one ploughing harrow in their wheat. This work they perform as foon as the weather breaks, and the fnow is all gone; they do it in a very clumfy manner, attending not the leaft to their lands being laid neat and regular. In September the corn is ripe: they ufually mow it, and the crops they get, notwithftanding the foil being good, fcarce ever amount to middling ones in England. I have been affured, that two quarters of bad wheat in quality, are a great crop. They have hardly any idea of fallowing, but in the fucceeding year plough up the ftubble for another wheat-crop, which they continue as long as the land will yield it, and then leave it to recover itfelf, fometimes, however, changing for beans. The wood-lands, when cleared, they plant with peafe, potatoes, cabbages, &c. the latter production is very ufeful to them, they keep under the fnow in winter very found.

As to inclofures, they have only a ring fence, and one or two near the houfe; not always that; fometimes none but what parts their marfh land from the weods.

Cattle,

Cattle, in summer, are turned into un-drained marshes and the woods, and in winter are three parts starved.

That I may give as clear an idea of this management in all its relations as I can, I shall insert the expences of settling the plantation of Reeves's on the bay of Fundy, as is was put into my hands by a gentleman on whom I can depend.

	l.	s.	d.
Freight, &c. of five persons from England, - - -	105	0	0
Patents, fees, &c. for nine hundred acres, - -	37	8	6
Dyking, - - - - - -	172	0	0
Building the house, barns, boat-houses, &c. - -	67	10	0
Stock of the farm, - - -	70	0	0
Grubbing two hundred and thirty acres of wood-land, at 25s. - - - - - -	287	5	0
Seed, and putting in the crop,	52	0	0
A schooner, seventy tons, at 40s. - - - - - -	140	0	0
A shallop, - - - - -	26	8	0
	957	11	6

Brought

	l.	s.	d.
Brought forward,	957	11	6
A whale boat, - - - -	10	10	0
Netts, lines, twine, and fun-dries, - - - - -	98	15	0
Seamen's wages for a feafon,	27	8	6
Bread, feventy hundred, at 15s.	52	10	0
Pork, three barrels, at 50s.	7	10	0
Beef, fix barrels, at 40s. -	12	0	0
Arms and amunition, - -	26	0	0
Furniture and fundries, -	156	0	0
	1348	5	0

The annual produce after a few years
was calculated at,

Six hundred quintals of cod fifh, at 14s. - - - -	420	0	0
Mackarel and fhads, fixty-feven barrels, at 20s.	67	0	0
Jamaica fifh, twenty-two quintals, 9s. - - - -	9	18	0
Refufe ditto, eighteen quintals, at 6s. 6d. - - - -	5	17	0
Ship timber and lumber, -	63	0	0
	565	15	0

B 4

It

It is much to be regretted, that the annual expenditure was not known; but if the high price of labour is confidered—the wages of the fifhermen—the repairs of the veffels—nets—implements—ammunition—wines—rum—tea—fugar, and other luxuries, &c. all thefe articles would certainly make a confiderable deduction from this annual product. As to the products of the land, they are more than confumed at home. Can any unprejudiced perfon fuppofe that the fum of thirteeen hundred pounds might not be expended on wafte lands in Great Britain to much better advantage? I will not fo far anticipate the fubject as to calculate here, but moft affuredly we may determine that, in point of *profit*, fuch a fum might be more beneficially expended in Britifh hufbandry, than in that of Nova Scotia.

I fay, in point of *profit*, as to that of pleafure, there are other circumftances to be confidered, which are material; thefe particularly concern the great plenty of game in the country, and the general freedom of all fporting and fifhing. It has been afferted, and not upon bad authority, that a boy of twelve or fourteen years of age, with his gun, would maintain ten or

twelve

twelve in family the year round, pork and bread excepted. Two boys have been known to catch above two hundred hares in one winter with twine fnares. Six boys, in three canoes, fhot, in four days, one hundred and fifty wild-geefe, and four hundred black ducks. To this may be added, that eels are in the little rivers fo plentiful, that they keep immenfe quantities of them frozen for winter provifion.

Thefe particulars, indeed, indicate, not only pleafure, but alfo a confiderable degree of profit; for a country, which will admit of fuch circumftances, muft yield no trifling advantages in houfekeeping: and however infignificant fuch a point my feem in a general account of a country, yet is it of importance in the eyes of thofe who quit their own to fettle in America. In Britain, the game laws are fo ftrict that unqualified perfons muft give up all thoughts of the pleafure of fhooting and fifhing, as well as the advantage in feeding their families, or be liable to fevere and infamous penalties; and that this monftrous contraft fends no trifling number of people to the colonies I have not a doubt.

In the preceding accounts the reader finds that the whole product of the new
plan-

plantation (and that a confiderable one) confifts in fifh and lumber. It is remarkable, that without the fifhery the inhabitants of this colony would ftarve ; their hufbandry is infufficient to feed them ; a circumftance ftrongly characteriftic of the merit of Nova Scotia as a colony. In this refpect the farmers fomewhat refemble the inhabitants of Devonfhire, Dorfetfhire, and Cornwal, before the northern colonies almoft beat the mother country out of her fhare of the fifhery; a very great portion of the Englifh Newfoundland fifhery was carried on by little farmers on the abovementioned coafts, who went out as foon as their fpring feed was over, and returned before harveft : but in Nova Scotia it is the principal dependance of the people for their fubfiftence ; and the only fale by which they can fupply themfelves with manufactures and other neceffaries.

Their other export is lumber to the Weft Indies, but of this the whole province does not fend out more than fells for five thoufand pounds, and fometimes not fo much. A part of the winter feafon is applied to cutting and fawing trees, but from the feverity of the feafon the progrefs made in this work is inconfiderable, and

yields

yields no great profit to the farmer. The distance of those islands, with the vast superiority of the more southern colonies in climate for the winter execution of this work, lessen the profit of the Nova Scotians greatly.

Neither the fishery nor the export of lumber prove advantageous enough to render the setlers comparable in ease and wealth to the people of New-England, New-York, &c. or, I may add (and this is what I mean particularly to inculcate) to the same class of men among our farmers in Britain ; except in the articles, not immaterial I allow, of shooting and fishing : but when the difference of climate is considered ; the agreeable and healthy life which is lead even in winter in England ; the friendly society enjoyed by our lowest classes of farmers in our country towns and village alehouses, upon market days and other meetings — the goodness of our roads, and the security of living, what can tempt any that feel such advantages to leave them in pursuit of imaginary happiness in the woods of Nova Scotia ? Where the winters are miserably severe, where society is scarcely any where to be found—without a road in the country, and where a hostile

2   tile

tile race of Indians, till very lately, rendered the whole colony unhappily infecure.
But the great fuperiority remains to be
mentioned: promotion, if I may fo ex-
prefs myfelf, is cheaper in England; for it
apears from the preceding calculation, that
a much larger fum is neceffary to go to,
and fettle, with any advantage in Nova
Scotia, even on the fmalleft fcale, than
would be fufficient to ftock a good farm in
England. The fifhing apparatus is expenfive; and if that employment is neglected,
the moft profitable branch in the country is
loft: the planters muft degenerate into
mere tartars, without a commodity for
fale wherewith to buy manufactures. Let
thefe circumflances be confidered, and I
think it muft be apparent, that many of the
emigrants who go to Nova Scotia with a
view to practife a hufbandry, &c. more
profitable than that of Europe, muft find
themfelves miferably deceived.

What fort of a country muft it be where
government is forced to give a bounty on
raifing corn to keep the people from ftarv-
ing? Yet this is the cafe with Nova Scotia.
On all wheat raifed it is one fhilling a
bufhel; on barley, oats, and pulfe, nine
pence, and on roots fix pence.

Relative

Relative to the iflands of Cape Breton and St. John I muft obferve, that the former has only a few plantations, made by connivance, by fifhermen, merely for the convenience of its fituation for the cod fifhery. But the ifland of St. John was granted to fome well-known noblemen, fince the peace, with a view to colonize the whole: the fcheme was originally formed by the late Earl of Egmont; but ho did not live to fee any fuccefs attend the plan, which yet was laid as well as moft could be for fuch climates, and the execution begun with great fpirit, at an expence that would have brought into culture no inconfiderable tract of wafte in England or in Scotland; and that the fuccefs would have been greater and infinitely more beneficial at home than in America, cannot for a moment be doubted. Several hundred of fettlers have been fixed there, yet they are at prefent fupplied with food from New-York: inftead of a beneficial fyftem of pafturage and planting hemp, they have already, like all thefe northern colonifts, taken to the fifhery, as the only means of paying for the neceffaries of life, in direct contradiction to the defigns of their patrons. This is, and ever will be, the confequence

fequence of colonizing in fuch northern latitudes, where agriculture muft ever be carried on with feeblenefs; where the climate
is to the laft degree rigorous; and where
every fpot is inhofpitable and frigid. To
plant colonies in fuch fituations, is acting
contrary to every rational idea of colonization.

I am fenfible that the original idea of
planting Nova Scotia was not fo much upon
a plan of *agriculture* as *defence*. The encroachments of the French made fettlements and fortreffes neceffary; and the
neighbourhood of Louifburg rendered a
fafe port, as a retreat for the navy, indif-
penfable: upon this plan garrifons were
neceffary: and thefe could not be fupported without an adjacent agriculture. There
is fomething rational in this, but it extends no further than the neceffity of the
cafe, and not to the immenfe expence which
the nation has fuffered on account of the
colony, amounting to confiderably more
than a million fterling; befides, this argument, fince the peace, has no longer any
validity, whereas we have acted as if it
continued in full force; and after feeling
the unprofitable expence of one fnowy defart, have planted a fecond. This conduct
would

would have been excufable had we poffeffed no other territories in America, but
while fuch immenfe diftricts remained uncultivated to the fouth, it was really inex-
cufable upon every principle of good policy.

CHAP.

CHAP. II.

C A N A D A.

*Soil and Climate of Canada—Agriculture—
Inhabitants—River St. Laurence—Nature of the Country not yet settled—Exports—Importance of this acquisition—
Observations.—*

CANADA is much colder in the winter than Nova Scotia, which may be
accounted for by the distance from the
sea; yet is the climate greatly preferable:
the air is clear and pure, and the inhabitants in general enjoy as good health as
any set of people in all America. That the
climate is better we may likewise gather
from the productions; pumpions and melons, apples and pears, are cultivated in
common; whereas in Nova Scotia, though
we cannot say the country is absolutely
without them, yet is the vegetation weak
in comparison. In this I speak of the
northern part of Canada about Quebec; for
as to the south of it, in the neighbourhood
of Montreal, it is far more mild, as appears

pears by feveral plants commonly found there and to the fouth, which will not live at Quebec.

- The north-weft wind blows, through winter, with a feverity that is fcarcely credible: it plainly comes through all walls that are not very thick; a candle is blown out when held againft a wall that is only a brick and a half thick: all the infide of fuch walls are covered with fnow blown through, on the fide againft the northweft; and the walls muft be of a vaft thicknefs, at the fame time that the houfe is well fheltered by wood and hill, for people within not to feel the wind blow on them. This dreadful north-weft is felt throughout the continent, even to Charles Town, in South Carolina; and it has been abfolutely afferted that it has blown over the whole Atlantic ocean, and been felt in Europe. It is this wind which renders the climate of all North America fo peculiar that no other is fimilar to it. Hence arifes the fevere frofts felt there in fuch fouthern latitudes, that the like is never known in Europe. Sharp frofts are fometimes felt in Florida, in latitude 30, which is that of Egypt and Morocco. This is owing to the north-weft winds.

They acquire their extreme coldnefs from the immenfe extent of fnowy continent over which they blow, poffibly from the North pole, whereas the continent of Europe and Afia ends in latitude 75, an open fea being to the north. This has been well explained by a late writer, from whom, candour demands I fhould acknowledge, that I borrowed the hint *.

This wind in Canada is more fevere than in Nova Scotia, the fnows are alfo as deep and as univerfal, but the air is clear, being free from the fogs which render the latter country fo extremely difagreeable. The winter is not, however, abfolutely without employment; wrapt up well in furs, winter expeditions are undertaken, and fawing and cutting lumber go on, though not with near fuch alacrity and effect as in the more fouthern colonies, where the workmen are employed as regularly in that feafon as in fummer.

The foil in Canada is of two forts, the ftoney, and the pure loam, or mould without ftones; both are cultivated, but the latter is much the beft; it is black or

---

* Dr. Mitchel's *Prefent State of Great Britain and North America.*

reddifh,

reddifh, and is certainly as fine land as any in the world; and were it in a more favourable climate would yield as rich productions. There are vaft tracts of it in Canada which would, in many parts of England, let at twenty-five fhillings an acre, but here are uncultivated ; all the fettlements and farms in this country being only on the banks of the rivers, principally on that of St. Lawrence; the cultivated country is only a narrow flip on each fide the river, fcarcely any where half a mile broad, unlefs it fpreads on account of other ftreams that fall into the principal one. In fome places, however, the cultivated country is fome miles broad, particularly near the three towns.

Refpecting the vegetable productions of this colony there are found almoft all the ufeful plants that are cultivated in Scotland, and many that fucceed better in England than in Scotland. The common crops are wheat, barley, rye, and oats; feveral forts of peas and beans; many forts of roots, particularly carrots, parfnips, and potatoes, but the latter not in plenty, from the French not much affecting them. Many of the farms have an orchard, though not fo commonly as in the old Englifh colonies to

C 2 the

the southward : apples, pears, and plumbs succeed well'; but peaches they get with difficulty, nor are they of a good flavour : mulberries will not grow here. Walnut trees, carried from France, dye every year to the root, but shoot out again in the spring.

Their husbandry is very bad ; the system is taking a crop and what they call a fallow, that is, they take a crop of wheat and after it leave the land at rest for a year, not for ploughing, but that the weeds may grow and be eaten off by the cattle: this method can arise from nothing but the plenty of land, for surely common sense might tell them, that a field, answering the purpose of a meadow, by the quantity of weeds on it, must be a strange preparation for corn. If they left it for ten or twelve years, till the grasses came so thick as to choak the weeds, it might, when ploughed up, become at once good corn land, as we find in many places is the case in England. In general they let the lands rest only one year, but some who have more land than the rest, leave it sometimes for two, three, or four years, before they sow it again : white clover, by that time, comes in great plenty.

No

No crop gets more than one ploughing, which is in April, after the frost breaks; then all their forts of corn are fown, wheat as well as the reft, confequently they have only a fpring wheat: however, a few far- mers have of late years got into the way of fowing the fame grain in autumn; they do not thereby get an earlier harveft, but the grain is weightier and better, and the crop more abundant. As foon as the weather breaks, all the ploughs in Canada are at work to get in the corn, waiting very rarely, and but on fmall fpaces of land, for carry- ing on the manure; and on one ploughing, which is performed with oxen or horfes in- difcriminately, they fow all forts of grain and pulfe. Their crops are as good as moderate ones in England; from four to fix or feven feptiers per arpent are commonly gained of wheat, that is, about two or two quarters and a half per Englifh acre: oats yield very large crops, they fow them for their horfes and other cattle; barley is a poor crop with them; and peas a very uncertain one, but fometimes they get a fine product of them.

Every farmer has annually a fmall piece of flax, but it is only for the ufe of his

C 3   family:

family: they have none that is good, whether owing to their management of it, or the climate, I know not. They have also a piece of tobacco in every farm, for the family: all smoak it here.

They have in all parts of Canada very fine meadows of natural grafs, of a fine fort *, with great plenty of white clover; not low marfhy fpots, but high upland meadows, the foil dry, found loam; thefe are great advantages to the farmers; they yield fine crops of good hay which is mown in Auguft.

The country inhabitants of Canada are all little farmers; very few of them having large farms, at leaft if we give that term only to the land they ufually keep in any culture. Villages are rarely met with, and the few there are confift only of here and there a mechanic, or a fchoolmafter: they are a chearful, hofpitable people. and have behaved themfelves with much good fenfe and politenefs to the Englifh that have fettled amongft them fince the conqueft. At Quebec and Montreal they are remarkably gay and focial, which indeed is the cafe in a good meafure in moft countries

---

* Poa Anguftifolia.

that

that are so cold as to confine the inhabitants to their houses for a long winter;
without a social disposition, such winters
would be insupportable.   They are further
a very happy people; yet their enjoyments
are by no means numerous, and the whole
country lies under two evils which almost
entirely prevent encrease; the want of
communication in winter with the rest of
the world; and the want of money for circulation.   This affects the whole colony
equally, and makes their share of chearful-
ness an absolute necessary of life.

Was it not for the river St. Lawrence the
whole country would be so destitute of
communication, as to be next to uninha-
bitable: but that noble river, which is navigable for the largest ships to Quebec, and
every where deep enough for all the inland
navigation of Canada, quite to the falls of
Niagara, is the great chanel of communication between the different parts of the
country.   Indeed Canada is but a narrow
slip of cultivated land along the banks of
this river, which to such parts answers
every purpose that can be wished, of travelling and the conveyance of merchandize,
and the produce of the farms to the
towns of Quebec, Montreal, and Trois Ri-

vieres,

vieres, in each of which are regular markets. No flight part of the demand in thofe markets is formed by the troops, who both enliven and enrich the colony. The unfettled country, which includes all but the banks of the river is a forefl, generally filled with various forts of pines, oak, birch, &c. many of the trees are large. In parts of thefe forefls the underwood is thick ; in others, there is none at all. The foil in them has the fame varieties as in the cultivated fields. Large tracts are excellent, and would, if cleared of wood, produce as good crops as any of the fields already in culture ; but there are not inhabitants enough to extend the cultivation ; and there are many reafons for this, which I fhall mention by and by. I may obferve that all that immenfe country to the fouth of the river St. Lawrence, which is part of New England and Nova Scotia, has very few tracts in it, by the report of the Indians, which are not capable of cultivation. It forms a fquare of three hundred miles every way, which is much larger than Great Britain ; and confifts of forefts on a good foil, or rich marfhes. Cultivation would improve the climate, drive away the fogs, and make the country much

more

more inhabitable than at prefent. But fuch improvements muft be fome centuries off, and in the mean time the whole will remain, except on the coaft and river, a mere inhofpitable defart, like Nova Scotia. The fouthern parts of Canada, north of the great lakes about Niagara, &c. poffefs a climate infinitely fuperior to that tract, and alfo the line of country from Crown Point to the river St. Lawrence, equals any part of North America for fertility of foil, and agreeablenefs; at the fame time that the climate is fo much fuperior to that even of Montreal, which I before obferved was preferable to that of Quebec. Were it not for the country to the fouth of the lakes drawing away the people, thefe territories would foon be cultivated.

For the further information of the reader I fhall tranfcribe the table of the annual exports from Canada fince the peace of 1763.

Skins,	£. 76,000
Whalebone and oil,	3,500
12000 quarters of wheat, at 20s.	12,000
Genfeng, fnake root, &c.	3,000
Timber and lumber,	11,000
	£. 105,500

Which

Which export, with the import of manufactures, &c. employ thirty-four ships, and about four hundred seamen. But the wheat has for the last three or four years been at thirty-two shillings a quarter. As far as the skins can be gained, this colony will admit of increase, but the common idea is, that it has for some time arived at its zenith, as the game, &c. from which they are taken, rather declines than increases; the wheat and lumber are the surplus of the colony consumption, raised by the hands which are fixed in their farms, and from habit, love of their native country, poverty, want of ability to move, or other motives, remain in it; but the export I do not apprehend is likely to increase, because new settlements are rare, but many families leave the country and move to the southward. This export · is all the means which the whole body of the inhabitants have of purchasing manufactures, wines, spirits, India goods, and sugar, excepting alone the expenditure of the military and civil government, a part of which may be reckoned *profit* to the colony, and supposed to go for the same commodities.

But notwithstanding the small prospect of improvement, yet is not Canada to be
esteemed

efteemed a flight acquifition to the Britifh empire. Indeed it is, with the territories on the Ohio, a very important one; and which, with good management on our parts, might be made of much greater confequence even to the commercial interefts of Britain, than the acquifition either of Guadalupe or Martinico, fuppofing there was a neceffity of giving up both thefe iflands, if Canada was retained; a fuppofition which may be ftarted, but which can never be believed. I have read many accounts of North America, in which the importance of this country has been pretty extenfively confidered, yet did I never meet with a juft idea of the main ftrength of the argument. Dr. Mitchel feems to have underftood it, but he wrote in fo confufed a manner, that it is difficult to gain his meaning.

The moft important commercial intereft of Great Britain is the fupplying her colonies with manufactures, in exchange for their ftaple commodities. This trade, far the greateft that is carried on by England, depends on the colonies having room, not for common hufbandry and farming, but for raifing immenfe quantities of ftaples, lumber, &c. to enable them to pay

for

for the Britiſh manufactures; a ſort of a-
griculture which we ſhall by and by find
requires very different *room* from the huſbandry of Europe, being incompatible with
a country that is fully, or even half peopled.
—It further depends on this plenty of land
being alſo great enough for every perſon
without much difficulty to become a planter or farmer; for if ſuch a difficulty ariſes,
the overplus of population muſt betake itſelf to common labour, which at once eſ-
tabliſhes manufactures, for people will not
ſtarve, and if they cannot have employment in one thing they muſt in another;
but, on the contrary, while land is very
plentiful no manufactures (further than for
private uſe, which ſhould not go by that
name) can be fixed, becauſe labour muſt
be immoderately dear, where every man
may with ſo much eaſe become a little farmer.

Now what I would deduce from this
circumſtance is, that the French policy in
hemming in our colonies to a narrow country along the ſea coaſt by that well known
chain of forts which they had built quite
from Crown Point to New Orleans, was
admirably calculated for the abſolute. de-
ſtruction of all our ſettlements, as *colonies*
ſupplied

fupplied by Britain with manufactures, for
they cut off the increafe of plantations fo .
effectually by their forts and the incurfions
of their Indians, that fome hundred thoufand people were, at the opening of the war,
deprived of their agriculture, and would
in a few years have all become manufacturers
for fale, had not the evil been deftroyed.
And if a different event of the war had
taken place to fecure them in their encroachments, that evil would have arifen
to a magnitude that would have explained
in a manner too ftriking to be doubted,
how the poffeffion of Canada might be of
more importance than a fugar ifland;
though one exported fix times more in value than the other.

It was faid, I remember, that confining
the French to their juft bounds would have
had the fame effect. But this was weakly
urged; for while they had Indians left
them, they would always have had it in
their power to prevent that neceffary ex-
tenfion of the agriculture of our fettlements,
upon which our whole interefts in America depend. The Indians the French col-
lected about Fort Duquefne, though near
two hundred miles from our fettlers, deprived us in fix months of near an hundred
miles

miles of territory ; for fo far did our back-
settlers quit their habitations upon the cruel
excurfions of their enemies.

It is therefore plain, that they who
reft the comparifon of Canada againft a
fugar ifland, merely on the ballance of an
account of exports and imports, much miftake the matter, fince they overlook therein the effential diftinctions which form the
real importance of this colony. But in the
prefent cafe there is fomething further than
mere extent and fecurity ; for the fouthern
diftricts of Canada, thofe of the lakes,
down to the Ohia, contain as valuable a
territory as any poffeffed by us in America.
The moft fertile part of that continent, in
a fine climate, and admirably adapted for
the production of hemp and tobacco, commodities, I will venture to affert, is of more
confequence to this nation than even fugar ; and yet I am very far from derogating
from the great and undoubted importance
of fugar colonies to Great Britain.

CHAP-

CHAP. III.

Defects in the Agriculture of Canada.

THE husbandry practised in this colony is in many respects so very defective, that I think it will not be an impropriety to point out the most material
branches of their management, in which
they act contrary not only to the common
ideas of good farmers in England, but also
to the dictates of the climate and other circumstances of the country.

First I shall remark that their system is
essentially faulty. It is this,

1. Wheat or other grain.
2. Fallow, that is weeds for one, two,
or three years.

There is no greater error in farming,
whatever may be the country, than taking
many successive crops of corn without the
intervention of a fallow, or some crop
which, from an extraordinary culture while

4   grow-

growing, anfwers the purpofe of a fallow;
but I fhall venture to affert that even this
fault is lefs than the management of the
Canadians: the food gained by their cattle
is too trivial to mention; but what condition of freedom from weeds can land be
in, when the crop is fown only on one
ploughing, and the land after that crop,
left to run to weeds for a twelvemonth?
Yet is this the management of thefe people.

Let me, inftead of fuch miftaken conduct,
recommend to them never to fail of
ploughing the land they defign for corn in
September; the fucceeding frofts and fnow
will meliorate it much; if their plan is
to leave it to weeds by way of a fallow after
the corn, let them never fail of fowing
plenty of white clover feed with the corn:
the country in general runs naturally to it;
it can never be fuppofed therefore to fail;
but when the ground is left to 'feed itfelf, it
is three, four, or five years, before a tolerable plant comes; in the management I
propofe, they would have a rich meadow
the firft year.

Secondly. Inftead of letting the land
reft only one year, I would advife them to

leave

leave it under clover three or four; during that, or even a longer time, it would conſtantly improve, until it gained a thick rich turf, after which the ploughing it up for corn would be attended with great advantage, at the ſame time that the meadow thus gained would pay the farmer as well as the beſt in his farm. Suppoſe the white clover left four years, the ſyſtem would then be

1. Corn.
2. Clover four years.
3. Corn.

But I ſhould propoſe improvements in the corn years of the ſyſtem. The Canada farmers are very inattentive to the change of their corn crops, making very little diſtinction between ſucceſſive ones of wheat, barley, and oats, and peaſe and beans; whereas they ought moſt certainly, according to the principles of the beſt Engliſh huſbandry, interchange them by following white corn with pulſe, and that again with white corn.

Thirdly, I muſt remark, that our French huſbandmen do not properly attend to the winter ſupport of their cattle : the climate agrees very well with cabbages of two or three ſorts, turneps, carrots, kale, &c.

plants which are hardy enough to stand extremely well the field culture in that climate. These would be of very high advantage in the winter support of their cattle, and would, with the help of a greater quantity of hay (gained by means of clover on their fallows instead of weeds) enable them not only to increase their profit by these cattle, but at the same time answer a purpose equally beneficial in raising manure, a business in which their long winters might be of great efficacy. In this climate, where the soil is so chilled with intense frost, and drenched in snow and rain, it must have a coldness in its nature much demanding that warmth which manure gives, and consequently no business would be more profitable than raising plenty of it. The population of the towns of Canada is insufficient to yield the famers much assistance in this way; nor indeed would it be of much consequence were this otherwise, unless the countrymen had better ideas of the nature of their business, since they do not carry away near so much from Quebec and Montreal as they might; for want of attention in them, no slight quantities are annually thrown into the river, which is utterly in-.

ex-

excufable confidering their having water carriage to every farm almoft in the colony.

Were the ideas of the farmers upon this object of keeping cattle, with a view to raifing the more manure, of the nature they ought to be, the articles of winter food for cattle above-mentioned, fuch as cabbages, turneps, and other roots, would be introduced in the arable fields interchangeably with corn, in the manner turneps are in the fyftems in England and Scotland: this would keep the lands in much better order than they are at prefent, befides being the means of raifing manure and making a greater profit from the increafe of cattle. Upon thefe principles the following fyftem might be recommended to the farmers of this country.

1. Wheat.
2. Peafe.
3. Oats.
4. Turneps.
5. Barley.
6. Cabbages.
7. Wheat.
8. White clover.
9. White clover.
10. White clover.

This

This fyftem for ten years would anfwer all
the purpofes of good hufbandry—would
keep the land clean from weeds—would
raife great plenty of winter food for cattle—
and improve by their manure the products
of corn.

Had I not extended this chapter to a
length I did not expect, I fhould expatiate
on other articles of their management,
which I have reafon to think not a little
faulty, particularly in their methods of
ploughing and laying their lands, which is
done here in a manner more aukward and
clumfy than can be conceived in England;
alfo in the way they have of getting in
their hay and corn harveft; but thefe and
other particulars may be efteemed too infignificant for particular notice.

CHAP.

C H A P. IV.

The agriculture of Canada compared with that of Britain.

I AM fenſible that the number of emigrants that go from Great Britain and Ireland to Canada is not conſiderable, nor to be compared with thoſe who every day go to our colonies to the ſouthward, yet as ſome future advocates, even for the northern ſettlements may ariſe—and as a worſe country than this, viz. the iſland of St. John, has lately been attempted to be ſettled, I think it may prove of uſe to draw a compariſon between the profit and advantages which may be expected from agriculture in Canada and in Britain, that all may, in future at leaſt, know (if they will leave their native country) which are the parts of America that emigrants had better go to.

Much of the happineſs, and many of the comforts of life among the farmers or planters of any country, depend on their raiſing a ſufficiency of ſaleable products, not only to pay the expences of cultivation, but

alſo

alfo to purchafe fnch commodities as they
cannot raife themfelves ; fuch for inflance
as many articles of cloathing, furniture, and
food, not to fpeak of luxuries, which hardly deferve that name from the generality of
the ufe.   Some idea may be formed of the
ftate of life in Canada from the exports being compared with the population.   No
lift of the inhabitants has been taken fince
it came under the dominion of Britain; but
I have reafon to think them not decreafed.
We are told by a good writer that before
the war they amounted to 100,000 *.   I
have already fhewn that they export to the
amount of 105,000 l. which may be called
20 s. a head for the people.   Now this is
the whole amount of the manufactures and
commodities which they confume, further
than what they grow and make at home;
an amount in a country that has only one
manufacture (of iron) ; which fhews how
flender thofe enjoyments of life muft be
which depend on foreign imports ; and that
fuch a dependance muft be abfolutely neceffary and effential, any one will fee who
confiders the climate.

---

* *Account of the European Settlements in America,*
vol. II. *pag.* 30.

But

But we are further to remember that only about 23,000 l. of this export is in the products that can have any thing to do with the farmers, viz. the corn and the lumber: the skins and furs, to the amount of 76,000 l. are almost all bought of the Indians for woollen goods, brandy, guns, and ammunition, consequently a great part of this sum goes to the Indians instead of the Canadians, a circumstance which will reduce the consumption of manufactures and foreign products in Canada to a sum far short of 20 s. a head, or even of 10 s. and will prove clearly enough that what we have here been calling the enjoyments of life dependant on importation, must be confined in a surprising degree.

Examining the affair in this light points out the nature of the country and of its agriculture. Land is in plenty, and so cheap, that every man may have as much of it as he can stock or cultivate; but labour must be extravagantly dear, as it is in every country where land is granted to all that will have it. Wood is plentiful; and food of most forts that are produced by the country, such as fish and fowl, very cheap, and flesh not very dear. In this case we see at once the state of a farmer, or a new settler;

he

he has land, and wood to build him a houfe, and after he has ftocked his farm with cattle, and implements, and feed, he has the product of it in corn and roots to feed himfelf and family; with fifh and fowl for the trouble of taking; his flax, and his family's labour fupply linen; and iron being the produce of the country, he may buy it with corn; fome coarfe woollens are alfo made, but the quantity is very trifling: there remains for him to purchafe rum or brandy, feveral articles of cloathing, guns, ammunition, parts of houfhold furniture, fugar, tea, wine, and India goods, if he confumes any; and in order to procure thefe he has no way to gain them but by his fhare of the export of wheat and lumber, that is 4s. or 5s. per head of his family, fuppofing the Indians carried off none of the import, but as they take off the moft, the fhare of the farmers muft be yet lefs.

It is very evident therefore that the life and enjoyments of a new fettler in Canada muft be ftrangely confined and wanting in what we fhould call the neceffaries of life; but this objection is not of weight with thofe whofe previous flate of life was inferior, fuch as difbanded foldiers, fervants, labourers, and fome others, fuch may certainly

tainly make a shift to get fixed in a farm, and find in it most if not all the necessaries of *their* life: but even these must be such as are on the spot; for it would answer to none to go thither in order to gain this. When a man receives his discharge in a country where he can have land for nothing, it is his business to take it, for another colony being far more advantageous is nothing to him, who may not have money to move himself one hundred miles, instead of five hundred, which may be necessary for him to go.

That the comparison between the number of people, and the exported produce, is, in respect of Canada, a just rule to judge of the consumption of foreign products, &c. will appear from reflecting, that in this colony they have no other means of gaining them: a case which is different in our maritime ones, where a trade is carried on, and other means of bringing money into the country besides their mere agriculture.

The circumstance that must keep down this colony, and make it unprofitable to settle in, is the want of a short and regular navigation. At first sight it might be urged, that if 12000 quarters of wheat

are

are exported, more might also be, and
then the farmer would find a sale for all he
could raise: but the situation of the colony
is such, that I should rather suppose those
12000 quarters, owing to an accidental
more than any regular demand—or to the
conveniency of loading ships with it going out with furs, &c. for the colonies to
the southward on the coast enjoy a navigation so superior, and are so much nearer
to market, that I should apprehend they
would entirely undersell the Canadians.

Let it be considered as an universal rule,
that agriculture can no where be a profitable employment—or one that will even
yield all the necessaries of life, where the
farmer has not a regular sale for every thing
he raises; for if he possesses not this, he
cannot with any advantage increase his
cultivation, upon however small a scale it
might have been before; nor can he without this scale command the money which
is necessary for purchasing those things
which his farm cannot produce. This is
equally a fact, whether his product be
wheat, tobacco, rice, or sugar. A regular market for all he raises is the soul of
the farmer.

This

This is the diſtinction that muſt ever be made; in thoſe colonies that have a market for the farmer's productions, he may practice his buſineſs with profit. But in thoſe that have it not, like Canada, he can only live; he cannot get money, nor can he, if he increaſes his culture, gain proportionably the comforts or agreeableneſſes of life.

From this ſtate of the caſe, how can it ever be adviſeable for any perſon employed in agriculture in Europe, to leave it for practiſing the ſame art in Canada? Whoever has in England, or Scotland, money enough to pay their paſſage and expences to Quebec, to ſtock a farm, and go thro' the expenditure of the firſt year, ſmall as it is, might certainly employ that money in farming at home to better advantage: ſince in the latter caſe they are in the way of improvement, and may by induſtry increaſe their capital while they live comfortably; but in the former, they can gain only a certain point, which is living comfortably, but as to increaſe or improvement very little is to be looked for. Yet in this we do not exclude exceptions, which there will ever be in all caſes; there are certainly men who make money in Canada—but
a few

a few inftances are not what fhould, in fuch an enquiry, be attended to, but the general nature of the country, and the fituation of the greater number.

' If money is to be expended on the paffage, flocking the farm, &c. in which works two or three hundred pounds would very foon be laid out, even for a fmall tract of land, in fuch cafe we may readily determine that the money might be laid out to far greater advantage in England, or in Scotland or Ireland : at the fame time that we deduce this, we muft alfo allow that there is a cafe in which Canada may be preferable to England, though not comparable to feveral other colonies : if a family in Britain have an opportunity of getting a free paffage to Quebec, which may happen from more accidents than one ; and they have a fmall fum of money to buy a few cattle and implements, when they arrive there, in that cafe they will be able to get into a bufinefs fufficient for their maintenance and fupport, which they could not be able to do in England. This is a cafe clearly in favour of Canada, but it is not one that can happen often.

CHAP.

CHAP. V.

NEW ENGLAND.

*Climate of New England—Soil—Present
state of the several counties of that province—Agriculture—Observations on the
exports of New England.*

THIS province lies between 41° and
45° north latitude, but like all the
territories of America, it must not have an
idea formed of its climate by a comparison
with the European parallels : that latitude
in the latter is the southern parts of France,
and the northern ones of Spain, countries
in which the climate is unexceptionable :
but in New England the winter is much
longer than it is here, and at the same time
severe beyond any thing we ever experience
in the sharpest frosts : the summer in heat
exceeds that of Spain, and it comes as it
does in most parts of North America, without the intervention of a spring : but what
is worse, they sometimes experience, tho'
not near so often as farther to the south,
sud-

fudden changes from hot to cold when the
north-weft wind blows; but in general the
weather is pretty uniform; in both fummer
and winter the fky is clear and ferene; and
for months together exhibits a pure azure
expanfe, without a cloud, or fpeck to be
feen. The climate has been vaftly im-
próved fince the country has been cleared
of wood and brought into cultivation.
The cold in winter is lefs intenfe, the air
in fummer purer, and the country in general much more wholefome. It is the
climate of this province which entirely regulates its agriculture, and therefore fhould
be well attended to, the great heat in fummer, and the fevere frofts in winter, with
the north-weft winds which blow with
fuch fharpnefs, thefe render the culture of
common wheat not near fo advantageous as
that of maize.

The foil of the province differs confiderably, as may be fuppofed in a country of
fuch great extent. The fouth and eaftern
parts are the moft fertile, fuch as Maffa-
chufets Bay, Connecticut, Rhode Ifland,
and the whole tract that borders on New
York, quite to the Lake Champlain. In
thefe territories are found very confiderable
tracts of fine and rich land. It confifts of
a black

a black mold on a red loam or clay : of
loams, some stoney, but not therefore un-
fertile ; and parts of clay alone which is not
their worst land.   The have also very good
sandy lands, which soil agrees best with
their capital production, maize.

New England being the oldest of our
American colonies, the best parts of it may
be supposed to be granted away or purchased, which is the case ; but it is not
thence to be apprehended that the greatest
part of this large province is cultivated :
in the southern divisions the country is
well settled, so as for many miles together
to have some resemblance of old England,
but even in these there are very large tracts
of forest left, which are private property,
and consequently cannot now be patented.
The richest parts remaining to be granted,
are on the northern branches of the Connecticut river, towards Crown Point, where
are great districts of fertile soil still unsettled.   The north part of New Hamp-
shire, the province of Main, and the territory of Sagadahock; have but few settlements in them compared with the tracts
yet unsettled ; and they have the advantage
of many excellent ports, long navigable
rivers, with all the natural advantages that
are

are found in other parts of this province.
I should further obferve, that thefe tracts
have, fince the peace, been fettling pretty
faft: farms on the river Connecticut are
every day extending beyond the old fort
Dummer, for near thirty miles; and will
in a few years reach to Kohaffer, which is
near two hundred miles; not that fuch an
extent will be one tenth fettled, but tho
new comers do not fix near their neighbours, and go on regularly, but take fpots
that pleafe them beft, though twenty or
thirty miles beyond any others. This to
people of a fociable difpofition in Europe
would appear very ftrange, but the Americans do not regard the near neighbourhood of other farmers; twenty, or thirty
miles by water they efteem no diftance in
matters of this fort; befides, in a country
that promifes well the intermediate fpace
is not long in filling up. Between Connecticut river, and Lake Champlain, upon Otter Creek, and all along Lake Sacra-
ment, and the rivers that fall into it, and
the whole length of Wood Creek, are numerous fettlements made fince the peace,
by the Acadians, Canadians, and others
from different parts of New England.
This whole neighbourhood is a beautiful
country,

country, and posseses as rich a soil as most in New England. Let me also remark here, that the new settlers in these parts have cultivated common wheat with good success, so that they have more fields of it than of maize, which is not the case in the southern parts of New England; to what this difference is owing I have not been informed.

In the province of Main, particularly on the rivers which fall into the sea near Brunswic, there are many settlements made by Germans who have come over since the war; they are in general in a thriving condition, as most of the settlers are in North America that are well situated for an immediate communication with the sea; ships come very regularly to all the ports on this coast to take in loadings of corn, salted provisions, and lumber for the West Indies; by which means the farmers (who also are engaged pretty deeply in the fishery on these coasts) have a ready opportunity of conveying all their surplus products to a regular market, the great thing wanted in Canada. But still these northern coasts of Main and Sagadahock, are under the fatal influence of that freezing climate, which is bad enough in the south

VOL. I.   E   parts

parts of New England, but here approaches
to the severity of Nova Scotia, though not
so much involved in fogs.

The particulars of the husbandry of this
province are extremely worthy of attention, because it is as it were between the
most northerly colonies, and the central
ones, which are of an acknowledged merit
in climate, &c. The crops commonly
cultivated are, first maize, which is the
grand product of the country, and upon
which the inhabitants principally feed. It
is not however to the exclusion of common
wheat, which in a few districts is cultivated
with success. It would be useless to give
a particular description of this plant, which
is so generally known. Its culture has
something particular in it, and therefore
should be mentioned more particularly. It
is a very large branching plant, which requires a great share of nourishment, so as
to be planted singly at the distance of four
or five feet square; it requires good land,
and much dung, if plentiful crops would be
gained; and the soil must be kept clean
from weeds, by frequent hoeings, besides
ploughing cross and cross between the
plants: this is practised only by good farmers, but it is pity it is not universal
among

among all the cultivators of this plant, for none in the world pays better for good treatment, proportioned to the value of its produce. Had Mr. Tull, the inventor of the horse-hoeing husbandry, known it, or rather had he lived in a country where it was commonly cultivated, he would have exhibited it particularly as the plant of all others which was most formed for his method of culture : even common farmers in some parts of New England have been struck with the excellency of the practice of ploughing between the rows of this grain, that they have been presently brought to practise it in common, so that it is now no longer an unusual method. One peck of the seed is the common quantity for an acre of land ; and the produce varies from twenty to forty bushels, but from twenty-five to thirty are very generally gained. The expences of this culture per acre have been thus stated.

	l.	s.	d.
Seed, - - - - - -	0	0	6
Culture, - - -	0	11	8
Harvesting, &c. - -	0	3	6
Conveyance to market, -	0	4	6
Sundries, - - -	0	2	6
	1	2	8

And

And the value, straw included, amounts
to, from 50 s. to 4 l. sterling, per English
acre, which is certainly very considerable:
but then their management in other respects renders the culture not so cheap as it
may appear at first sight, for the New England farmers practise pretty much the same
system as their brethren in Canada; they
have not a just idea of the importance of
throwing their crops into a proper arrange-
ment, so as one may be a preparation for
another, and thereby save the barren expence of a mere fallow. Maize is a very
exhausting crop; scarce any thing exhausts
the land more, and this to so great a degree, that their being obliged to depend on
this for their food, renders them more
than any other circumstance unable to
raise hemp and flax in sufficient quantities
for exportation, or even for rigging their
own ships, and cloathing themselves with
linen. Nor have they sufficient quantities
of rich land upon which they can practise
a management that would include both.

Besides maize, they raise small quantities of common wheat; but it does not
produce so much as one would apprehend
from the great richness of the soil: this is
owing to the peculiarity of the climate, for

we

we have lands in Europe that, to appearance, could bid fairer to produce large
crops. But as I before obferved, the new
fettlers in the north-eaft part of the province have found that wheat is to be raifed
with no contemptible fuccefs.

Barley and oats are very poor crops, yet
do they cultivate both in all parts of New
England : the crops are fuch as an Englifh farmer, ufed to the hufbandry of the
eaftern parts of the kingdom, would think
not worth ftanding ; this I attribute entirely to climate, for they have land equal
to the greateft productions of thofe plants.
Their common management of thefe three
forts of grain, wheat, barley, and oats, is
to fow them chiefly on land that has laid
fallow for two or three years, that is, left
undifturbed for weeds and all forts of
trumpery to grow; though at other times
they fow oats or barley after maize, which
they are enabled to do by the culture they
give the latter plant while it is growing :
all their corn here is in general fown in
fpring, from the common idea that the climate will not admit of an autumnal fowing : but this is with exceptions; for of
late years fome of the more intelligent
gentlemen farmers have, in various inftances,

E 3 broken

broken through the old methods, and fub-
flituted new ones in their room. Thefe
have, in various parts of the province, fub-
flituted the autumnal inftead of the fpring
fowing, and with great advantage. In
fome parts of Connecticut and Rhode Ifland, they have introduced the Englifh fyftem of making clovers a preparation for
corn; they leave the grafs upon the land
as many years as it will yield tolerable
crops, and then plough it up, and fow
wheat, which is found a much better management than the common one. The
clover affords good crops of hay once a
year, befides an advantageous eatage for
their cattle, which is much better than
leaving the land to cover itfelf with weeds.

Summer fallowing is in fome parts of
the province not an uncommon practice,
but it is not executed fo well as in England; they give this preparation to land
that is pretty much exhaufted, and which
they defign for maize or for hemp, which
latter alfo requires the addition of much
manuring. What they produce is good;
though not equal to the Ruffian, or even
to that of old England; but its requiring
the very beft rich lands in the province,
and alfo dunging, prevents them raifing
even

even enough for their own use, as their numerous shipping demands large supplies of it. They have been urged by several counties, even to a large amount, to go largely into the culture of hemp, which would certainly be a very national object, since there is no staple that any colony could raise would be more advantageous to Great Britain, or save her the expenditure of larger sums of money.

Flax they raise with much better success, as it does not demand near so rich a soil as hemp; but the more southern colonies much exceed New England, even in this article, for what is there raised is not sufficient for the home consumption of this very populous colony, whereas more to the south they export considerable quantities of flax seed.

In the best cultivated parts of New England, turneps are introducing in the field culture, but not in the manner they ought to do. This is an article that demands their attention greatly, but as I shall be more particular on them when I speak of the defects of their husbandry, I shall not enlarge on it here.

Pease, beans, and tares, are sown variously through the province, but scarcely

E 4   any

any where managed as they are in the well cultivated parts of the mother country. But every planter or farmer grows enough of the food for fattening hogs, for supplying his own family, and driving some fat ones to market. Hogs are throughout the province in great plenty, and very large, a considerable export from the province constantly goes on in barrelled pork, besides the vast demand there is for the fishery, and the shipping in general.

Apples may be mentioned as an article of culture throughout New England, for there is no farmer, or even cottager, without a large orchard : some of them of such extent, that they make three or four hundred hogsheads of cyder a man ; besides exporting immense quantities of apples from all parts of the province. The orchards in New England are reckoned as profitable as any other part of the plantation. Among the other productions of this province, I should not forget the woods, which, in the parts not brought into culture, are very noble ; they consist of oak, ash, elm, chesnut, cypress, cedar, beech, fir, ash, sassafras, and shumac. The oak is very good, and employed chiefly in ship building ; and the fir yields very greatly for masts, yards, and

plank,

plank, even the royal navy is supplied from hence with masts of an extraordinary size; and the export of lumber to the West-Indies is one of greatest articles in the province.

A large portion of every farm in New England, consists of meadow and pasture land; wherein it much resembles the better parts of the mother country. In the low lands, the meadows are rich, yielding large quantities of hay, which, though apparently coarse, is yet much liked by all cattle; the common herbage of many of these is a grass which has made much noise in England under the name of Timothy grass. Two or three tons of hay an acre are not an uncommon produce in these meadows. The farmers find great advantage in keeping a large part of their farms for pasturage, as they are thereby enabled to support large herds of cattle, and flocks of sheep, which much improve their farms.

The cattle commonly kept here are the same as in Great Britain: cows, oxen, horses, sheep, and hogs; they have large dairies, which succeed quite as well as in Old England; oxen they fat to nearly as great a size; their mutton is good; and the wool
which

which their sheep yield is long but coarse, but they manufacture it into coarse cloths, that are the common and only wear of the province, except the gentry, who purchase the fine cloths of Britain : no inconsiderable quantities of these coarse New England cloths are also exported to other colonies, to the lower people of whom, especially to the northward, they answer better than any we can send them. The horses are excellent, being the most hardy in the world ; very great numbers are exported to the West-Indies and elsewhere.

It is proper to observe, that the unsettled parts of the province, which northwards extend almost from the coasts to the river St. Lawrence, are, with an exception, of some open meadows and marshes, one continued and thick forest of the above-mentioned trees, but particularly of pines ; and though such parts are not brought to that value and population as the rest, yet are they to be esteemed highly valuable, and a great treasure for future exportation, whenever the legislature shall in their wisdom give a bounty sufficient to enable the New Englanders to undersell the Baltic in the ports of Great Britain ; an object of infinite importance, than which there is scarcely any

any in the œconomy of our colonies that demands more earnest endeavours. This vast forest, which is in size equal to that of the whole island of Great Britain, and extends into the greatest parts of Nova Scotia, belongs to the crown, but grants are made constantly to all such persons as apply for land, of such parts of it as they demand, under condition that they settle it in a given time and proportion; also under a reserve of all timber fit for masts for the royal navy. If there is a navigation, and application is merely made for grants in any other parts, the rest of the timber is of no slight value to the new settlers, as it yields a certain price, and is a commodity regularly exported from the province.

I shall conclude this account, with a table of the exports of this province since the peace.

Cod-fish dried, 10,000 tons, at 10 l. £.	100,000
Whale and cod-oil, 8500 tons, at 15 l. -	127,500
Whale-bone, 28 tons, at 300 l. - - -	8,400
Pickled mackrel and shads, 15,000 barrels at 20 s.	15,000
Masts, boards, staves, shingles, &c. - - -	75,000
Ships about 70 sail, at 700 l. - -	49,000
Turpentine, tar, and pitch, 1500 barrels, at 8 s.	600
Horses, and live stock, - - -	37,000
Pot ash, 14000 barrels, at 50 s. - -	35,000
Pickled beef and pork, 19,000 barrels, at 30 s.	28,500
Bees-wax, and sundries, - -	9,000
. Total £.	485,000

I

Upon

Upon this table I muft obferve, that the fifhery amounts to 250,900 l. of it; or rather more than half the total, which fhews what a great proportion of the people of this colony are employed in it. The other half is the produce of their lands, for fo both fhips and pot-afh muft be efteemed. Cattle and beef, pork, &c. came to 65,500 l. all the reft is timber, or what is made of timber; this is a proportion that gives us at once a tolerable idea of the colony. We are not from hence to fuppofe, that the great body of the landed intereft in this country has, like Canada, no other refource to purchafe foreign commodities with, than this fmall export. The cafe is very different, New England enjoys a vaft fifhery, and a great trade, which brings in no flight portion of wealth. The moft confiderable commercial town in all America is in this province; and another circumftance is the increafe of population. Thefe caufes operate fo as to keep up a confiderable circulation within the colony. Bofton and the fhipping are a market which enriches the country intereft far more than the above mentioned export, which, for fo numerous a people, is very inconfiderable. By means of this internal circulation, the

farmers

farmers and country gentlemen are en-abled very amply to purchase whatever they want from abroad.

CHAP. VI.

State of the inhabitants—Country gentle-
men—Farmers—New settlers—Lower
classes.

THERE is in many respects a great resemblance between New England and Great Britain. In the best cultivated parts of it, you would not in travelling through the country, know, from its ap-ance, that you were from home. The face of the country has in general a cultivated, inclosed, and chearful prospect; the farm-houses are well and substantially built, and stand thick; gentlemen's houses appear every where, and have an air of a wealthy and contented people. Poor, strolling, and ragged beggars are scarcely ever to be seen; all the inhabitants of the country ap-pear to be well fed, cloathed, and lodged, nor is any where a greater degree of in-dependency, and liberty to be met with:

nor

nor is that diftinction of the ranks and claffes to be found which we fee in Britain, but which is infinitely more apparent in France and other arbitrary countries.

The moft ancient fettled parts of the province, which are Rhode Ifland, Connecticut, and the fouthern part of New Hampfhire, contain many confiderable land eftates, upon which the owners live much in the ftyle of country gentlemen in England. They all cultivate a part of their eftates; and if they are fmall, the whole: this they do by means of their ftewards, who are here generally called overfeers: the reft is let to tenants, who occupy their farms by leafe, in the fame manner as it is in the mother country; the rents paid for fuch farms being the principal part of the landlords income.

Here therefore we fee a fketch of one clafs of people, that has a minute refemblance to the gentlemen in England who live upon their own eftates, but they have in fome refpects a great fuperiority: they have more liberty in many inftances, and are quite exempt from the overbearing influence of any neighbouring nobleman, which in England is very mifchievous to many gentlemen of fmall fortunes. Further,

ther, they pay what may be almoſt called no taxes ; for the increaſe of people and farms is ſo great, that the public burthens are conſtantly dividing ; beſides their being in all inſtances remarkably low. This is an advantage to be found no where but in America, for all the reſt of the world groans under the oppreſſive weight which bad governments and abſolute monarchs have laid on mankind. They have alſo the advantage of living in a country where their property is conſtantly on the increaſe of value. Trade, navigation, fiſheries, increaſing population, with other cauſes, have operated ſtrongly to raiſe the value of all the eſtates under cultivation, whoſe ſituation is favourable, for in proportion as the wild country is taken up good lands and convenient ſituations riſe in value; till we ſee they come, near the great towns, to as high a value as in the beſt parts of Great Britain, for near Boſton there are lands worth twenty ſhillings an acre. Another circumſtance, in which the eſtates of the gentlemen in New England have a great advantage, is that of being exempted from the payment of tythes, and rates for the ſupport of the poor, which in Britain make a vaſt deduction from the product of an
eſtate.

eftate. The plenty of timber, and the cheapnefs of iron, and all materials for building, are alfo advantages to all country eftates of a moft valuable nature; in England this article, which is what goes under the general name of repairs, fwallows up a large portion of rent, and with thofe already mentioned, and land-tax, leaves him, out of a large nominal rental, but a fmall neat income.

With thefe advantages, the New England gentlemen are enabled to live upon their eftates in a genteel, hofpitable, and agreeable manner; for the plenty of the neceffaries of life makes houfekeeping remarkably cheap, and counter-balances the fmall rents they get for fuch parts of their eftates as they let. This circumftance is owing to the eafe of every man fetting up for a farmer himfelf on the unfettled lands: this makes a fcarcity of tenants; for thofe who have money enough to ftock a farm, have enough to fettle a tract of wafte land, which is much more flattering than being the tenant of another: one would fuppofe that fuch a circumftance would prevent their being a tenant in the country; but this is not the cafe, low rents and accidents fometimes induce them to live rather than to fettle: nor, upon the whole,

whole are tenants common in New England, there are more estates that are under
the management of over-seers than that are
let to tenants.

Upon the whole, we may determine that
the country gentlemen of New England
are in many respects very fortunately situated, and as well stationed in all respects
for living comfortably and at their ease, as
any set of people can be : and this circumstance does not extend merely to the points
which I have now mentioned, but to another which deserves attention; it is the
growth of timber and increased value of
forest land: in New-England, any gentlemen may have a grant of whatever land he
pleases upon complying with the common
terms of settlement, which are the grant of
fifty acres for every white person fixed on
the estate; this to a person in the country, .
is a condition so easily performed that they
have it in their power to command almost
what part of the ungranted land they please:
this is an advantage unparalleled in any country of the world except our other colonies.
By this means the gentlemen of New England have an opportunity of constantly en-
creasing their estates. Those of fortune
erect saw mills on their new grants, by

which means they are enabled to make a very confiderable profit by the woods at the fame time that they lay the foundation of future eftates for their pofterity.

Some modern writers, very well informed in the affairs of our American colonies, have been particularly attentive to the circumftance of the mortgages which the merchants and others of London have on their eftates. This wants an explanation: the country gentlemen of New England are as free from this as any men in the world: it concerns only thofe who have dealings with London, thefe are the tobacco and rice planters; but as to the people of property in New England it is not the cafe with, I may fay, any man in the province that is not engaged in trade.

The next clafs of the country inhabitants of which I am to defcribe is the farmers; but I muft previoufly obferve, that by farmers we are to underftand not only the men who rent lands of others, but alfo the little freeholders who live upon their own property, and make much the moft confiderable part of the whole province. Thefe are the pofterity of former fettlers, who having taken in tracts of wafte land proportioned to their ability, have died

and

and left it to their descendants equally divided among all the children, by the gavel-kind custom, which is prevalent throughout this province. These countrymen in general are a very happy people; they enjoy many of the necessaries of life upon their own farms, and what they do not so gain, they have from the sale of their surplus products: it is remarkable to see such numbers of these men in a state of great ease and content, possessing all the necessaries of life, but few of the luxuries of it: they make no distinction in their agriculture from the tenants of the gentlemen, only live more at their ease, and labour with less assiduity. I should observe that this set of men near resemble a similar class which we knew in England very generally, before our wealth grew so considerable as to destroy all moderation; the great, when grown wealthy as well as powerful have purchased all such little freeholds as joined their estates, and thereby exterminated one of the most useful sets of men that could be found in this or any kingdom, an event which the law of gavelkind secures the New Englanders from.

These freeholders of small tracts of land which compose the greatest part of the pro-

F 2 vince,

vince, have, almoſt to a point, the neceſſaries of life and nothing more, ſpeaking
however according to our ideas of life in
Europe. Their farms yield food—much
of cloathing—moſt of the articles of building—with a ſurplus ſufficient to buy ſuch
foreign luxuries as are neceſſary to make
life paſs comfortably: there is very little
elegance among them, but more of neceſſaries—a greater capability of hoſpitality,
and decent living than is to be found among
the few remains of their brethren in England: a claſs which taxes, tythes, rates, and
repairs, with the increaſed expences of living, have almoſt driven from the face of
the earth. It is not therefore difficult to
draw a parallel between the little freeholders of Old and New England: in the former, a variety of cauſes have almoſt ſwept
away the race ; whereas in the latter they
flouriſh as much as ſuch a ſet of men can
any where flouriſh.

Before I take my leave of the two different ranks of landlords in New England,
let me obſerve that there is a very material
difference between the country gentlemen
of this colony, and the mother country, in
reſpect of that branch of luxury which
induces men to leave their eſtates, in order

to

to fquander the rents of them in a capital.
Of late years there are few men in England who call themfelves gentlemen, that
do not at leaft pay an annual vifit to London with their wives and families, and
fpend as much in one month upon pleafure,
as they do in the other eleven upon utility:
In a word, the country gentry of fmall fortunes in England ftarve upon their eftates, in
order to make a figure at the Pantheon and
Almack's; and if their rental is fomething
above mediocrity, will not content themfelves without a town houfe, in which to
fpend the better half of the year. This
is a cuftom which waftes and deftroys half
the eftates in the kingdom, and makes
beggars of many families that might with
prudent management live genteely and in-
dependently in the country.

To enter into a full account of the confequences of this branch of luxury, would
be unneceffary; fuffice it here to obferve,
that the gentlemen of New England are
almoft intirely free from a profufion, which
could not but be fatal to their eftates. It
is very rarely that any families from the
country make a winter refidence at Bofton
for the fake of the fmall degree of pleafure
which that capital affords. I know there

F 3   are

are inftances of it, but in general the thing is otherwife. The country gentlemen live the year round upon their eftates, going to town only when bufinefs calls them. And thereby they efcape an expence which is equally ufelefs and confuming.

The new fettlers upon fixing themfelves in their plantations enter at once into tho clafs of thefe freeholders; but from poverty in the beginning of their undertakings fall naturally into a clafs below them, unlefs they begin with a confiderable fum of money that raifes them in the confideration of their neighbours. There are many of thefe who begin with fuch fmall poffeffions, that they are fome years before they can gain the leaft exemption from a diligence and active induftry that equals any of the farmers of Great Britain. Such men, although they may be in the road of gaining as comfortable a living as any of the old freeholders, yet rather fall into an inferiority to them; not from the manners or conftitution of the colony, but from modefty and the natural exertions of a domeftic induftry.

Refpecting the lower claffes in New England, there is fcarcely any part of the world in which they are better off. The price of labour is very high, and they have with this

this advantage another no lefs valuable, of
being able to take up a tract of land whenever they are able to fettle it.   In Britain a
fervant or labourer may be mafter of thirty
or forty pounds without having it in their
power to lay it out in one ufefal or advantageous purpofe ;. it muft be a much larger
fum to enable them to hire a farm, but in
New England there is no fuch thing as a
man procuring fuch a fum of money by
his induftry without his taking a farm and
fettling upon it.   The daily inflances of this
give an emulation to all the lower claffes,
and make them point their endeavours with
peculiar induftry to gain an end which they
all efteem fo particularly flattering.

   This great eafe of gaining a farm, renders the lower clafs of people very induftrious ; which, with the high price of labour, banifhes every thing that has the leaft
appearance of begging, or that wandering,
deftitute ftate of poverty, which we fee to
common in England.   A traveller might
pafs half through the colony without finding, from the appearance of the people,
that there was fuch a thing as a want of
money among them.   The condition of
labourers in England is far from being comfortable, if compared with their American

brethren,

brethren, for they may work with no flight diligence and industry, and yet, if their families are large, be able to lay up nothing against old age: indeed the poor laws are very deftructive of any fuch provident conduct. Thofe laws have the effect of deftroying prudence without giving an adequate recompenfe; the condition of the aged or difeafed poor who depend on their fupport is in many cafes lamentable; or at leaft much inferior to what their own previous induftry would have procured them had they not been feduced by the idea of this worfe than no dependence. And without extending our reflections to this part of their lives we may determine that the pay they receive for their work does not rife proportionably with the price of all their neceffaries; the confequence of which is to them great oppreffion. On the contrary, the New England poor have no delufive poor laws to depend on: they aim at faving money enough to fix them into a fettlement; their induftry rarely fails of its end, fo that the evening of an induftrious life is univerfally that of a little planter in the midft of all neceffaries. The public confequence of this may be eafily deduced; it is a very high price of labour, and an amaz-

ing

ing increase of people; since marriages must abound greatly in a country, where a family, instead of being a burden, is an advantage.

I have more than once mentioned the high price of labour : this article depends on the circumstance I have now named ; where families are so far from being burthensome, men marry very young, and where land is in such plenty, men very soon become farmers, however low they set out in life. Where this is the case, it must at once be evident that the price of labour must be very dear; nothing but a high price will induce men to labour at all, and at the same time it presently puts a conclusion to it by so soon enabling them to take a piece of waste land. By day labourers, which are not common in the colonies, one shilling will do as much in England as half a crown in New England. This makes it necessary to depend principally on servants, and on labourers who article themselves to serve three, five, or seven years, which is always the case with new comers who are in poverty.

C H A P.

C H A P. VII.

Remarks on the errors in the rural manage-
ment of New England.

CHAPTERS of fuch a nature ought
not to be efteemed impertinent in
fuch a work as this, wherein I particularly
mean to explain every thing in my power
concerning the country management of
America, from its being fo little known
in England. And it is of confequence to
underftand the defects of their agriculture,
as well as the advantages of it, fince we
are almoft equally concerned in both.

The cultivated parts of New England
are more regularly enclofed than Canada,
but the planters do not fufficiently attend
to this circumftance; many eftates, and
farms are in this refpect in fuch condition,
that in Great Britain they would be thought
in a ftate of devaftation; yet here it all
arifes from carelefsnefs. Live hedges are
common, yet the plenty of timber in many
parts of the province is fuch, that they
neglect planting thefe durable, ufeful, and
excellent fences, for the more eafy way of

pofts

posts and rails, or boards, which last but
a few years, and are always out of repair.
This is a negligence, and a want of foresight that is unpardonable: but though the
new settlers see the inconvenience of it on
the lands of the old ones, and find live
hedges in many places substituted, yet do
they go on with the practice, as if it was
the best in the world. In many plantations, there are only a few enclosures about
the houses, and the rest lie like common
fields in England, the consequence of
which is much useless labour in guarding
crops from cattle.

Respecting their system, a distinction is
to be made between the parts which have
been many years in culture, and which,
from the neighbouring population, are
grown valuable; in these the lands are
much better managed than in the frontier
parts of the province, where land is of
little value, and where all the new settlers
fix. In the former, the farmers lay down
a system which they seem tolerably to adhere to, though with variations. They
sow large quantities of maize, some wheat,
barley, oats, buck-wheat, pease, and beans,
turneps, and clover: hemp and flax in
small parcels. And these they throw after
one

one another, with variations, so as to keep
the land, as well as their ideas permit,
from being quite exhausted; which they
effect by the intervention of a ploughed
summer fallow sometimes. When the
land has borne corn for several years, till it
threatens to yield no more, then they sow
clover among the last crop, and leave it as
a meadow for some years to recover itself.
But all this system proceeds too much on
the plan of the worst farmers of Great
Britain, to get corn from their fields as
long as ever they will bear it.

Instead of such management, I shall venture to recommend the following system.

   1. Summer fallow.
   2. Maize.
   3. Pease or beans.
   4. Barley or oats.
   5. Turneps.
   6. Wheat.
   7. Clover for three, four, or five years.
   8. Wheat.

I think such a system is well adapted to
their climate and soil. But I am sensible
many objections will be made to it; particularly there being twice as much wheat
as maize: in this point I am doubtful.
                   They

They fay they cannot grow good wheat; that they *do not* grow good wheat I am fenfible, but I attribute it to their throwing it into fuch fyftems as this, 1 maize, 2 maize, 3 wheat, 4 oats, 5 wheat, &c. &c. In which cafe, the wheat may be thin, fhrivelled, and hufky, without its being the fault of the climate; I am of opinion, under fuch culture, it would be the fame in Britain. But if in this point I fhould be miftaken, let the fixth crop be changed for maize. In this fyftem I confider maize, barley, oats, and wheat, as crops that exhauft the land; but peafe, beans, turneps, and clover, as fuch as rather improve than exhauft it, provided they are cultivated in the manner they ought.

Maize is reckoned a great exhaufter in New England, and they have fome reafon for the idea, though I think they carry it too far. The culture is fomething fimilar to that of hops; being planted in fquares of about five feet, and when up, the plant is earthed into little hillocks: they ought, during the whole growth, to proceed on the exact principles and practice of the Tullian culture, of horfe-hoeing it incef-fantly, and cutting up fuch weeds as grow

about

about the plant, out of the reach of the horse-hoes; these are not many, as the plants standing in squares, the horse-hoes work both ways. The misfortune is, they do not always keep the plantations of maize clean, or the earth so loose in the intervals as it ought to be, in which case one may easily conceive that the land may be left totally exhausted; but this effect would be vastly lessened by being more assiduous in the culture, while the crop was growing —absolutely to destroy all weeds, and keep the vacant spaces in garden order: points in which the New England farmers (some few excepted) are not by any means perfect.

Turneps, and other articles of winter food for cattle, they are extremely inattentive to; the great want of the country, which almost prevents their planting hemp in quantities, is the want of dung, and yet they will not take the only method of gaining it, which is the keeping great stocks of cattle, not ranging through the woods, but confined to houses or warm yards. This can only be done by providing plenty of winter food: at present, they keep no more than their hay will feed, and some they let into the woods to provide for themselves,

felves, not a few of which perifh by the
feverity of the cold. Great ftores of turneps, or other roots, and perhaps cabbages
better ftill, would make their hay and
ftraw go much further, and by means of
plenty of litter, for which this country is
in many refpects very well provided, they
might raife fuch quantities of manure as
would double the fertility of all their
lands, and give them the command even
of hemp in much greater quantities than it
is now raifed. A more general culture of
the various forts of clovers, would alfo increafe the means of keeping cattle, and
confequently raifing more dung, which is
in all parts of the world, whatever may be
the climate, the only means of getting
good arable crops. Befides, turneps, or
other roots, cabbages, clover, &c. in their
growth, and the culture which fuch receive as ftand fingle, much improve the
land, as all good farmers in England have
well known thefe hundred years. Nor
have the New Englanders any reafon to
fear the having too much cattle for the
conftant export of beef, pork, and live
ftock of all kinds, to the Weft Indies,
which is a market that will never fail them,
let their quantity be almoft what it may.

And

And this mention of cattle leads me to obferve, that moft of the farmers in this country are, in whatever concerns cattle, the moft negligent ignorant fet of men in the world. Nor do I know any country in which animals are worfe treated. Horfes are in general, even valuable ones, worked hard, and ftarved: they plough, cart, and ride them to death, at the fame time that they give very little heed to their food; after the hardeft day's works, all the nourifhment they are like to have is to be turned into a wood, where the fhoots and weeds form the chief of the pafture; unlefs it be after the hay is in, when they get a fhare of the after-grafs. A New Englander (and it is the famequite to Penfylvania) will ride his horfe full fpeed twenty or thirty miles; tye him to a tree, while he does his bufinefs, then re-mount, and gallop back again. This bad treatment extends to draft oxen; to their cows, fheep, and fwine; only in a different manner, as may be fuppofed. There is fcarce any branch of rural œconomy which more demands attention and judgment than the management of cattle; or one which, under a judicious treatment, is attended with more profit to the farmer in all countries; but

the

the New England farmers have in all this matter the worst notions imaginable.

I must, in the next place, take notice of their tillage, as being weakly and insufficiently given: worse ploughing is no where to be seen, yet the farmers get tolerable crops; this is owing, particularly in the new settlements, to the looseness and fertility of old woodlands, which, with very bad tillage, will yield excellent crops: a circumstance the rest of the province is too apt to be guided by, for seeing the effects, they are apt to suppose the same treatment will do on land long since broken up, which is far enough from being the case. Thus, in most parts of the province, is found shallow and unlevel furrows, which rather scratch than turn the land; and of this bad tillage the farmers are very sparing, rarely giving two ploughings if they think the crop will do with one; the consequence of which is their products being seldom near so great as they would be under a different management. Nor are their implements well made, or even well calculated for the work they are designed to perform; of this among other instances I may take the plough. The beam is too long; the supporters ought to be moveable, as they are in ploughs in England, and in Scotland ; the plough share is too narrow, which is a common fault; and the wheels are much too low ; were they higher, the draft would be proportionably lighter. In other parts of the province, I have indeed seen better ploughs, but they are in few hands, and, besides, are not quite free from these defects.

The harrows are also of a weak and poor construction ; for I have more than once seen them with only wooden teeth, which however it may do for mere fand in tilth, muft be very inefficacious on other foils, but the mifchief of ufing fuch on one fort of land, is, that the flovens are always ready to extend them for cheapnefs to the reft. The carts and waggons are alfo in fome parts of the province very aukward ill made things, in which the principles of mechanics are not at all confidered. There are however fome gentlemen near Bofton, who having caught the tafte of agriculture, which has for fome years been remarkable in England, have introduced from thence better tools of moft forts, and at the fame time a much better practice of hufbandry ; and if they took pains to fpread this about the province, it could not

fail

fail of being attended with very beneficial effects. Societies for the encouragement of agriculture seem to be the only means of bringing it to bear, by means of premiums and bounties.

Another article, which I shall here mention, is that of timber, which already grows so scarce upon the south coasts, that even fire-wood in some parts is not cheap; and is forced to be brought from Sagadahock: this has been owing to the planters upon their first settling, ravaging rather than cutting down the woods: and what is a striking instance of inattention to their real interest, is the new settlers going on in the same manner, although they cannot but see and know the effects of it in the parts first settled. They not only cut down timber to raise their buildings and fences, but in clearing the grounds for cultivation they destroy all that comes in their way, as if they had nothing to do but to get rid of it at all events, as fast as possible. Instead of acting in so absurd a manner, which utterly destroys woods of trees, which require an hundred years to come to perfection, they ought in the first settling and cultivating their tracts of land, to inclose and reserve portions of the best woods

for

for the future ufe of themfelves, and the general good of the country ; points which they
have hitherto feemed to have very little at
heart. Indeed, this violent and unlicenfed
deftruction of timber, has been carried to
a degree in our colonies, that calls for a
preventive from the public : for it is clear
to common fenfe, that if the legiflature
does not interfere in this point, the whole
country will be deprived of timber, as faft
as it is fettled ; which ought not to be
the cafe while any attention is given
to the public interefts.   For nothing
is of more importance to this country, though a colony, than timber : the
plenty which has hitherto abounded, makes
the planters fo regardlefs of their effential
interefts, as to think it a commodity of
little or no value. Which muft be attended with worfe confequences than almoft
any part of the ill management, which they
have hitherto been attended with.

Let me, before I quit this fubject, obferve further, that the New Englanders
are alfo deficient in introducing thofe new
articles of culture, which have become
common in different parts of Great Britain ; among others, let us inftance carrots, parfnips, potatoes, Jerufalem arti-
chokes,

chokes, beets, lucerne, fainfoine, and particularly cabbages; thefe articles are many
of them better adapted to the climate of
New England than of Great Britain; yet
are they not attended to half fo much: but
the farmers of this country would find
their intereft more in the introduction of
thefe articles, than could ever happen to
any people in the mother country, where
land is fo fcarce, that they cannot afford
to make trial of any thing that they
are not previoufly certain will anfwer;
whereas in thefe colonies the cafe is different; land cofts nothing; they have e-
nough of various foils to try every thing,
without the lofs of the land bringing them
into thofe difficulties which it muft ever
do in countries where a confiderable rent,
tythe, and poor's tax are paid. But this
circumftance, which is fuch an undoubted advantage, in fact turns out the contrary; and for this reafon, they depend on
this plenty of land as a fubftitute for all
induftry and good management; neglecting the efforts of good hufbandry, which
in England does more than the cheapnefs
of the foil does in America.

C H A P.

C H A P. VIII.

Comparison between the benefits resulting from agriculture in Great Britain and New England.

I Have given in the preceding passages what I may venture to say is a fair and candid account of New England. I may be in numerous passages mistaken, bu: I have not purposely given a better or worse account of things than the fact has really been; this observation is necessary, in order to prepare the reader for the comparison which I am going to draw. The case is not indifferent; nor is it so strongly decisive in favour either of one or the other, as to make the argument depend upon a few strong outlines, that appear clear to the reader the instant they are produced, which is the case with Canada and Nova Scotia. On the contrary, New England very much resembles, in several essential circumstances, Great Britain. For instance; it is a country which produces all the necessaries, but none of the luxuries of life. It is a country which depends as much or

more

more upon navigation, commerce, and fisheries, than Britain does; agriculture not yielding those rich products which form the foundation in other countries of the most beneficial branches of commerce. Besides this, the face of the country in some particulars, the ranks of the people, the number of gentlemen living on their estates, the freedom of the lower classes, with various other circumstances, give an uncommon resemblance between Great Britain and New England, which may well make it a matter of difficulty to judge between them; to which if we add that both enjoy liberty, both civil and religious, we shall find that a cool, dispassionate, and candid examination is necessary, and by no means a hasty or incautious one.

The great points in favour of New England are the enjoyments of plenty of land— a freedom from heavy taxes,—from tythes, —from poor rates ;—with an open market for all commodities raised. On the contrary, Great Britain lies under the disadvantage of having no land for new grants— is much burthened by taxes—and also by that of tythes—and poor rates: in this comparison the benefit is all on the side of New England ; but in others there are

points

points much more favourable to the mother country : *Firſt*, the climate is more favourable than that of New England to huſbandry ; for though the fruits of ſome kind in America are far beyond what we have in Britain, yet in the articles of farming produce this advantage extends to nothing of importance. Wheat is a crop far more valuable than maize, but cannot be gained in New England upon comparable terms with what it is in Britain ; nor does maize produce nearly like it in quantity, nor any thing like in value. This ſuperiority runs through all the products of a farm, and alſo in the price of them : which in a compariſon of the two countries ſhould never be forgotten. The exporting price of wheat, for three or four years after the peace of Paris, in the colonies was 20s. a quarter, while in England, it was from 44s. to 50s. This principal grain regulates the reſt in moſt parts of the world, as it does in both Britain and America ; the caſe is the ſame with barley, oats, peaſe, beans, hay, butter, cheeſe, and every article the farmer carries to market. If the monſtrous difference of theſe prices be conſidered, it will ſurely be thought a counterballance to many other advantages. I am

ſenſible,

senfible, that wheat in America, has of late
years been at 26s. to 32s. a quarter; but
then it has in England been from 50s. to
56s. fo that the fuperiority has continued:
we may fafely fuppofe the fame difference
of price has run through other articles of
corn; indeed we know it has, and alfo,
that in all products which arife in whatever
manner from grafs lands, the fuperiority in
the price of England is far greater; upon
the whole, this difference may be reckoned
at 50 per cent.

Now if a calculation is made of this fuperiority or even of 40 or 30 per cent. I
am clear it will be found to more than
ballance the difference of the farmers expences in rent, tythe, and rates; and alfo
the advantages which the New Englanders
have in plenty of timber and fome other
articles of inferior importance.

But further, the American has in one
inftance an inferiority which is great and
marked; it is the price and nature of the
labour which he employs: he pays more
than treble the rate of Great Britain, or
elfe fubmits to be ferved in a manner which
is open to an hundred inconveniencies.
This is an article of fuch confequence as
to ballance many others.

As

As far therefore as the comparifon concerns the fubftantial farmers in either country, the renters in Britain, and the renters
or owners in New England, that rank neither with the lower claffes nor with the
gentlemen, I think the advantage lies clearly
in favour of the former; and no flight
proof that this determination is juft, is the
difference of wealth between thefe two
fetts of men; the farmers in Britain of the
rank now under confideration are incom-
parable richer than the fimilar inhabitants
of New England; among whom very few
are to be found that can be called men of
wealth or even property : they live in a decent comfortable manner, but rarely acquire wealth.

I do not apprehend the parallel turns out
the fame with the lower clafs of farmers,
for I do not think a more miferable fet of
men are to be found than the little farmers
in Britain; they work harder, fare worfe,
and are in fact poorer than the day labourers they employ, whereas in New England,
the little freeholders and farmers live in the
midft of a plenty of all the neceffaries of
life; they do not acquire wealth, but they
have comforts in abundance: I freely acknowledge

knowledge the fuperiority of the colony in this article.

In that of the poor, and the labourers, the comparifon is equally in favour of New England : in this refpect common and almoft univerfal experience tells us, that in all countries which have long been wealthy, in which a great commerce, flourifhing manufactures, and eftablifhed luxury are fixed, that in fuch countries the poor are always in a ftate of oppreffion and of mifery : It would be too much to fay that this *muft be* fo, but the fact is, that it always *is* fo ; and, we fee in the cafe in queftion of Great Britain, that the poor in general are in a ftate of poverty; and it is neceffary they fhould, or the trade and manufactures of the country would fink, for their profperity depends on that low price of labour which keeps the labouring poor below the proportion of the high price of every thing elfe.

The laft circumftance of this parallel is the country gentlemen of two, three, or to five hundred pounds a year land eftate ; and here I muft obferve that the comparifon turns out utterly in favour of the colony. Indeed the high prices of every thing at home, owing to the plenty of money, has
almoft

almoſt ruined ſuch people, ſo that very few will ſoon be found; they muſt either ſtarve, or convert their eſtates into money, and apply it in ſome line of induſtry to make more than common intereſt; they muſt become traders, or farmers if they do not ſuffer themſelves to be eclipſed by every country grocer, or woolman. But this is not the caſe in New England; there, four or five hundred pounds a year is a great eſtate—not that there is not much larger, but it is ſufficient for all the comforts and conveniences of life, and for ſuch a portion of the luxuries of it, as are indulged in by any neighbour, though their eſtates may be larger than his. In a word, his ſituation is the very reverſe of that of his brethren in Britain, inſomuch that no change can be imagined more beneficial (in point of the expenditure of his income) than for ſuch a country gentleman to ſell his eſtate in England, and with the money of the ſale to buy in New England; though we ſhall by and by come to colonies that are preferable. By ſuch a conduct he leaves his country after making the only advantage in his power of the cheapneſs of money, by getting a great price for his land; and he goes immediately into another in which he

finds

finds money dear; fo that he profits doubly
by the change.

As to gentlemen whofe fortunes are confiderable enough to fupport them in the enjoyments of the age, they of courfe will
remain fixed, becaufe they can get nothing
by moving which they have not at home;
with the circumftance of living in the midft
of the luxury and elegance of the firft
country in the world—luxuries which they
do not behold like their little neighbours,
with envious eyes, but which they enjoy in
common with the rich and great.

Upon the whole there are fome claffes,
whofe emigrating to New England need
not furprize us, but there are others among
whom it happens very irrationally.

CHAP.

CHAP. IX.

NEW YORK.

Climate of New York—Soil—Productions—
Husbandry—Curious accounts of a new set-
tlement—Present state of the inhabitants—
Exports.—

THE colony of New York lies between
latitude 41° and 44°, which tho'
partly the same parallel as New England,
yet is it attended with a different climate in
some respects; but in every circumstance
superior, since there are productions that will
not thrive in New England, which do admirably here; not owing to the greater heat
(for New England is as hot as New York)
but to a better and more salubrious air.
The spring in New York is earlier, and the
autumn late; the summer is long and
warm; indeed sometimes the heat is great,
but rarely oppressive; the winter is severe
but short; it is not so sharp as in New England, and they have in general a clear
bright sky. In winter the snow lies deep,
and for two or three months; and they
travel

travel on it in fledges both here and in New England, in the manner that is common in the northern parts of Europe.

Sometimes indeed the cold is extraordinary great; of which Dr. Mitchel gives an inflance. By the obfervations, fays he, made, in January 1765, by the maflers of the college at New York, Fahrenheit's thermometer fell 6 degrees below o, which is 21 degrees below 15, the greateft cold in England.—Water then froze inftantly, and even ftrong liquors in a very fhort time.—And we are told it is not uncommon there to fee a glafs of water fet upon the table, in a warm room freeze before you can drink it, &c.*

The foil of the province is in general very good; on the coaft it is fandy but backwards, they have noble tracks of rich black mold, red loam, and friable clays, with mixtures of thefe foils in great varieties; at fome miles diftance from the fea, the country fwells into fine hills and ridges, which are all covered with foreft trees, and the foil on many of thefe is rich and deep, an advantage not common in poor countries. The river Hudfon which is navigable to Al-

---

* *Prefent State.*

bany,

bany, and of such a breadth and depth as to carry large sloops, with its branches on both sides, intersect the whole country, and render it both pleasant and convenient. The banks of this great river have a prodigious variety ; in some places there are gently swelling hills, covered with plantations and farms ; in others towering mountains spread over with thick forests : here you have nothing but abrupt rocks of vast magnitude, which seem shivered in two to let the river pass the immense clefts ; there you see cultivated vales, bounded by hanging forests, and the distant view completed by the *Blue Mountains* raising their heads above the clouds. In the midst of this variety of scenery, of such grand and expressive character the river Hudson flows, equal in many places to the Thames at London, and in some much broader. The shores of the American rivers are too often a line of swamps and marshes ; that of Hudson is not without them, but in general it passes through a fine, high, dry, and bold country, which is equally beautiful and wholesome.

In general the soil of this province exceeds that of New England : besides the varieties I have already mentioned, there is

on

on Long Island sands that are made quite fertile with oyster-shells, a fish caught there in prodigious quantities : they have the effect of shell marle in Scotland. The productions of New York are the same in general as those of New England, with an exception of some fruits that will not thrive in the latter country ; but almost every article is of a superior quality: this is very striking in wheat, of which they raise in New England, as I have already observed, but little that is good, whereas in New York their wheat is equal to any in America, or indeed in the world, and they export immense quantities of it ; whereas New England can hardly supply her own consumption.

They sow their wheat in autumn, with better success than in spring : this custom they pursue even about Albany, in the northern parts of the province, where the winters are very severe. The ice there in the river Hudson is commonly three or four feet thick. When professor Kalm was here, the inhabitants of Albany crossed it the third of April with six pair of horses. The ice commonly dissolves at that place about the end of March, or the beginning of April. On the 16th of November the yachts are put up, and about the beginning or middle of April they are in motion again. If wheat will do here in autumn, where the ground is sometimes frozen four feet deep, one would apprehend it would succeed even more to the north.

Wheat in many parts of the province yields a larger produce than is common in England : upon good lands about Albany, where the climate is the coldest in the country, they sow two bushels and better upon one acre, and reap from 20 to 40: the latter quantity however is not often had; but from 20 to 30 bushels are common, and this with such bad husbandry as would not yield the like in England, and much less in Scotland. This is owing to the richness and freshness of the soil. In other parts of the province, particularly adjoining to New Jersey and Pensylvania, the culture is better and the country more generally settled. Though there are large tracts of waste land within twenty miles of the city of New York.

Rye is a common crop upon the inferior lands, and the sort they produce is pretty good, though not equal to the rye of England. The crops of it are not so great in produce

produce as thofe of wheat on the better lands.

Maize is fown generally throughout the province, and they get vaft crops of it. They chufe the loofe, hollow loams, or fandy lands for it, not reckoning the ftiff or clayey ones will do at all for it: half a bufhel will feed two acres, and yield an hundred bufhels in return: about Albany, where they have frofts in the fummer, maize fuits them particularly, becaufe tho' the fhoots are damaged, or even killed by the froft, yet the roots fend forth frefh ones. Maize, from the greatnefs of the produce, may eafily be fuppofed a rich article of culture, and efpecially in a province that has fo fine an inland navigation through it as New York. It is alfo of great advantage in affording a vaft produce of food for cattle in the winter, which in this country is a matter of great confequence, where they are obliged to keep all their cattle houfed from November till the end of March, with exception indeed of unprovident farmers, who truft fome out the chief of the winter, to their great hazard.

Barley is much fown in all the fouthern parts of the province; and the crops they fometimes get of it are very great, but the

grain

grain is not of a quality equal to that of
Europe. They make much malt and brew
large quantities of beer from it at New
York, which ferves the home confumption,
and affords fome alfo for exportation. Peafe
are a common article of culture here, and
though uncertain in their produce, yet are
they reckoned very profitable; and the ftraw
is valued as winter food. Thirty bufhels
per acre they confider as a large crop, but
fometimes they get fcarcely a third of that.
Oats they fow in common, and the products
are generally large; fixty bufhels an acre
have been known on land of but moderate
fertility. Buckwheat is every where fown,
and few crops are fuppofed to pay the farmer better, at the fame time that they find
it does very little prejudice to the ground,
in which it refembles peafe.

Potatoes are not common in New England, but in New York many are planted;
and upon the black, loofe, frefh woodland
they get very great crops, nor does any pay
them better if fo well, for at the city of
New York there is a conftant and ready
market for them; I have been affured that
from five to eight hundred bufhels have
been often gained on an acre.

There are many very rich meadows and
paftures·

pastures in all parts of the province; and upon the brooks and rivers, the watered ones (for they are well acquainted with that branch of husbandry) are mown twice and yield large crops of hay. In their marshes they get large crops also, but it is a coarse bad sort; not however to a degree, as to make cattle refuse it, on the contrary, the farmers find it of great use in the winter support of their lean cattle, young stock, and cows.

The timber of this province consists chiefly of oak, ash, beech, chesnut, cedar, walnut, cypress, hickory, saffafras, and the pine; nor is there any preceptible difference in their value of the wood here and in New England; though it declines, for ship building when you get further to the south; with some exceptions however, for there are other species of trees even in the most southern colonies that are equal to any for that purpose. New York not being near so much settled as New England, timber is much more plentiful, so that the planters and new settlers make great profit by their lumber. Upon most of the streams that fall into the river Hudson, there are many saw mills for the mere purpose of sawing boards, planks, and other forts of lumber,

which

which goes down in immenſe quantities to New York, from whence it is ſhipped for the West Indies. We ſhall by and by ſee that this is a very great article in the profit of every planter. Among all the woods of this province, are found immenſe numbers of vines of ſeveral ſpecies, and quite different from thoſe of Europe, ſome of the grapes reſembling currants rather than ours. Wine has been, and is commonly made of them, but of a ſort too bad to become an article of export.

Hemp is cultivated in all parts of the province, but not to a greater amount than their own conſumption : flax is however a great article in the exports ; it ſucceeds extremely well, and pays the farmer a conſiderable profit. Lintſeed oil is another article of export, the ſeed for which is raiſed by the planters ; but more is exported unmanufactured. Turnips alſo are grown in large quantities, and by ſome planters upon a ſyſtem much improved of late years. The fruits in this province are much ſuperior to thoſe in New England ; and they have ſome, as peaches and nectarines, which will not thrive there. Immenſe quantities of melons, and water melons are cultivated in the fields near New York, where they come to

as

as great perfection as in Spain and Italy;
nor can it well be conceived how much of
thefe fruits and peaches, &c. all ranks of
people eat here, and without receiving any
ill confequence from the practice. This is
an agreeablenefs far fuperior to any thing
we have in England; and indeed, the fame
fuperiority runs through all their fruits, and
feveral articles of the kitchen garden, which
are here raifed without trouble, and in profufion. Every planter and even the fmalleft
farmers have all an orchard near their houfe
of fome acres, by means of which they
command a great quantity of cyder, and
export apples by fhip loads to the Weft
Indies. Nor is this an improper place to
obferve that the rivers in this province and
the fea upon the coaft are richly furnifhed
with excellent fifh; oyfters and lobfters are
no where in greater plenty than in New
York. I am of opinion they are more
plentiful than at any other place on the
globe; for very many poor families have
no other fubfiftence than oyfters and bread.
Nor is this the only inftance of the natural
plenty that diftinguifhes this country: the
woods are full of game, and wild turkies
are very plentiful; in thefe particulars New
York much exceeds New England.

H 4　　　　　Thefe

These upon the whole are circumstances which contribute much to the plenty and happiness of living in this country; and among other causes, contribute very greatly to the plenty and general welfare of all ranks of the people, nor should I here omit making some observations on the state of the settlers and other inhabitants.

To what causes it is I know not, but New York is much less populous than New England to the north, and Penfylvania to the south: there is no circumstance that results from nature, or from the government of the province that can account for this; but to whatever cause it may be owing, certain it is, that we ought to esteem it as fortunate for such persons as now chuse to settle there. There are vast tracts of un-patented land yet remaining on the river Hudson and its branches, which abound in every beneficial circumstance that can render a new country desirable to settle in.

This however, will not, in all probability last long, for the new settlements in-crease every day; so that in a few years there will not be many such spaces abound-ing in wood and navigable water unoccu-pied.

But there is one mistake made by most

new

new settlers, especially on the river Hudson; they have in general an idea that the only good soils are the deep black loam, or clays; and accordingly reject all the tracts that consist of a thin reddish loam on rock; but I have been assured by some intelligent gentlemen, that experiment has proved this soil, though so thin, fertile to a great degree in most of the productions which are common in the whole province: they have mentioned particularly, barley, pease, potatoes, turneps, clover, and even wheat. And as a confirmation that this opinion was just, I was favoured with the following particular of the produce of a field of this soil, which having been rejected by several new settlers, was planted by the person to whom I am obliged for this intelligence. The piece of land contained sixteen acres, the soil a light thin loam, of a reddish colour, on a lime-stone rock.

First year.

Grubbed, ploughed, and prepared for potatoes, and planted without dung: produce 11000 bushels, which were sold at 10d. per bushel, which is 453l.

Second year.

Ploughed once, and sown with wheat, produce 512 bushels, which sold for 85l.

I

Third

Third year.

Planted again with potatoes, produced 8490 bushels, which sold for 10d. a bushel, or 354 l.

Fourth year.

Sown with wheat again, produce 600 bushels, which sold for 120 l.

Fifth year.

Sown with barley, produce 730 bushels, . which sold for 73 l.

Sixth year.

Ploughed once, and sown with peafe, the produce 630 bushels, which sold for 53 l.

With this crop of peafe clover was sown, and left an excellent pasture, which was reckoned as profitable as any other piece of land in the whole plantation.

First year,	-	- -	£. 453
Second do.	-	- -	85
Third do.	-	- -	354
Fourth do.	-	- -	120
Fifth do.	-	- -	73
Sixth do.	-	- -	53

Total £. 1138

Which is near £. 11 15 0 per acre per annum.

Now

Now upon this account I have several remarks to make, which I think important, as it shews what may be done in this country, by good husbandry, even when no manure is used. The reader doubtless observes, that the *system* of management in this field ran upon the principle of an intervening crop of potatoes or pease between every two of wheat and barley. This is the husbandry which I would always recommend, but which is diametrically opposite to the practice of the New York planters; who make not the least scruple of taking six or eight crops successively of maize, wheat, rye, barley, or oats, without ever thinking of the least necessity of introducing pease, buckwheat, turneps, clover, or any other plant which in its nature or culture would prove a preparation for corn. The idea exemplified in the preceding sketch shews quite a different conduct.

In the next place I must observe, that the register of this field shews strongly the importance of cultivating potatoes on fresh woodlands; the products here reaped from them exceed infinitely those of any other crops, which should animate the farmers of this province to extend the culture of them;

2

them ; but the importance of planting them does not only rest in the amount of the produce, however considerable, they prepare the ground for corn better than any other plant, of which no bad idea can be formed from the crops which here succeeded them. There is a notion, common in many parts, that the lands even in New York are far inferior to those of Europe in general, but I am apt to believe that this is very much owing to the husbandry here being so much inferior. The instance I have now given of a bad soil, not esteemed here, but well managed, shews what might be done if the same attention was given to the culture of the earth, that is common in Britain.

The same gentleman to whom I am indebted for the preceding account, gave me another of the expences and product of a considerable plantation on the river Hudson. This I shall insert with pleasure ; for such accounts are what I have most aimed at gaining for all the colonies, not always with success indeed, but it is only from such that we can form a just idea of the advantages and disadvantages of American husbandry. Such accounts of agriculture in Europe are common in numerous books,
while

while the management and flate of the
agriculture of the colonies has been little
attended to, for which I am clear no good
reafon can be affigned.

The plantations in queftion confifted of
1600 acres, fituated partly on the banks of
the river Hudfon, and partly on each fide
a fmall river that runs into it; the purcha-
fer was not the firft fettler, for the land
was marked out, a houfe built, and fome
offices, with a fmall tract of land cleared:
nothing, however, was done either expen-
fively, or with good judgment; and the
place was in a ftate of neglect when purchafed. The price was 370 l.

A fmall faw-mill, and additional offices
were built on it immediately, which with
fome other improvements, of no great a-
mount, came to 260 l.

Eight hundred acres were grubbed, and
the trees fawn and rived into plank, board,
fhingles, and ftaves: the whole expence of
which was 1162 l. Many of the trees were
oak and elm, of great fize; alfo fome limes
of extraordinary growth.

Eight new inclofures were made, the
fences, pofts, and rails and ditching, with
all expences, came to 32 l.

The

The stock fixed on the plantation was as follows :

	£.
Eight negroes, at 34l. - - - -	272
Four indented servants, at 11 l. each, for 3 years,	132
Two hired by the year at New York, 12l. -	72
Three German emigrants, at 9 l. - - - -	81
Servants provisions, and cloathing for negroes, besides what produced, - - - -	56
Implements of husbandry, expences of, exclusive of timber, - - - - -	87
Salary of overseer, 3 years, - - -	110
Seed for the first crop, - - - -	90
Sundry expences, - - - - -	113
Cattle, - - - - -	230
Provisions, &c. for 3 years, - - -	300
	£. 1543

The produce of the three years, in various articles, came to the following sums.

Lumber.

	l.	s.	d.
17,000 feet of boards, at 5l. 2s. 6d. per 1000.	87	2	6
970 plank, at 3s. 8d. - - -	177	16	0
220,000 shingles, at 12s. per 1000 -	132	0	0
60,000 staves, at 4l. 10s. per 1000. -	270	0	0
260 pieces of timber, at 7s. 6d. -	97	0	0
Sundry articles of various kinds, -	187	10	0
	951	8	6

Recapitulation.

	l.	s.	d.
Purchase, - - - - -	370	0	0
Saw-mill, &c. - - - -	260	0	0
Clearing 800 acres, - - -	1162	0	0
Eight inclosures, - - - -	32	0	0
Stock, - - - - -	1243	0	0
Provisions, - - - - -	300	0	0
Total	3367	0	0

The annual after expence was :

	l.	s.	d.
Intereſt of capital, - - - - -	168	7	0
Repairs, - - - - - -	12	0	0
Incloſing, - - - - -	10	0	0
Negroes, - - - - -	16	0	0
Servants wages, - - - -	135	0	0
Implements, - - - - -	13	0	0
Sundry expences, - - - -	100	0	0
	454	7	0

Produce 1ſt year.

	l.	s.	d.
4 acres of potatoes, 260 buſhels per acre, 1040 buſhels at 8d. - - -	34	13	0
82 acres Indian corn, 30 buſh. per acre 2460 buſhels at 1s. 6d. - -	184	10	0
10 acres peaſe, failed, - - -	0	0	0
22 of wheat, 22 buſhels per acre, at 3s.	72	12	0
	291	15	0

Produce 2d year.

	l.	s.	d.
6 acres potatoes. 200 buſhels per acre, 1200 buſhels, at 10d. - - -	50	0	0
135 acres Indian corn, 32 buſh. per acre, 4320 buſh. at 1s. 6d. - -	324	0	0
90 acres wheat, 20 buſh. per acre, 1800 buſh. at 3s. - - -	270	0	0
40 acres peaſe, 15 buſh. per acre, 600 buſh. at 1s. 3d. - - -	37	10	0
40 acres barley, 2 do. potatoes, 16 turneps, 35 oats, 32 clover, 20 Indian corn, } for plantation, -	0	0	0

416 acres in culture.   £. 681 10 0

Pro-

Produce 3d year.

	l.	s.	d.
8 acres potatoes, 300 bush. per acre, 2400 bush. at 10d.	50	0	0
170 acres of Indian corn, 35 bush. per acre, 5950 bush. at 2s.	595	0	0
60 acres wheat, 16 bush. per acre, 960 bush. at 3s.	144	0	0
80 acres peafe; 40 failed, 40 at 10 bush. 400 bush. at 1s. 3d.	25	0	0
Cattle,	87	10	0
150 acres clover, 2 potatoes, 20 barley, 20 oats, 10 Indian corn, 2 wheat, 38 turneps, } for plantation,	0	0	0
560 acres in culture.	£. 901	10	0

	l.	s.	d.
First year,	291	15	0
Second,	681	10	0
Third,	901	10	0
Lumber,	951	8	6
	2826	3	6
Capital,	3367	0	0
Product first three years,	2826	3	6
Remains,	540	16	6
Three years interest,	504	0	0
	£. 1044	16	6

800 acres were foon in culture, which were
ufually employed in the product of

8 acres

3 acres potatoes, - - - -	£. 50
100 do. Indian corn, - - -	300
100 do. wheat, - - - -	300
40 do peafe, - - - - -	60
400 do. clover,	
20 do. barley,	
20 do. oats,	
80 do. turneps,	
32 do. fundries, including orchard and yielding,	
Cattle, - - - - - -	200
Fruit, - - - - - -	25
Annual lumber, - - - -	60

$$\begin{array}{r} 995 \\ \text{Expences,} \quad - \quad - \quad - \quad - \quad - \quad 454 \\ \hline \text{Profit } £. \ 541 \end{array}$$

This profit is, befides the annual improvement of wafte, from which the lumber is cut, and alfo the advantage of the furrounding waftes, which are granted as faft as the family increafes; but which will not admit of calculation, becaufe waftes are converted to profit merely in proportion to the ability, that is the money, of the planter.

The firft obfervation I fhall make on this account, is the lumber paying nearly the expence of clearing, which is an high advantage, and certainly owing to the expedition of the faw-mill: in many parts of the northern provinces, where a faw-mill is not ufed, the expence of clearing is infinitely the greatest part of a new settler's work. But it is plain from every article in this account, that the great advantage in settling, is the command of a large sum of money, that the planter may go spiritedly to work, and make his ground produce him something considerable immediately, which can never be done if he has not money enough to clear away the woods speedily. Half this capital I am clear would not yield a proportionable profit; on the contrary, it might not afford half such interest for the amount. It is by means of this advantage, that near two thirds of the whole expenditure is repaid by the product of the three first years, which would be far enough from the case, if the sum of money at the beginning of the undertaking had been much less. If the planter's time and trouble, for three years, be not reckoned, as indeed it need not in reason be, then the sum of 1044 l. might be reckoned the original capital, which would make the annual profit on the undertaking immensely great.

But the great superiority of the account of this improvement, over those that can be made in the cultivated parts of Europe, is the *increase* of cultivation. The account

here

here is stated at 800 cultivated acres, and 60 l. a year from lumber; but this does not include the annual increase of the cleared land, which may be carried on as fast as the planter's money will allow. Instead of 60 l. a year in lumber, it might be 2 or 300 l. by having hands enough, and the land, when cleared, all brought into culture, at the same profit as the first 800 acres; the quantity of land to be had does not stop, let him be as able and industrious as he will. This advantage I think greater even than the making the profit above stated.

For here let us consider, that in the cultivated parts of Britain, or any other European country, a farmer, who is on such a farm as 3000 l. will stock, supposing him to make as great an advantage as this planter, lies under two disadvantages; tho' he has this neat income of 541 l. per annum from his business, he lives in a country where such an income is very easily spent, even by a farmer, and actually is spent by many farmers, without their making in any respect the appearance of gentlemen, which is owing to the luxury of the age, and the high prices of every thing in the country. Secondly, if on the contrary he

I 2

does

does not spend such an income, but lives
frugally on a part of it, and is desirous of
expending the remainder to the best advantage, he cannot throw it into an annual
increase of his business, because he is on
every side surrounded by the farms of his
neighbours; and though he may now and
then hire other farms, it is not to be depended on; and if they do not join his
old one he will be better without them;
besides the circumstance of such farms
being probably either too large, or too
small for the money he has to spare: so
that the only advantage he can, in a general way, put his savings to, is the common interest of four or five per cent.

The case of the New York planter is very
different. For first he makes his income of
541 l. a year, in a country where money
is so dear, and most things so cheap, that
he may live upon a part of it in a way far
more genteely, upon a comparison with all
his neighbours, than he could do with
twice the total in England, the consequence
of which must naturally be a far greater
probability of a person's saving at least a
part of his income, than if he lived where
the whole of it would hardly support him.
Secondly, upon the supposition of his spend-

ing

ing only a part of his income, he has the advantage of being able to throw the remainder, like a merchant, immediately into bufinefs, and to make it pay him as good intereft for his money as his original ftock. He has only to increafe his fervants, his cattle, and his works proportioned to the fum of money he has annually to lay out, which gives a proportioned increafe of land under culture, and confequently an increafe of crops to fell : this refults from his fettling in an uncultivated country, and is upon the whole, fo great an advantage, that it overbalances an hundred inconveniences. For by means of this circumftance, the planter is able to make a continued compound intereft of all the money he can raife, at the rate of from 40 to 100 per cent. till he has enlarged his cultivation fo much as to be incapable of management. The immenfe increafe of compound intereft is well known, yet ought not the reader to ftartle at the propofition : fuppofe the planter lives upon, or, more properly fpeaking, fpends in manufactures, wine, tea, fugar, fpices, and fpirits, 24 1l. per annum, he has then 300 l. per annum for improvements ; which 300l. the firft year, will clear a certain portion of wafte

I 3 (the

(the lumber nearly paying the expence)
cultivate, stock, and convert it to saleable
crops. From that time, this portion of
land becomes equally profitable with the
rest of the farm, and yields a proportionable advantage: this profit is the next year
added to the 300 l. and a still larger piece
taken in, which still yielding its profit, like
the rest, the accumulation continues; and
the annual amount of savings grows incef-
santly; being, to all intents and purposes,
plainly a compound interest.

But here let me observe, that this prodigious advantage is not annexed to the
mere settling in New York; on the contrary, the cultivated parts of the province
are in this respect exactly upon a par with
Britain; for fixing in a plantation, in that
part of the province, would be fixing in a
spot surrounded with other plantations, and
consequently possessing no great part of this
advantage which I have been endeavouring
to explain. It is only in the back country, which is yet forest, that new settlers
can find plenty enough of land to be secure
of those additions to their farms, which
are attended, when made, with such benefit. Nor is it only in this respect that the
waste country is the most eligible to settle

in;

in; there is fo much greater choice of land through fuch parts of the province than in the other, and the land of courfe fo much better, that although plantations are often to be bought cheap in the cultivated parts, yet is it more advifeable for thefe reafons to fettle in the back country; always provided there is a navigation near the farm, for all land products are in America, too cheap to bear a land carriage.

This comparifon between New York and Britain is fo much in favour of the former, that I think it is neceffary to make fome obfervations upon that part of the ftate of agriculture in Britain, which gives fuch a fuperiority to America: not that I fhall enter into a full calculation of this point. But at prefent I muft obferve, that the reafon of this inferiority of Britain is not a want of land—for the waftes of this country including thofe of Scotland and Ireland, amount probably to more than a third of the whole territory; nor is it a want of fertility in thofe lands, but it is the mifchief of being in hands that will neither cultivate them themfelves, nor yet let others. A man may in New York, &c. have land in fee-fimple for demanding it, and complying with certain reafonable con-

ditions,

ditions, which leave him abfolute mafter of the foil for ever. In Britain he may apply for wafte land, and he will be anfwered that he fhall have a leafe of 21 years, perhaps only of 7 or 14; and upon fuch a leafe he is to build, without a ftick of timber, and enter into very great expences: this at once banifhes the fcheme in any prudent perfon, and makes any common hufbandry more profitable. Thus is it found, that when the waftes in a country are in private hands, they are like to remain fo, except what a few fenfible active individuals do upon their own eftates, which bears fcarcely any proportion to the quantity that remains wafte. This is of moft pernicious influence upon the public good, which is fo intimately concerned in all waftes being cultivated. No man ought in fuch a wealthy, induftrious country as Britain, where every product of the earth bears fuch an high price, to be allowed to keep wafte lands in his poffeffion above a certain number of years; if by a given time they are not in culture, or at leaft a confiderable part of them, and the work going on, then they ought to be forfeit and affigned in the American manner to whoever will comply with the terms of the grant. Doubtlefs, this will appear

to

to the generality of the people in this country as a very wild fcheme; and fo it may
be, but neverthelefs the evil is not lefs real,
nor does it lefs demand a remedy. Were
the waftes of Britain to be granted away
in fmall portions, in the fame manner as
thofe of America, we fhould fee them
peopled, and as well cultivated as the reft
of the kingdom; notwithftanding the general want of timber on them, and their
not being equal in fertility to the woodlands of America. And here I muft further
obferve, that this ftate of the cafe fhews
the great reafonablenefs, and even importance of ftrenuoufly infifting on the new
and old fettlers in all parts of the continent,
performing their conditions of taking no
more land than they people in the required
proportion. Letting any perfons take up
more land than they can moderately people,
is bringing the fame mifchievous confequence on America, that we experience in
Britain; for the waftes in America that are
private property, are of little more ufe to
the public than if tHey did not exift.

The account of a fettlement given above,
is not to be fuppofed a picture of the profit,
which every one makes by going to New
York; I would on no account, have it
imagined

imagined that this is the cafe: this was executed by means of a large fum of money, for fo 3000l. muft be reckoned in America; and not only by a fum of money, but alfo by the exertion of much better hufbandry than is common in the colonies. So far from every fettler making a profit like this, not one in forty equals the proportion of it. In general, the fettlers come with a fmall fum of money, very many of them with none at all, depending on their labour for three, five, or feven years to gain them a fum fufficient for taking a plantation, which is the common cafe of the foreign emigrants of all forts. It is common to fee men demand, and have grants of land, who have no fubftance to fix themfelves further than cafh for the fees of taking up the land; a gun, fome powder and fhot, a few tools, and a plough; they maintain themfelves the firft year, like the Indians, with their guns, and nets; and afterwards by the fame means with the affiftance of their lands; the labour of their farms, they perform themfelves, even to being their own carpenters and fmiths: by this means, people who may be faid to have no fortunes, are enabled to live, and in a few years to maintain themfelves and families

milies comfortably. But such people are
not to be supposed to make a profit in cash
of many years, nor do they want, or think
of it. And as to the planters who begin
their undertakings with small sums of money ; though they do better, and even make
a considerable profit by their business, yet
are they very far from equalling what I have
now described ; this is for want of money,
for I might add, that not one new settler in
a thousand is possessed of a clear three thousand pounds.

The conclusion which I deduce from
these particulars is, that new settlements
in New York are undertaken to good advantage, profit in money considered, only by
those who have a good sum of money ready
to expend ; and by this term, I mean particularly men who have from two to five
thousand pounds clear; in Britain such people cannot from the amount of their fortune get into any valuable trade or manufacture, unless it is by mere interest, or
being related to persons already in trade.
But it is evident, that in New York, they
may, with such a sum of money, take,
clear, stock, and plant a tract of land that
shall not only amply support them in all
the necessaries of life, but at the same time
yield

yield a neat profit fufficient for the acquifition of a confiderable fortune.

I fhall next lay before the reader the
exports of this province as taken on an
average of three years fince the peace.[*]

Flour and bifcuit 250,000 barrels, at 20s. £.	250,000
Wheat 70,000 qrs. - - - - - - -	70,000
Beans, peafe, oats, Indian corn and other grains,	40,000
Salt beef, pork, hams, bacon, and venifon,	18,000
Bees wax 30,000 lb. at 1s. - - - - -	1,500
Tongues, butter, and cheefe - - - - -	8,000
Flax feed, 7000 hhds. at 40s. - - - -	14,000
Horfes and live flock - - - - - - -	17,000
Product of cultivated lands, - - - -	418,500
Timber planks, mafts, boards, flaves, and } shingles - - - - - - - - -	25,000
Pot afh, 7000 hhds. - - - - - - -	14,000
Ships built for fale, 20, at £700. - - - -	14,000
Copper ore, and iron in bars and pigs - -	20,000
£.	526,000

Let me upon this table obferve, that far
the greater part of this export is the produce of the lands including timber; and
even the metals may be reckoned in the
fame clafs; this fhews us that agriculture
in New York is of fuch importance as to
fupport the moft confiderable part of the
province without the affiftance of either

---

[*] *American Traveller*, p. 73.

the

the fishery or of commerce; not that the
city of New York has not traded largely,
perhaps equal to Boston, but the effects
of that trade have been chiefly the introduction of money by the means of barter,
besides the exportation of their own products : whereas New England's exports
consist five parts in six of fish, and the other
products of the fishery; a strong proof that
agriculture is far more profitable in one
country, than in the other; for settlers in
colonies will never take to the sea, in a
country whose agriculture yields well; but
in very bad climates, and such as destroy
instead of cherishing the products of the
earth, any branch of industry pays better than
cultivating the earth. This is a distinction
that ought to be decisive with those who
have a choice to make which of these colonies they will go to; for men do not usually settle themselves in countries where
they are to make their livelihood by en-
countering a boisterous sea, and leading a
life of perpetual hardships and violent labour: This is very different from the employment of those who support themselves
in so fine a country as New York, by agriculture.

C H A P.

CHAP. X.

*Propositions for the improvement of the hus-
bandry of New York—Bad management
—Better system—Vines—Winter food of
cattle, &c.*

THE rural management in most parts
of this province is miserable: se-
duced by the fertility of the soil on first
settling, the farmers think only of exhausting it as soon as possible, without attending to their own interest in a future
day: this is a degree of blindness which in
sensible people one may fairly call astonishing. The general system is to crop their
fields with corn, till they are absolutely
exhausted; then they leave them, what
they call fallow, that is, to run to weeds
for several years, till they think the soil has
recovered somewhat of its fertility, when
they begin again with corn, in succession,
as long as it will bear any, leaving it afterwards to a fallow of weeds. If no spontaneous growth came, but such as cattle
would freely eat, the evil would not be
great,

great, becaufe then the land would not
have more to fupport than it would gain
by the dung, &c. of the flock fupported.
But the contrary is the cafe : an infinite
quantity of rubbifh comes which no beaft
will touch, this feeds the land in fo conftant a fucceffion, that the foil is never
without a large crop on it. The extent to
which this practice is carried would aftonifh
any perfon ufed to better hufbandry : it is
owing to the plenty of land ; the farmers,
inftead of keeping all their grounds in good
order, and a due fucceffion of valuable
crops, depend on new land for every thing,
and are regardlefs of fuch management as
would make their old fields equal the value of the new ones.

Inftead of this, the New York farmers
fhould imitate the conduct of thofe of Britain : they fhould never *exhauft* their lands;
and when they were only *out of order* they
fhould give them what ought to be efteemed the moft beneficial fallow; that is,
crops which, while growing, receive great
culture, at the fame time that they do not
much exhauft the foil ; fuch as all forts of
roots, and pulfe, and every kind of leguminous plant, with the various kinds of
clovers. By introducing thefe in proper
fuc-

fucceffion, the land is never exhaufted.
In the remarkable inftance given of a plantation managed on this fyftem, we find
a crop of this nature introduced between
every two of maize, wheat, barley, or oats,
and in every round of the fyftem, feveral
years under clover, which is inftead of
the fallow of weeds of the generality of
the New York farmers.

The benefit of purfuing this plan is very
great; for the lands, when laid down to
clovers, maintain more cattle on fifty acres
than with weeds they would on four hundred; this quantity of cattle improves the
ground by the fummer feeding, and enables the farmer to raife great ftore of manure in the winter, by which means his
crops of corn, &c. are by much more a-
bundant. It further keeps the whole
plantation in a ftate of profit; whereas
in the common method only a part, and
that not the largeft, is valuable at once,
his dependence for product being only on
the new broken up-lands.

Another part of hufbandry, in which the
New York farmers are very defective, is
the management of their meadows and
paftures: they make it a rule to mow
every acre that is poffible for hay; and as
long

long as they get a tolerable *quantity*, they are ftrangely inattentive to the quality; weeds, ruſhes, flags, and all ſorts of rub-biſh, they call good hay, and ſuppoſe their cattle have not more ſenſe in diſtinguiſhing than themſelves. This is owing alſo to their graſping mere extent of land, and caring but little for the good huſbandry of it. Many of their meadows are marſhes, which, with little trouble, might be drain-ed, and at once improved prodigiouſly, yet are ſuch undertakings very ſeldom ſet about: others of the up-land ſort are e-qually filled with various weeds, from the ſlovenly manner in which they are laid down, or left to clothe themſelves; but the appearance of theſe do not at all ſtartle men whoſe ideas of agriculture are ſo little poliſhed.

In reſpect to the management of cattle, and the raiſing manure, the farmers of New York are equally inattentive with their neighbours of New England.

I before obſerved, that vines of ſeveral ſorts grew ſpontaneouſly in all the woods of this province; and that wine, though bad, had been made of them: their being bad has no weight with me, ſince wild vines in no part of the world produce good wine; but if they would plant vineyards of them, and cultivate them with the same care as is taken in wine countries, I have no doubt but they would produce excellent wine. Some endeavours have been made in this branch, by several patriotic persons in this province; but they have all been on the scent of bringing vines from other countries, scarce any of which ever thrive, and some of them will not live: the frosts are so excessive cold in winter, that these foreign vines, used to so different a climate, either come to nothing, or produce a grape very different from what they do in their own country. The instance of the great success with which the Dutch planted French vines at the Cape of Good Hope, proves nothing in this case, because the climate in general, at that Cape, is not only one of the finest in the world, but the winters are mild, and in every respect different from the peculiar climate of North America.

But good culture, and a proper choice of a high dry situation, of which there are plenty in this province, and even rocky ones, would in all probability be attended with success, and make these native grapes yield a wine that would add infinitely to the

the value of the exports of the province. This is an object of too much importance to be left to the dilatory proceedings of the planters themfelves; they are in general engaged in a plain line of hufbandry, from which moft of them have not the rapacity or knowledge to deviate, and the reft want money for it. But the government fhould order a vineyard to be planted under the direction of an overfeer fkilled in this branch of agriculture, and alfo by the fame means take care that it was cultivated in perfection. The expence of this would not be great.

CHAP. XI.

NEW JERSEY.

Climate, foil, and productions of New Jersey — Agriculture — Defects — Improvements proposed — The people.

THE climate of New Jersey much resembles that in the southern parts of New York; they have sharp frosts in the winter, though rather less so than in that province, and the heat is sometimes very great in summer; but the air is clear, dry, and pure, and much superior to the more southern sea coasts, where are many swamps; in New Jersey scarce any of these are to be found, and consequently it is much the more healthy to the inhabitants.

There is another difference in the climate of these two provinces, which has an intimate connection with husbandry, the winters being so much milder, as to allow the cattle being left out all winter. Mr. Kalm took notice of this (which I before remarked was not the custom in New York.)

Not-

Notwithstanding, says he, it snowed several days and nights together, and the snow lay six inches high upon the ground, yet all the cattle are obliged to stay, day and night, in the fields, during the whole winter. For neither the English nor the Swedes had any stables, but the Germans and the Dutch had preserved the custom of their country, and generally kept their cattle in stables during winter. Almost all the old Swedes say, that on their first arrival in this country, they made stables for their cattle, as is usual in Sweden; but as the English came and settled among them, and left their cattle in the fields all winter, as is customary in England, they left off their former custom, and adopted the English one. They owned, however, that the cattle suffered greatly in winter, when it was very cold, especially when it froze after rain; and that some cattle were killed by it in several places, in the long winter of the year 1741. About noon the cattle went into the woods, where there were yet some leaves on the young oak; but they did not eat the leaves, and only bit off the extremities of the branches, and the tops of the youngest oaks. The horses went into the maize fields, and ate the dry

K 3   leaes

leaves on the few ſtalks which remained. The ſheep ran about the woods and on the corn-fields. The chickens perched on the trees of the gardens at night, for they had no particular habitation. The hogs were likewiſe expoſed to the roughneſs of the weather within a ſmall incloſure *.

The ſoil in general is ſandy, and upon the whole inferior in fertility to both New York and Penſylvania; it is an error in ſeveral writers, who have treated of the agriculture, &c. of theſe provinces, to claſs them together; for the ſoil on the ſides of the river Delaware, which parts this province from Penſylvania, is quite different; on the New Jerſey ſide it is all ſandy, and on the other ſide it is loam and clay.

The products are the ſame with thoſe of New York, both in corn, and roots, and fruit, excepting that peaſe are found to thrive much better in the latter; and the peaches of New Jerſey are of a finer flavour than thoſe of New York.

On the moſt ſandy parts of the province, and which to appearance are very poor, they cultivate maize to advantage; and on

* *Kalm's Travels into North America*, Vol. II. p. 51.

this

this fand it grows eight feet high ; but in
the cultivation of it they are very inattentive to its nature; fowing rye broad caft
between the rows, which precludes that
weeding and hoeing, which is fo neceffary
to this plant. The afparagus plant is a
common weed in maize plantations here,
which, fowing rye, prevents the farmer
from eradicating. Others, yet more flovenly, mark out the hillock for fowing the
maize, and leave the intervals of five or fix
feet untouched. About New Brunfwic,
Amboy, &c. and many tracts on the river
Rareton, the foil is much richer, and the
maize is finer : about this part the country
is in general beautifully variegated, and almoft entirely cultivated.

Buck-wheat is very generally cultivated
in New Jerfey, they find it pays them
even as well as wheat, by its fuperior produce: they never give any other preparation to
the land for it than one or two ploughings,
and harrow in the feed, about a bufhel and
half to the acre, which yields them, if
the feafon is wet, for dry years do not fuit
it, from 30 or 40 bufhels on good land,
and very feldom lefs than 28. They make
bread, or, more properly fpeaking, cakes of
it, which are eaten by every body, but its

K 4   prin-

principal ufes here, as in Europe, are for fattening poultry and hogs.

Rye is a common crop in New Jerfey, which is rather furprifing, for wheat yields as good products. What is extraordinary, the farmers in this country fow lefs feed rye than in England, where two bufhels are the common quantity for an acre, but here they fow only one; they commonly receive twenty in return. Barley is cultivated in common over the whole province; they fow two bufhels an acre, and receive from 30 to 50 bufhels; this feems to be the grain which thrives better in the province than any of the European ones.

All the bread-corn of this country yields fufficient, in the very worft feafons, to feed the inhabitants; and not only to feed them, but at a reafonable and equable price: the bread eat by the loweft ranks, whether of maize, wheat, or rye, is of the fineft fort that can be gained from the grain; nor is the crop in general ever known fo fcanty as materially to affect the market price, which is greatly owing to the conftant and regular exportation which always goes forward.

Cabbages are lately cultivated here by almoft every planter in the province, the

fort

fort is the great white winter cabbage; it is not found only in gardens, but whole fields of it are common; it is eat in large quantities in every family, but the cows get no flight portion of the crop; for hogs alfo they are much efteemed. There are no tracts of good land in this province, without having portions affigned to the culture of hemp; which does extraordinary well here. To the north of New Jerfey, the pieces fown with this plant are but fmall, but here, large fields of it are every where to be feen, which is a profpect that ought not a little to endear us to this country, for no ftaple produced in America, not even fugar, is more valuable. Unfortunately they no-where produce more than is fufficient for home confumption; but this I apprehend, is owing to a want of fufficient encourage-ment; no object can demand it more, or pay us better for it, yet has not the legiflature hit upon the proper · effective means for extending the culture, fo as the mother country, as well as the na-vigation of New York and Philadelphia, may profit by it: an object which one can-not apprehend fo difficult as this negligence might make us believe.

In

In the moſt ſouthern parts of the province, ſaffron is commonly planted; but the drug produced is not reckoned ſo good as that which is the product of England: this is not to be attributed to either ſoil or climate, for both ſuit it in an extraordinary degree; but they are not careful enough in the culture, nor in the manufacture of the commodity after it is produced: they do not weed the crops with that aſſiduous care which the planters of Cambridgeſhire and Flanders exert, and which ſeems to be eſſential to the ſucceſs; nor are they equally attentive to curing, drying, and caking of it.

They have, in various parts of New Jerſey many tracts of meadow land, much of which is marſhy; they mow them twice a year, about the latter end of May, and the end of Auguſt or beginning of September; they get large crops of hay, ſome yield three tons an acre at the two mowings, but it is of a coarſe ſort: however the produce is of great value in a country where the general fault is the not laying in ſtore of winter proviſion for cattle. But there is a general fault here in the management of all graſs lands, which is letting poor and indifferent ſorts of graſs occupy ground that would yield much better ſorts: the marſhes produce

duce nothing but the *Carex*. Another circumstance which should not be forgotten,
is the planters neglecting the artificial grasses,
which they might have upon their uplands,
from their dependence upon these marshes;
this has another bad consequence in making the farmers adopt a worse system than
they otherwise would; for such farmers as
have some marsh land, have no notion of
sowing the clovers upon their arable fields,
by way of a fallow; which one would suppose they must do, rather than leave them
to rest without any other crop than weeds.
This dependence on marsh land, however, by
no means proves answerable to their cattle,
for in no province are all the four-footed
animals worse treated.

Every farm in New Jersey has a large orchard belonging to it, some of them of a
size far surpassing any thing in England.
The common fruits are apples and peaches,
with some cherries and pears; the peaches
are of a fine flavour, and in such amazing
plenty that the whole stock of hogs on a
farm eat as many as they will, and yet the
quantity that rot under the trees, is astonishing. Apples are not suffered to go to such
waste as they make cyder in vast quantities, and also export them by ship-loads to
the

the West Indies. This favourable climate to fruit is a circumstance of great importance to all ranks of people, especially the lower ones that settle there; since it gives them a plenty of one article of food, very wholsome in this climate, without the least expence or trouble. Water melons also are in such plenty, that there is not a farmer, or even a cottager without a piece of ground planted with them: in some parts of the province they have whole fields of these and gourds. The country people eat them as they do in Naples and the Ecclesiastical State, at all times of the day while they are at their labour, when thirsty; in the same manner as a labourer in England would drink ale or small beer; with this difference, that the fruit never intoxicates, and if taken with any tolerable moderation is perfectly wholesome.

In a word, I must observe, that the plenty of all the productions of nature which contribute to the food of mankind, which abounds in this province, is equal to what can be expected or wished for by any one: this is owing to the regularity of the summer season; the summer frosts are of no account, they have no cold nights, the rains are not excessive, nor are they hardly ever

ever troubled with a drought; thefe important circumftances are of fuch effect, that the farmers are reaping or gathering fome crop or other in every month from May to November.

In refpect of timber, their woods yield them all the trees that are found to the northward : with the circumftance of being plentifully ftored with fome of the moft valuable forts ; among thefe the white cedar figures particularly; being the moft ufeful of all their trees. They ufe it in building preferably to oak, from its lafting longer, and the fhingles made of it furpafs all others; they are more durable at the fame time that they are lighter, circumftances invaluable in fhingles, where they have fcarcely any other covering to their houfes. All the churches, and the houfes of the principal people have no other roofs.
Of this tree is alfo made the beft rails for fencing; nor are the pofts of it bad, as it long refifts putrefaction ; great numbers of hoops are alfo made of it, and likewife ftaves. But confidering the value of this tree, the people of New Jerfey are very deficient in their care of it ; the farmers and fettlers feem to make little account of it, but deftroy all with the fame relentlefs

feverity

severity that is common throughout all our colonies. The saffafras in much less valuable, yet they leave that standing singly about their cleared fields.

Having thus particularized the principal products of the country, I shall, in the next place, offer a few remarks on the defects in the management of the farmers which are most striking; since it is only by properly attending to these, that future improvements are to be expected. First I shall observe, that their culture of maize deserves much reprehension: so luxuriant a vegetable demands great attention in the management while growing, particularly in the articles of keeping the plants quite clean from weeds, and ploughing the spaces between the rows often enough to keep them fine and well pulverized; instead of which I have before observed, that they sow rye in them, or else leave them to a crop of weeds; this is miserable management, and such as tends strongly to keep the ground in that bad state, which is a general enemy to all improvement; maize is of itself a very exhausting plant, and requires all the nourishment that can be given to it, this nourishment is not manure only, but the hoeings and ploughings which surround the

plant that keep the land loose, and kill all
the weeds, and for this purpose there is no
article of culture that is better adapted than
one which will admit being planted at the
distance of six or eight feet *square*; for if
the rows only were so far asunder, and the
plants thicker together, they then could receive only the common horse hoeing, which
would not be near so efficacious : it was
certainly with this intention that good farmers first used this method of planting, nor
could there well be a greater perversion of
the method than keeping to the distances,
and instead of ploughing, cropping them
with rye.

I need not observe here, that in all countries one great principle of husbandry is the
procuring and using as much dung and manure as possible; the farmers of New Jersey cannot raise hemp for exportation in
large quantities, for want of more manure;
yet do they give into one practice which is
very negligent : they leave the straw of most
the buck-wheat they cultivate about their
fields in heaps, they find their cattle will
not eat it, and so think there is no other use
for it ; but surely these men might reflect
on the importance of *litter*, as well as *food*
for cattle; in the consumption of their hay

8   and

and other straw they might certainly use
far more than they have, or perhaps can
have; but to possess it on their own farms
without using it, is unpardonable; nor is it
a universal practice, which keeps the whole
country in countenance, for there are some
planters who have better ideas, use all their
straw carefully for litter; and the advantage
which these men reap from the practice
ought surely to make the rest follow their
example. There is no error in husbandry
of worse consequence than not being sufficiently solicitous about manure; it is this
error that makes the planters in New Jersey,
and our other colonies, seem to have but
one object, which is ploughing up fresh
land. The case is, they exhaust the old as
fast as possible till it will bear nothing more,
and then, not having manure to replenish
it, nothing remains but taking new land to
serve in the same manner. Whereas would
they be properly attentive, raising as much
manure as possible, at the same time that
they introduced their crops in a proper
system, so as to keep the land clean and in
heart; in this case they would find no such
necessity of changing the soil: and by the
use of clovers in the manner they are sown
in Britain, all their lands would be in pro-

fit,

fit, and perhaps equally profitable; inſtead of which they have now only a part under the plough that pays them any thing, and the reſt are over-run with weeds and trumpery. One would imagine that the error of ſuch a conduct would ſoon be diſcovered and rectified of itſelf; but the American planters and farmers are in general the greateſt ſlovens in chriſtendom; plenty of land ruins their huſbandry in every reſpect of general conduct—neatneſs—good management—ſpirited attempts, &c. Kalm confirms theſe obſervations, and carries the cauſe back to the firſt coming of the ſettlers; he ſays, " After the inhabitants have converted a tract of land into fields which had been a foreſt for many centuries together, and which conſequently had a very fine ſoil, they uſe it as ſuch, as long as it will bear any corn; and when it ceaſes to bear any, they turn it into paſture for the cattle *(that is, leave it to whatever ſpontaneous growth of weeds comes)* and take new corn-fields in another place where a fine ſoil can be met with, and where it has never been made uſe of for this purpoſe. This kind of agriculture will do for ſome time; but it will afterwards have bad conſequences, as every one may clearly ſee. The depth and rich-

VoL. I.　　　　　L　　　　　neſs

ness of the soil they found here who came
over from England (as they were preparing
land for ploughing which had been covered
with woods from times immemorial) mis-
lead even the English, and made them care-
less husbandmen. It is well known that the
Indians lived in this country for several centuries before the Europeans came into it;
but it is likewise known that they lived
chiefly by hunting and fishing and had
hardly any fields. They planted maize,
and some species of beans and gourds, and
at the same time, it is certain that a plantation of such vegetables as serve an Indian
family during one year, take up no more
ground than a farmer in our country *(Sweden)* takes to plant cabbage for his family
upon, at least a farmer's cabbage and turnep
ground taken together is always as extensive, if not more so than the corn-fields and
kitchen gardens of an Indian family. Therefore the Indians could hardly subsist for one
month upon the produce of their gardens
and fields. Commonly, the little villages
of the Indians are about twelve or eighteen
miles distant from each other. From hence
one may judge how little ground was formerly employed for corn-fields, and the rest
was over grown with thick and tall trees;
and

end though they cleared, as it is ufual, new
ground as foon as the old one had quite loft
its fertility, yet fuch little pieces as they
made ufe of were very inconfiderable when
compared with the vaft forefts which remained. Thus the upper fertile foil increafed confiderably, for centuries together;
and the Europeans, coming to America,
found a rich and fine foil before them, lying
as loofe between the trees as the beft bed in
a garden. They had nothing to do but to
cut down the wood, put it up in heaps, and
to clear the dead leaves away. They could
then immediately proceed to ploughing,
which in fuch loofe ground is very eafy;
and having fown their corn, they got a moft
plentiful harveft. This eafy method of
getting a rich crop has fpoiled the Englifh
and other European inhabitants, and induced them to adopt the fame method of
agriculture which the Indians make ufe of;
that is, to fow uncultivated grounds as long
as they will produce a crop without manuring, but to turn them into paftures as foon
as they can bear no more, and to take in
hand new fpots of ground covered fince
time immemorial with woods, which have
been fpared by the fire or the hatchet ever
fince the creation. This is likewife the

L 2   reafon

reason why agriculture and the knowledge of this useful branch is so imperfect here, that one can learn nothing on a large tract of land, neither of the English nor of the Swedes, Germans, Dutch, and French, except that, from their gross mistakes and carelessness for futurity, one finds opportunities every day of making all sorts of observations, and of growing wise at the expence of other people. In a word, the corn-fields, the meadows, the cattle, &c. are treated with equal carelessness, and the English nation so well skilled in these branches of husbandry is with difficulty found out here. We can hardly be more lavish of our woods in Sweden and Finland than they are here : their eyes are fixed upon the present gain, and they are blind to futurity. Every day their cattle are harassed by labour, and each generation decreases in goodness and size, by being kept short of food as I have before mentioned. On my travels in this country, I observed several plants which the horses and cows preferred to all others : they were wild in this country, and likewise grew well on the driest and poorest ground, and where no other plants would succeed. But the inhabitants did not know how to turn this to their advantage,

vantage, owing to the little account made
of natural hiftory, that fcience being here
(as in other parts of the world) looked upon
as a mere trifle, and the paftime of fools.
I am certain, and my certainty is founded
upon experience, that by means of thefe
plants, in the fpace of a few years, I have
been able to turn the pooreft ground, which
would hardly afford food for a cow, into
the richeft and moft fertile meadow, where
great flocks of cattle have found fuperfluous
food, and are grown fat upon. I own that
thefe ufeful plants were not to be found on
the grounds of every planter; but with a
fmall fhare of natural knowledge, a man
would eafily collect them in the places
where they were to be got. I was aftonifhed
when I heard the country people com-
plaining of the badnefs of the paftures;
but I likewife perceived their negligence,
and often faw excellent plants growing on
their grounds which only required a little
more attention and affiftance from their un-
experienced owners."

The principal improvements wanting
in the agriculture of this province, are
the introduction of fuch general good
management upon the common crops of
the farmers, as to enable them to raife a

L 3   ftaple

staple on some parts of each farm; suppose hemp and flax: at present their conduct is in general so bad, that very many planters cannot raise an acre of hemp, &c. this is owing to the neglects which prevail so much throughout their management; and especially to the badness of their systems: On the contrary, they should adopt the best British husbandry of introducing crops which yield both winter and summer food for cattle, between such as are found most to exhaust the land; an idea, which would in the execution, bring with it a remedy for almost all the inconveniencies they feel at present, suppose they proceed in some such system as this:

1. Maize,
2. Roots for winter food of cattle, or cabbage,
3. Barley or oats,
4. Clovers,
5. Wheat,
6. Buck-wheat,
7. Barley or oats,
8. Roots,
9. Roots,
10. Hemp;

varied in different fields, so that the total quantities of each article might be proportioned

portioned to the fize of the plantation. Two crops of roots both well manured would be a preparation that would bring hemp on all the good and tolerable land in New Jerfey. In this fyftem dung would not be wanting, becaufe there is fo much food for cattle cultivated, that great flocks might be kept, which with a due management of litter would enable the planter to keep his fields always in heart, inftead of the feventh crop of barley, perhaps maize might be thrown in again : it is true, it is a great exhaufter, but then it yields fuch an immenfe quantity of excellent fodder, that, with a proper attention to cattle and dung, I don't know whether it may not more than make amends for that quality. The reader will obferve, that if this fyftem is changed for fuch as are common in Jerfey, of corn in fucceffion till a piece of land is worn out, fo far from being able to have a portion in hemp, they cannot plainly do well even by their corn, fince only the firft crops on a piece of new land enjoy a tolerable preparation. Nothing but fuch an improvement in the general management of common hufbandry in our old colonies, can ever make hemp an article of exportation in them : and a circumftance which is conti-

nually

nually acting even against that, is the vast increase of people, which has of late years so raised the price of grain among them, as to make the culture of it much more profitable than formerly; this perhaps may rise higher still, and if that is the case, it may come to be more profitable than even hemp; which is not so rich a product to the farmer as those may think, who consider only the many hundred thousand pounds that are paid by England for it. Hemp is not near equal to tobacco in profit.

The inhabitants of this province consist almost entirely of planters; and though there are many considerable estates for that country among them, yet in general they are little freeholds, cultivated by the owners; they have no town of any note, New York and Philadelphia being their places of export and import, Perth Amboy not being yet considerable; this circumstance keeps them very much at home and pretty free from luxury, that is from the pleasures of a capital: they live in a very plentiful manner, which indeed they could hardly fail of doing in so plentiful a country; for no where on the coast are the necessaries of life in greater plenty. Fish, flesh, fowl, and fruits, every little farmer

has

has at his table in a degree of profusion; and the lower classes, such as servants and labourers, atizans, and mechanics in the villages are all very well cloathed and fed; better than the same people in Britain. Tea, coffee, and chocolate, among the lowest ranks, are almost as common as tea in England; they are universal articles in every farmer's house, and even among the poor.

CHAP.

C H A P. XII.

PENSYLVANIA.

*Climate of Pensylvania—Soil—Productions
—Agriculture—Defects—Improvements.*

THE climate of Pensylvania has a
strong distinction between the maritime and back parts; the former, for
near a hundred miles, is much like New
Jersey, or rather hotter; but the latter is
more temperate and pleasant, neither so
cold in winter, nor so hot in summer, being in all respects as agreeable and healthy
a climate as can any where be found in
America. The heat in this province is
not sufficient for rice, nor is there that
plenty of swamp land (happily for the inhabitants) that is found more to the south;
tobacco grows well in many parts of it, yet
did it never become a staple, not however
owing to the climate, for in Canada they
have some tobacco. But for wheat and all
kinds of plants, cultivated in Europe, with
fruits, few parts of America exceed the
back country of Pensylvania; that is to
say,

ſay, the hilly (not the mountainous) tracts. The air is very clear and healthy ; the ſky ſerene ; and in general the climate agrees perfectly well with European conſtitutions. In the worſt parts of the province, the winters, though ſevere, conſidering the latitude, do not generally laſt above two months, that is, the ſeaſon of froſt and ſnow. In ſummer, the heats here are great, and almoſt without intermiſſion ; but in the hilly parts theſe heats are, as I before obſerved much moderated : it is owing to this warm ſun, that melons, water-melons, pumpions, and other fruits which here require hot-beds, and ſome that cannot be raiſed with them, grow abroad, and in the common fields in a plenty, and of a flavour much ſuperior to what is found more to the northwards ; and though no better treated than turneps, they are ripe ſo early as July. Cherries are ripe by the twenty-fifth of May, and wheat is commonly reaped before the end of June. The months of September, part of October, April, May, and the firſt half of June, are the fine and agreeable months in this country.

A conſiderable part of the ſoil of this province is a ſand, or light ſandy loam ; theſe prevail chiefly in the maritime parts ;
with

with variations however, for in some large tracts it is a strong loam, and in others clay. In the back parts of the province there are immense tracts of a black mould, and rich loam; and in general the new forest land has several inches, whatever may be the soil, of a light black mould, which is certainly formed in long process of time, by the putrefaction of vegetable substances. The finest parts of the province are the level tracts that join upon the Allegany mountains.

The productions of this country, in corn, timber, and fruits, are nearly the same as those of the Jerseys; only exceeding them in quality and plenty. Vines are in greater abundance, and mulberry trees among the most common in the province. The fruits are finer, and if any thing in greater plenty: hogs are frequently fattened with peaches; for in the orchards they fall in such quantities, that great numbers are left to rot upon the ground.

Wood grows very scarce near Philadelphia, however plentiful it may be in the remoter parts of Pensylvania: the first settlers, with the usual foresight of the Americans, destroyed the timber, as if it was impossible they should ever want any; which,

which, with the continued confumption
ever fince, for building, firing, and by iron
works, have fo leffened it, that wood is
almoft as dear at Philadelphia, as it is in
fome parts of Britain; indeed in winter,
firing is one of the moft expenfive articles
of houfekeeping in that capital. The beft
fuel here is the hickory, a fpecies of the
walnut; then they prefer the white and
black oaks. Notwithftanding the want of
wood here, there are not far from Philadelphia fome very confiderable woods;
but being the private property of people
of fortune, they were referved for many
years, in expectation of that high price
which the commodity now fetches. Within thefe ten years much has been felled,
but there yet remains large tracts full of
very fine timber, which is every day cutting down.

In the productions commonly cultivated,
wheat is the grand article of the province.
They fow immenfe quantities, about the
latter end of September generally; rifing
from two to three bufhels of feed an acre,
which on good lands yield from 25 to 32
bufhels per acre; on fields of inferior quality, or fuch as are almoft exhanfted by
yielding corn, they get from 15 to 25
bufhels,

bufhels, and fometimes not fo much as 15, but this never happens without its being owing to previous bad management. Some few planters have fummer fallow for wheat, in the Englifh manner, but the common preparation is the ground lying what they call fallow, which is the fame management as that of Jerfey and New York; viz. leaving the land, after it is exhaufted by yielding corn, to recover itfelf under a crop of fpontaneous growth, weeds or whatever trumpery comes: or elfe they fow it in fucceffion, after wheat or other corn. It is owing to this general bad management that they get not greater crops; for in the back parts of the province are as fine lands for yielding this grain as any in the world; but foil alone will not do, good culture is no lefs requifite.

Nor is it to be forgotten here, for one fhould not praife or condemn in wholefale, that fome planters have introduced the Englifh way of fowing wheat on clover lays, which has been found one of the greateft improvements that ever were introduced; for by this hufbandry, the lands, at a fmaller expence than ufual, are made to yield much better crops. I may alfo remark, that this moft beneficial practice

en-

encreafes in Penfylvania. It is to be attributed to more enlightened knowledge
fpreading in the province, from the voyages
to Britain being more frequent, and from
books of hufbandry being more read in
proportion to the encreafe of wealth and
luxury : the fame caufes will doubtlefs by
and by operate, however gradually, in introducing other practices, which in Europe
have been found beneficial. I have been
informed, that a gentleman in the back
parts of this province, has introduced the
culture of wheat by the drill plough, which
was invented by Mr. Tull, an Englifh writer, and fince perfected in France by M.
du Hamel : it anfwered greatly ; but the
culture of maize is the completeft horfe-
hoeing hufbandry of all others.

They fow large quantities of rye on their
fandy lands, and on other fields, when they
are exhaufted with wheat ; rye is reckoned
to pay them in fome parts of the province,
as well as wheat.

Barley is alfo a common grain in this
country, though not fo general as in Britain, where it yields the univerfal drink
of all ranks of people ; whereas in Penfylvania, the quantities of cyder made is
prodigious, and rum is confumed in great
quan-

quantities; not however that beer is unknown, oh the contrary they make much,
and cultivate hops alfo with fuccefs. Of
barley they fow four or five bufhels on an
Englifh acre, generally in April, and it is
ripe the end of July. Oats are managed
in the fame manner: the preparation for
both thefe grains is common with that of
wheat, fave their giving wheat the preference in foil, and earlinefs in the fyftem.
They fow them on the American fallow of
weeds; after one another, and very often
after wheat and maize. Barley yields, on
good land, from 30 to 40 bufhels, and on
bad from 20 to 25. Near the Allegany
mountains, on fome frefh land, from 50 to
65 bufhels of barley have been known; a
crop often exceeded in England, where
good management more than ballances the
advantages of foil and climate; 35 bufhels
of oats are reckoned a very good crop.

Maize is not cultivated in fuch quantities in fome parts of Penfylvania, as in more
northern colonies, where wheat is not fo
common. Here is a field of it near every
farm houfe, but fmall in proportion to
what is found in New Jerfey, New York,
&c. for the plain reafon, that they cannot
raife wheat to equal advantage. But in
fome

fome parts of this province, particularly the
fandy ones, there are large quantities; they
cultivate it nearly on the fame principles
as in New Jerfey, that is, in a moft incomplete manner: for even rye is fometimes fown in the intervals, which is fuch
a piece of bad hufbandry, as ought to be
banifhed by every man who would pride
himfelf on having ideas of modern culture.
Wheat thriving fo well in Penfylvania,
makes them neglect maize; which is a
much lefs valuable grain: this is a diftinction which fhould always be made; it is
not that maize is not a profitable crop in
itfelf, but their lands will yield one which
is much more beneficial. This will be the
better underftood, when I add, that Indian corn yields but 2s. 7d. a bufhel, when
wheat is at 7s. 6d. both Penfylvania currency; a difference that at once accounts
for the preference in a country that will
yield wheat.

Much greater quantities of hemp and
flax are raifed in this colony than in any to
the northward: this is owing to a more
favourable climate, and to a better foil;
for in the parts of Penfylvania, adjoining
to the Allegany mountains, are very large
tracts of land, which are as favourable to

the production of these plants as can be
wished: it is not want of good land in
certain quantities, nor of climate, that prevents the export of hemp, but the demand
for it at Philadelphia, which exceeds, for
home consumption, what the province can
raise. Improvements might be made, of
which more hereafter, that would enable
Penſylvania to export hemp; but with
out a change in certain branches of rural œconomy, they never will raise this
commodity for exportation. A people
increaſing at ſuch an amazing rate, makes
the neceſſaries of life ſo dear, that no
other huſbandry anſwers ſo well, that
is, they poſſeſs not a ſtaple that will pay
them for a neglect of wheat and common
proviſions. Hemp and flax would be as
proper ones as could be propoſed to this
colony, but they do not pay well enough
to make them ſuch objects as tobacco is in
Virginia; and while that is the caſe, we
may be certain it will never be planted.
Of flax ſeed there goes annually to Ireland
large quantities.

And here I ſhould remark, that they
have in this province a native flax, which
promiſes to be a treaſure. It is a
ſort of *dogs-bane*. The country people
uſe

ufe it inftead of flax, for various domeftic purpofes ; preparing the ftalks of it
in the fame manner as we prepare flax or
hemp. They fpin and weave feveral kinds
of ftuffs of it : it was of this plant that the
Indians made a kind of linen bags, fifhing
net twine, and other manufactures, long
before the Europeans fettled on this continent. It is an idea which ought to be
purfued ; what is at prefent ufed, is nothing but the quantity gathered wild as a
weed ; why not take the hint, and make it
an article of culture ? I have not a doubt
but it would fucceed well, and anfwer all
the purpofes of the real flax, with this infinite advantage, that it is congenial to the
climate, and confequently would thrive
far better than flax, which has been imported here from Europe. Nothing can
argue lefs attention to the agriculture of
thefe colonies, than overlooking the natural productions of the continent, in favour of the tranfplanted ones, which it
would be folly to fuppofe could thrive fo
well ; for the climate of North America
is quite peculiar : even in the fouthern latitude of Philadelphia, which in Europe
hardly knows what a froft is, the cold is
fo fevere, that fhips cannot ftir from that

port

port for at least one month of the winter.
Let us compare this with the same parallel
in Europe, and we shall find the amazing
difference of the two hemispheres. This
ought to teach them the value of those
productions, which are indigenous in the
country : hemp, flax, and vines, are all instances, and striking ones.

Cabbages and turneps are commonly
cultivated in Pensylvania, partly for the
table, and partly for cattle, but by no
means for the latter in the quantities they
ought to be : they raise both of an immense
size, and without any very extraordinary
culture, though they seldom attempt them
without dung. One reason why they are
bad husbandmen, in this respect, is the fa-
vourableness of the climate, which is such
as to allow cattle to be out all winter, and
to pick up their living in the woods ; such
a circumstance must necessarily render the
farmers negligent in raising winter food
for cattle, which for so many reasons is a
point in husbandry so necessary in all sorts
of countries, since none I ever yet heard
of, is, from heat of climate alone, so rich
as to dispense with the want of dung. Another great disadvantage of this neglect of
turneps and cabbages, is the want of them
among

among the fucceffive crops of corn which the Penfylvanian farmers croud upon their land in much too quick a fucceffion,

Mulberry trees are among the moft common productions of the province of Penfylvania; indeed, they are fo plentiful, that filk might be made in any quantities, provided the country was populous enough; but agriculture anfwers fo much better in a country where land is had almoft for nothing, that people cannot make profit by filk worms; at leaft they think fo: yet for curiofity, fome families have kept them, and wound off large quantities of filk, more than fufficient to fhew that any quantities might be made, if the people could or would find time for the bufinefs. Nor do I think that any employment of their time would pay them better; efpecially confidering that fix weeks in a year is all that is required for making filk.

Buck-wheat is not fo commonly cultivated in Penfylvania, as more to the northward; what the reafon for this is I know not, fince it agrees perfectly well with the climate, and produces larger crops than in New York: perhaps they find wheat fo much more profitable than any other pro-

M 3

duct,

duct, that they cultivate it on land, which
more to the northward would be differently employed. They sow about a bushel
and half to the acre, which yields sometimes more than forty bushels, but generally from 30 to 36.

In several parts of Pensylvania, they are
very well acquainted with the husbandry
of watering meadow lands, by conducting
brooks over them; which they do in a
very artificial manner, bringing the water
in little streams along the sides of the hills,
and letting it into the meadows at command. By this management, which agrees
wonderfully in so hot a climate, they mow
three crops a year, whereas without water
they would mow them but once, and at
that mowing not get so much as by the
worst of the present three. This is an improvement well known in many parts of
Europe, particularly on the Thames in
England; in Flanders, in Lombardy, and
in several of the provinces of Spain, but
it is no where practised to more advantage
than in Pensylvania; which is surprising,
considering the very low state in which
most other parts of husbandry is found.

Many of the planters, especially in the
back parts of the province, where the wild

tracts

tracts are adjoining, keep great stocks of
cattle: some of them have from forty to
sixty horses; and four or five hundred
head of horned cattle, oxen, cows, bulls,
calves, and young cattle; they let them
run through the woods, not only in summer, but also in winter; which is a circumstance that makes them very inattentive to the providing winter food: sheep
also they have in great numbers, and tho'
the wool does not equal the best in England or Spain, yet is it much better than is
produced in many of our counties, and
makes cloth that answers exceedingly well
for the general wear of the province, fine
as well as coarse cloths; and accordingly,
almost all the farmers, and their servants,
with the lower classes of other sorts, are
clad in it; they have no lands in the whole
province but what do excellently for feeding sheep, even the very worst tracts maintain great numbers. Sheep are kept in
such numbers, that wool might be a valuable article of exportation unwrought,
and by a proper policy in the mother country, wool might become as good an import from the colonies as any other.

The farmers make their fences like those
to the northward, of planks and posts; but

in thofe parts of the province which have been long fettled, wood is too fcarce for this method, and they have fubftituted live hedges, not however with judgment, for they have taken the privet for this purpofe, which badly anfwers it for want of fpines; they have plenty of hawthorn, but have not yet fagacity to ufe it. They are in general, throughout the province, very carelefs of their fences, which is the confequence of having fuch plenty of land: confiderable plantations, that are not yet all under culture, have no other ring fence than marks fet upon the trees, fo that the cattle turned into the woods may wander into thofe of other men, and others cattle make equal trefpaffes; and if the farm joins the wild country, it is the fame. Some men are even fo carelefs, that when they take in a new field for corn, they will plough, fow, and fometimes reap it before they go about the inclofure, fubmitting to the depredations of cattle, rather than have the trouble of fencing it. There is nothing can give a man, that only travels through a country, fo bad an opinion of the hufbandry of it, as to fee two circumftances; firft, the fences in bad order; and, fecondly, the corn full of weeds. In many parts of Penfylvania, sylvania, a country in which nature has done so much, man will do so little, that both these are almost every where to be seen by every traveller.

Pensylvania is not without negroe slaves for cultivation, though the number bears no proportion to the white servants; it may also be proper to remark, that there are in this province, and it is the same in others, a difference in the white servants; they have, throughout the province, the same sort of servants that perform work in England, that is, hired by the year, in which case, they are washed, lodged, and boarded, but find their own cloaths; an able bodied man, in husbandry, will get from 10 l. to 16 l. a year sterling. Maids will will get so high as 5 l. to 7 l. Another sort of white servants, which are unknown in Britain, are the new settlers that are poor. Very many of these cannot even pay their passage from Europe, which amounts to 10 l. sterling, and agree therefore with the captain of the ship, that he shall sell them for a certain number of years to be servants, in which case the farmers buy them, that is, pay their freight, &c. and this usually puts something also in the captain's pocket, beyond what he
would

would otherwise have. If the paſſenger has
ſome money, but not enough, he is then
ſold for a ſhorter time to make up the ſum.
There are laws in the province to regulate
this kind of ſervitude, which ſeems very
ſtrange to us; the maſter is bound to feed,
clothe, and uſe the ſervant as well as others.
Others that have money enough to pay for
their paſſage, eſpecially Germans, yet will
not pay, but chooſe to be ſold in order to
have time to gain a knowledge of the lan-
guage and the manner of living in the country. Both theſe ſorts of ſervants are greatly
preferred to the common hiring method;
for the wages do not amount to much more
than half the other, and at the ſame time
there is a ſecurity of keeping them, which
with common ſervants is not the caſe; nor
are theſe near ſo induſtrious. Theſe diftinctions in ſervitude are met with in our
other colonies, but they do not occur ſo
often, becauſe for one new comer in them,
there are twenty at Philadelphia.

The agriculture of the province is not
equal to what the preceding productions
would admit of; and to which they might
be encouraged by ſoil, climate, and getting
labour more plentifully than many other
colonies. I have in two or three inſtances
mentioned

mentioned bad management, and shall in speaking of their general conduct shew others.

Their system which is a point of so much importance is like that I have mentioned more than once to the northward. They sow a piece of land with wheat till it will bear wheat no longer, then they sow barley on it till it will bear that no longer, and perhaps after that they will do the same by various crops of oats, buck-wheat, pease, &c. The following is the system that was pursued in a large new field in a plantation near Durham about fifty miles to the north of Philadelphia, the account was given me, among several others concerning the same plantation, by a person on whose accuracy I can depend.

1. Wheat,
2. Wheat,
3. Maize,
4. Wheat,
5. Wheat,
6. Barley,
7. Barley,
8. Barley,
9. Oats,
10. Barley,
11. Buck-wheat,

12. Barley,

12. Barley,
13. Oats,
14. Peafe.

This is not only a proof of the planter's bad hufbandry; it is alfo a proof of what excellent land it muft be to yield fuch a fucceffion of crops in plenty, enough to induce a man to fow them. After this fyftem for fourteen years, it was left what they call a fallow for feven years more; that is, the land unploughed for whatever fpontaneous growth comes; for fome years there is nothing but weeds, but there afterwards appears fome graffes thinly fcattered which cattle eat, many forts of fhrubs and trees alfo fpring up, which the cattle feed on alfo, and if the land was fo to be left for twenty or thirty years longer, it would become a foreft.

This abfurd way of having an eye to nothing but exhaufting the land as quick as poffible by conftant crops of corn, is pernicious to their interefts: it is owing as I before faid, to plenty of land, for new fettlers always take up as much as they poffible can, and far more than they know how to ftock or cultivate: they can afford no care for manuring, nor yet to clear two pieces of ground for corn as long as one

will

will bear it. They clear a field and have
not ftrength of ploughs and cattle, and men
to crop more than that; they therefore ftick
to it as long as they can get any corn, and
when the land will no longer bear it, they
clear another piece and ferve that in the
fame manner, till they have run through
their whole ground, and then they go back
again to the piece they cleared firft, which
by that time is half foreft, and half weeds
and grafs; this they clear again and fow it
as before with corn as long as it will yield
any. It is very evident that this muft neceffarily be the fyftem while the fettlers
fpend half their fortune in buying the land,
that is, in paying the province fees for it:
if a man has an hundred pounds in his
pocket, and was able with it to cultivate
properly forty or fifty acres; and he takes
three or four hundred, which in patent
fees cofts him half his fortune, he then
plainly leffens his ability to cultivate, while
his cultivation ought to increafe greatly.
The writers on the fubject of hufbandry
give very numerous inftances of this in
England, where farmers are too apt to hire
much more land than they have money to
ftock well and manage properly; no wonder therefore that in America we fhould fee,
the

the fame error, where all forts of people
turn farmers—where no mechanic or arti-
zan—failor—foldier—fervant, &c. but
what if they get money take land, and turn
farmers.

There are very few defects in rural œconomy, but many inftances are here to be
produced; and many of which flow from
the fame caufe as their bad fyftem, viz.
taking too much land for their money;
among which we are to rank their neglect
of the native products of the country, which
might be turned to profit, fuch as flax, vines,
mulberries, &c. The extreme carelefsnefs
every where feen in the whole management
of cattle, their flovenly fences, their utter
inattention to raifing manures, with other
circumftances, not of equal importance.

In this condemnation however, there is
a tract of country around Philadelphia
which is to be exempted: land here is of
fuch value that they think it worth cultivating with fome care. There are feveral
eftates in that neighbourhood, which are
let for twenty fhillings an acre; and which
even at that rent have been fold at twenty-
five years purchafe. But all this is the
neighbourhood of that flourifhing and
wealthy city: it does not hold to any great
distance

diſtance from that place. I muſt alſo exempt the lands of certain gentlemen who
are fond of improvements, and who manage
them in a manner ſuperior to the generality
of farmers, to whom it is a great reflection
that they do not copy ſuch better methods.
Theſe inſtances however are not ſo common
as one could wiſh.

Duly conſidering the ſtate of huſbandry
in this colony, I ſhall venture to propoſe
ſome improvements which I think would
greatly further the intereſts of the inhabitants.

Their ſyſtem is the firſt thing that demands attention, becauſe a thouſand evils
flow from this alone: inſtead of exhauſting
their lands with perpetual corn crops, as
long as it will bear them, they certainly
ought to throw in corn with ſuch moderation as never to exhauſt the ſoil ; to inter-
mix crops of peaſe, buck-wheat, turneps,
cabbages, potatoes, clover, and lucerne
among thoſe of maize, wheat, barley, oats,
and flax ; this would keep the land clean
and in heart ; and when they had kept it in
a ſyſtem of corn as long as they wanted it,
throw in the artificial graſſes, that they
might have at once a good meadow, inſtead
of that miſerable management which they
cal

call a fallow. The land, in their fystem, after it is done with corn, is of no more value than the fky to them, for some years at least; but in the fystem now propofed, they would get meadows that would feed large herds of cattle, or yield at least a ton, or a ton and half of hay per acre immediately. The great advantage of purfuing a fystem of this nature, even upon their own principles, would be, that it admits their fpreading their culture for fresh land in the manner they do at prefent; it only obviates the mifchief arifing from exhaufting it, and leaving it of no value.

In this propofition I mentioned lucerne, a grafs which I am confident would anfwer with them to a great degree, and for feveral reafons. They know not how to raife dung, from the circumftance of their cattle running abroad all the winter; for where cattle are not confined, no dung can be made. The want of dung makes them folicitous for fuch land, and at the fame time much confines their culture; with plenty of it, all their crops would be far more confiderable : another point to be mentioned, is the heat of the climate, in a great meafure, burning up the paftures, (except the watered ones) in all the maritime

time half of the province.: now to remedy all thefe inconveniencies, I propofe lucerne. In that climate, the common broad caft culture would do for it, and perhaps beft. They fhould ufe it for foiling (as the Britifh farmers call the operation) their horfes, cows, and other cattle, under cover all fummer through, keeping them well and regularly littered with ftraw; and if they formed compofts of the dung thus raifed, with marle or loam, in the manner it is practiced in the Weft-Indies, it would be fo much the better.

In this conduct they would, on a fmall quantity of land, be able to keep a large ftock of cattle, which is alone a circumftance of great confequence in any country, and the quantity of dung they would be able to raife, if they ufed litter plentifully, would be of the higheft importance in the management of their farms.

A union of this method with the improvement of their fyftem, mentioned above, would not only vaftly increafe their products of corn, making one acre yield as much as two or three, but would alfo enable them at the fame time to raife ftaples for exportation in a greater plenty than they do at prefent, flax feed being the

VOL. I.   N   only

only one which they raife in their fields;
both flax and hemp might then be valuable articles with them.

In the next place let me obferve, that
their inattention to vines is very inexcuf-
able. In the back country they have hilly,
and even rocky dry tracts of ground, that
would in all probability anfwer perfectly
well for them; their argument, that the
wine made from thefe grapes at prefent is
bad, is not a conclufive one : when planted
in vineyards, and properly trained and
dreffed, with the intervals between the
rows, cultivated as in Europe, the produce
might, and probably would be of a different flavour from the uncultured grapes
now found under the drip of foreft trees.
It is at leaft a point that fhould be tried ;
for though the reafoning of the Penfylvanian farmers will never convince the world,
fair experiment would; the importance of
the object loudly fpeaks the expediency,
not to fay, neceffity of the trial. Another
objection made here, is the want of hands;
but that is obviating every day by extreme
increafe of population : nor do we know,
with any accuracy, that the vineyard culture in America would not anfwer the prefent price of labour; it is to be remember-
ed

ed that they do not require attendance during the whole year, but only at an inconfiderable part of it.

Another improvement which might be made, is the introduction of filk: mulberries are in great plenty throughout the province, and filk has been wound off there, equal to the fineft that comes from India or Italy. The people do not in the leaft pretend that the climate is improper, their only argument is, that the price of labour is too high. But this is as miftaken as any thing that could be urged, for fervants are in no countries hired to make filk; it is a work executed at a certain feafon of the year, which lafts only for fix weeks, by the females of a family, by the young, and aged, that cannot perform laborious work: this is the courfe of the bufinefs in the filk countries of Europe. Silk is a commodity that is never to be adopted, as the principal means of fupporting a people, the time requifite for it is too fhort, as it leaves a fufficiency for other articles. Nothing can therefore be more abfurd than to urge the high price of labour as a reafon why filk cannot be made in this province. Labour is yet dearer in Georgia, but filk is there made in large quantities.

The

The native flax is another article which ought to be attended to by fensible planters in this province. It is amazing to think that more experiments have not been made on it: it is certainly an article that promises great advantages: but trials of a nature more accurate and fcientific than what is to be expected from the planters and farmers of this country. Perfons fhould, by government, be appointed to examine into this matter, and to try what a proper cultivation will do in improving this production.

Thefe and other articles of improvement, for the province of Penfylvania, deferve much more attention than they have hitherto met with. Why cannot the gentlemen of Philadelphia, and its neighbourhood, who are lovers of agriculture, form themfelves into a fociety for the encouragement of that noble art? They might, in monthly meetings, be able to fettle a plan of operations, which would, in a few years, by means of an annual fubfcription, given in bounties and premiums, alter the face of things. They might reduce thefe doubtful points to certainty; they might introduce a better fyftem of rural œconomy, and

and be in a few years of infinite fervice to
their country.

Before I conclude this chapter, I fhall
infert a table of the exports of the province.

Bifcuit flour, 350,000 barrels, at 20s. - - £. 350,000
Wheat, 100,000 qrs. at 20s. - - - - 100,000
Beans, peafe, oats, Indian corn, and other grain, 12,000
Salt beef, pork, hams, bacon, and venifon, 45,000
Bees wax 20,000 lb. at 1s. - - - - - 1,000
Tongues, butter, and cheefe, - - - - - 10,000
Deer, and fundry other forts of fkins, - - 50,000
Live ftock and horfes, - - - - - - 20,000
Flax feed, 15,000 hhds. at 40s. - - - - 30,000
Timber plank, mafts, boards, ftaves, and } 35,000   fhingles - - - - - - - - }
Ships built for fale, 25, at £700. - - -, 17,500
Copper ore, and iron in pigs and bars, - - 35,000

Total £. 705,500

Upon this account I muft obferve, that far
the greateft part is the cultivated produce
of the lands; which is the very contrary
to New England, whofe lands yield nothing to export. In proportion to this
circumftance, is the value of a colony, for
it is the nature of colonization, that the
people ought, on firft principles, to fupport themfelves by agriculture alone.
Wheat appears to be the grand export of
this province: that, and other articles of
food, amount to above half a million, which

N 3   is

is a vast sum of money to export regularly, besides feeding every rank of people in
the utmost plenty; but of late years this
has risen to much more, for wheat, instead
of being at 20 s. a quarter, is at above 30s.
No circumstance in the world can be more
strong, in proof of the temperature, moderation, and healthiness of the climate,
than this of exporting such quantities
of wheat, which, throughout the globe,
thrives no where in climates insalubrious
to mankind: though nearly a universal
grower, yet it is an article of export only
in good and wholesome climates: consider
our European experience, the exports of
wheat are from England and Poland to the
coast of Africa. All the intermediate
countries, from extremity to extremity,
are temperate and fine climates. Barbary,
though hot, is one of the best in the world;
provided (as in all cases of climate) you fix
in the tracts that lie properly with respect
to other circumstances, such as a freedom
from low marshy coasts, which in all countries, especially hot ones, are the most un-
wholesome in the world: hilly and mountainous tracts are generally wholesome and
temperate.

This

This export, of more than seven hundred thousand pounds worth of products, shews of what vast importance this colony is of to Britain; but I must observe, that in a national light it is much to be regretted, that a larger portion of this sum is not in what are commonly called *staples*; that is, products which cannot be raised in proper quantities in the mother country; or which she is forced to buy of foreigners, such are copper, iron, naval stores, flax seed, &c. The Pensylvanian export of these is,

Skins, - - - -	£.	50,000
Flax feed, - - -		30,000
Timber, - - -		35,000
Ships, - - - -		17,500
Copper and iron, - -		35,000
	Total £.	167,500

As to wheat and provision, that part of them which goes to the West-Indies is in the light of a staple, but all that comes to Europe rivals the exports of Britain, and are to be confidered differently. This is a fresh proof of the neceffity of regulating the husbandry of Penfylvania, fo as to enable the farmers to raife more of these

N 4   valuable

valuable products, which are of so great account to the mother country. This is a distinction which is very essential, and which good management may make as much for the advantage of Britain as of the colony *.

CHAP. XIII.

The inhabitants of Penfylvania—Method of living—New settlers—Mode of settling waste tracts—Plantations—Comparison between the husbandry of Britain and Penfylvania.

THIS country is peopled by as happy and free a set of men as any in America. Out of trade there is not much wealth to be found, but at the same time there is very little poverty, and hardly such a thing as a beggar in the province. This is not only a consequence of the plenty of land, and the rate of labour, but also of the principles of the Quakers, who have a con-

---

* For understanding the importance of staples well, consult *Political Essays concerning the Present State of the British Empire.*

sider-

fiderable fhare in the government of the country. It is much to the honour of this fect that they fupport their own poor in all countries, in a manner. much more refpectable than known in any other religion.

There are fome country gentlemen in Penfylvania, who live on their eftates in a genteel and expenfive manner, but the num-. ber is but fmall; many are found, who make much fuch a figure as gentlemen in England of three or four hundred pounds a year, but without fuch a rental; for money is fcarce in this country, and all the neceffaries and conveniencies of life cheap, except labour. But in general the province is inhabited by fmall freeholders, who live upon a par with great farmers in England; and many little ones who have the neceffaries of life and nothing more.

In the fettled parts of the colony, there are few fituations to be found that are without fuch a neighbourhood as would fatisfy country gentlemen of fmall eftates, or country parfons in Britain. There are, befides Philadelphia, many fmall towns in which are found focieties that render the country agreeable; and the country itfelf is fcattered with gentlemen at moderate diftances, who have a focial intercourfe with each other,

other, befides occafional parties to Philadelphia.

The moft confiderable of the freeholders
that do not however rank with gentlemen,
are a fet of very fenfible, intelligent, and
hofpitable people, whofe company, in one
that is mixed, improves rather than leffens
the agreeablenefs of it; a circumftance
owing to many of them being foreigners,
which even gives fomething of a polifh to
the manners when we find ourfelves in the
midft of a country principally inhabited
by another people. The little freeholders
(there are not many farmers, except near
Philadelphia) are in eafe and circumftances
much fuperior to the little farmers in England.

The method of living in Penfylvania in
country gentlemen's families, is nearly like
that of England : the only bufinefs is to ride
about the plantation now and then, to fee
that the overfeers are attentive to it; all the
reft of the time is filled up with entertaining
themfelves; country fports, in the parts of
the province not fully fettled, are in great
perfection; they have hunting, but their
horfes are unequal to thofe of England;
fhooting and fifhing are much more followed, and are in greater perfection than

in

in England, though every man is allowed
both to shoot and fish throughout the province, except the latter in cultivated
grounds. They have partridges, phea-
sants, bustards, wild turkies, wild geese,
ducks, and other water fowl, wood pigeons,
&c. And the rivers are most of them very
full of fish, especially in the back country,
to which parties are made in boats with
nets; in which excursions shooting is
joined: the fish they take are brought home
alive in well-boats, and put into their
stores: every planter has his pond at least,
but generally a chain of them, on a brook,
which always supplies fresh water; in these
stores, as they call them, are kept the products of their river-fishing, ready at all
times for the table.

Their meals are three times a day, and
served quite in the English taste: coffee,
tea, and chocolate, are of the best sorts,
cheap enough to be commanded in plenty
by every planter, especially coffee and chocolate; sugar also is cheaper than in England; these, with good bread and good
butter, give a breakfast superior to what
gentlemen of small estates usually make in
England. For dinner and supper they are
much better supplied, as may easily be

8   sup-

suppofed, when the plenty is confidered that abounds in an American plantation: game, variety of fish, venifon almoft every where, poultry in prodigious plenty and variety, meat of all kinds, very good, and killed on every plantation of any fize; feveral forts of fruits, in a plenty furpaffing any thing known in the beft climates of Europe, fuch as melons, water-melons, and cucumbers, in the open field; apples, pears, cherries, peaches, nectarines, goofeberries, currants, ftrawberries, and rafberries, gathering fome every month, from May till October. Their grapes, though plentiful to excefs, are inferior. Thefe are circumftances that make it neither difficult nor expenfive to keep an excellent table. The wine commonly drank is Madeira, at not more than half the price of England; freight is cheaper, and there is none, or a very trifling duty. French and Spanifh wines are alfo drank; rum is very cheap; and good beer is brewed by thofe who are attentive to the operation.

From hence it is fufficiently clear, that the time paffed at the table need not be a barren entertainment. To this we muft add reading, which fills up fome hours very agreeably; great numbers of books, in-

including all the new publications, are imported from London at Philadelphia; besides which, that city, which has a college and a literary society itself, employs several printers, and sends forth news-papers every day. If to this we add, that there are many families in which music is well understood—that Philadelphia abounds with schools of all sorts, and has a college—that the roads for communication are good—the post regular—and carriers numerous; it will upon the whole be thought that gentlemen of education and ideas may, without any violence on themselves, pass their time on a plantation in Pensylvania, not only in plenty, but agreeably. It must be at once apparent, that a given income would go much further here than in Britain; this is so strongly a truth, that an income of four or five hundred pounds a year, and a plantation, can hardly be spent without extravagance, or indulging some peculiar expence; whereas that income from an estate in Britain will hardly give a man the appearance of a gentleman.

The new settlers upon the uncultivated parts of the province, are either such as go backward to the waste country, and

take

take up what land they pleafe, paying the
fixed fees to the proprietors ; or fuch as buy
uncultivated fpots of other planters, who
have more than they want, or chufe to
fell : in this cafe, they make as good a
bargain as they can ; but the land is dearer
than that which is had of the proprietors.
It is remarkable to fee the fmall tracts that
men will buy with a view to fupport a
whole family.

The progrefs of their work is this ; they
fix upon the fpot where they intend to build
the houfe, and before they begin it, get
ready a field for an orchard, planting it immediately with apples chiefly, and fome
pears, cherries and peaches. This they fecure by an inclofure, then they plant a piece
for a garden; and as foon as thefe works are
done, they begin their houfe : fome are
built by the countrymen without any
affiflance, but thefe are generally very bad
hovels ; the common way is to agree
with a carpenter and mafon for fo many
days work, and the countryman to ferve
them as a labourer, which, with a few
irons and other articles he cannot make,
is the whole expence : many a houfe is built
for lefs than twenty pounds. As foon as
this

this work is over, which may be in a month
or fix weeks, he falls to work on a field of
corn, doing all the hand labour of it, and,
from not yet being able to buy horfes, pays
a neighbour for ploughing it; perhaps he
may be worth only a calf or two and a
couple of young colts, bought for cheapnefs; and he ftruggles with difficulties till
thefe are grown; but when he has horfes to
work, and cows that give milk and calves,
he is then made, and in the road to plenty.
It is furprifing with how fmall a fum of
money they will venture upon this courfe
of fettling; and it proves at the firft mention how population muft increafe in a
country where there are fuch means of a
poor man's fupporting his family: and in
which, the larger the family, the eafier is
his undertaking.

When a fettler is poffeffed of a tolerable
fum of money, as from one hundred to
two hundred pounds, or fuch as begin
with from two to fix or feven hundred, they
reap equal advantages from this plenty of land
and the neceffaries of life, for their money
goes fo much farther; and they are able to
live much better, and in all refpects more
comfortably than upon equal fums in Europe;

rope; that this is the case will be seen from
the following account of a new settlement
formed on the river Scoolkuyl, between 30
and 40 miles beyond Reading near the Kit-
talanny mountains, in one of the most
healthy and beautiful countries in the province. The tract of land was 5000 acres,
which, being part of a large grant not settled,
were purchased. The person who settled
here went from the West of England, his
whole fortune being twelve hundred pounds:
it was some years after the event that this
account was taken; but though it may not
be minutely accurate, yet is it sufficiently
so to explain the expences of forming a
settlement, and also the advantages of laying out such a sum of money.

Freight and expences of three persons from Bristol, - - - - -	£. 57
Expences of a residence at Philadelphia for about half a year, - - -	25
Purchase of 5000 acres - - -	267
N. B. A part of it unprofitable waste.	
Building a very neat house fit for a small family; the expression, such as in England, would let for 20l. a year.	96
Furniture, - - - - - - -	90
Barn, stables, and other offices, - -	22
Two negroes - - - - -	56
Wages for five years, of six German servants bought, - - - - - - -	120

Carried forward 733

```
                    Brought forward,          £. 733·
Cloathing and expences one year,   -  -   ·        32
Implements of husbandry      -       -     ·       70
A boat  ·  -   -   -   -   -   ·  ·   -            10
Arms, ammunition and sundries      ·    ·          9
A year's house-keeping and family expences        112
Live stock, 8 horses, at 4l.   -   -   £. 32
            10 Cows, at 3l.    -   -       30
            30 Young cattle, at 20s.       30
            70 Swine      -    -    ·      16
            50 Sheep      -    -    -      10
            Poultry      -    -    -        5
                                        ———123
Cash reserved for feeding the land, orchards, }
   gardens, and incidental expences    -     }    111

                                           £. 1200
```

The annual expences of the family, &c. were afterwards :

	l.	s.	d.
Labour, in cloathing negroes, wages paid (besides the six Germans) and labourers, - - - -	27	10	0
House-keeping and family expences, -	60	0	0
Repairs of implements and new ones bought,	16	10	0
Expences in building and additions to furniture, &c. - - - -	20	0	0
Province taxes, &c. - - - -	11	11	0
Sundry expences. · - - -	20	0	0
	£. 155	11	0
To which should be added interest of 1200 l. at 5 per cent, - - -	60	0	0
	Total 215	11	0

The product was extremely various, but for several years it ran nearly as follows, none being reckoned but what was sold off the plantation, the increase of cattle was all the time considerable, besides the family living off the land; the 60l. for housekeeping being only for manufactures, India goods, rum, &c.

	l.	s.	d.
220 quarters. of wheat, -	220	0	0
40 quarters of Indian corn, -	14	0	0
100 qrs. of barley, pease, and beans,	46	0	0
Product of cattle sold, - - -	34	0	0
Fruit and cyder, - -	10	0	0
Sundry sorts of lumber, - -	13	0	0
	337	0	0
Expences, - - -	215	0	0
Neat profit. - - £.	122	0	0

Which with the 5 per cent is 182 l. which on 1200l. is 15 per cent. This appears to me to be very considerable, for besides this amount of profit there is to be reckoned the increasing value of the estate, from buildings, fruit-trees, improvements, and the stock of cattle which on all American farms presently quadruple their numbers. What these

thefe articles amounted to cannot be faid,
but muft certainly be confiderable ; this circumftance with that of living in fo plentiful and agreeable a manner, are the
greateft advantages of this country : one
point is however to be attended to, which
is the ability of employing the profit made
in increafing the bufinefs, hiring more fervants and breaking up more land, which
would prefently increafe the profit confiderably.

I am of opinion that 15 per cent is much
exceeded by many farmers in England,
upon a capital of 1200l., but they do not
befides, live in the manner of the Penfylvanian planter, who has at leaft the advantages in houfe-keeping that are enjoyed in
England by a country gentleman of four
hundred pounds a year : this makes a vaft
difference ; and the Britifh farmer lies under the difadvantage like all his brethren of
not being able to increafe his bufinefs : but
what an amazing advantage compared with
this, is the cultivated fpot being in the
midft of 5000 acres all belonging to the
planter, who enlarges his improvements
gradually as fuits him ! this can no where
be had in a country that is all parcelled out
into eftates, except a purchafe is made of a

tract

tract of waste land; which is of a very different price in Britain and America.

Another account I gained of a new settled plantation, was one on a much smaller scale. It was of 300 acres of waste.

	l.	s.	d.
Patent fees on the grant, - - -	30	0	0
Buildings, - - - - -	45	0	0
Implements, - - - -	17	10	0
Two servants bought, - - -	26	0	0
House-keeping, &c. - - -	36	0	0
Furniture, - - - -	25	0	0
Orchard and seed, - - -	13	10	0

	l.	s.	d.			
2 horses, at 3l. 10s.	7	0	0			
4 cows, at 2l. 10s.	10	0	0			
10 swine, at 5s. - -	2	10	0			
Poultry - - -	0	10	0			
				20	0	0

£. 213 0 0

The annual expences were reckoned.

	l.	s.	d.
Taxes and repairs, - - -	3	0	0
Implements, - - - -	5	10	0
Wages and cloathing, - -	16	0	0
Housekeeping, &c. - - -	27	0	0
	51	10	0

The products annually sold in corn and lumber amounted to about 127l. This is very considerable, but the planter and a son both worked almost as hard as his servants.

8   In

In a few years he got almoft the whole grant into culture; purchafed more land, had near a dozen fervants, and above 200 head of cattle. Such a rife is not to be experienced in cultivated countries.

In no territory in the world, I apprehend, can a man with two or three hundred pounds, enter into hufbandry, with fuch a profpect of making a fmall fortune : in England, the fum is nothing; but where there is fuch a plenty of frefh land to be taken up, the cafe is different ; a man's expences are few, he is enabled to fave fomething every year, and every fhilling he faves he can throw into an increafe of culture, which is the greateft inducement to induftry in the world.

My enquiries into the domeftic œconomy of this province has brought me acquainted with another inftance which I fhall lay before the reader. Such accounts form but very unentertaining reading for people who look for amufement alone ; but I cannot help efteeming them as the only means of gaining that fort of intelligence which is truly ufeful. The following inftance was of a perfon who left Scotland a few years ago in order to fettle in this province.

Freight

	l.	s.	d.
Freight from Glafgow to Philadelphia, -	25	0	0
Patent, fees, &c. of 1000 acres, - -	37	10	0
Building a houfe, a barn, a ftable, a cow-fhed, a fruit houfe, a cyder aparatus, a poultry building, a hog-yard and a boat-houfe, - - - - -	136	0	0
Inclofing 86 acres with pofts and planks in three divifions, - - - -	16	0	0
Inclofing 111 acres with live hedge and bank in three divifions, - -	21	0	0
Planting an orchard of 16 acres, containing 16,000 apple trees, 2000 pears 3000 cherries and 3000 peach-trees, -	22	10	0
Expence of the garden, - - -	11	10	0 .
Six negroes, - - - - -	185	0	0
Cloathing and food of ditto for a year, -	22	0	0
One fervant, a foreigner, bought for three years, at 4l. 10s. - - -	13	10	0
Two ditto for 4 years, at 3l. 5s. -	26	5	0
Cloathing a year, - - - -	14	10	0
Furniture, - - - - -	36	0	0
Arms, - - - - - -	6	13	6
Ammunition, - - - -	2	17	0
A fchooner, - - - -	15	0	0
A boat, - - - - -	6	5	0
Implements of planting, - -	38	0	0
A year's houfe keeping - - -	36	0	0
	659	5	0

Live ftock.	
10 cows, at 3l. - - £.	30
10 horfes, - -	50
60 fheep, - -	18
Swine, - -	14
Poultry, &c. - -	2
	114 0 0
Sundries. - - - -	30 0 0
	£ 803 5 0

Product

Product of the firſt year.

	l.	s.	d.
15 acres of wheat, at 2½ qrs. per acre, 37½ qrs. at 20s.	37	10	0
60 acres Indian corn, 40 buſhels per acre, 2400, at 1s.	120	0	0
Cattle,	15	0	0
Lumber	10	10	0
	£. 183	0	0

Product of the ſecond year.

	l.	s.	d.
20 acres of wheat, 2 qrs. per acre, 40 qrs.	40	0	0
40 acres Indian corn, 30 buſhels per acre, 1200 buſhels, at 1s. 3d.	75	0	0
10 acres of barley, 3 qrs. per acre, 30 qrs. at 8s.	12	0	0
15 acres of peaſe and beans, 3 qrs. per acre, 45 qrs. at 10s.	22	10	0
Fruit and cyder,	10	0	0
Lumber,	15	0	0
Cattle,	20	0	0
	£. 194	10	0

Leſt any perſons ſhould be miſled by
theſe accounts of produce, the firſt and ſecond years, I muſt obſerve that many planters receive very little produce the firſt and
ſecond and ſome even the third years,
which is owing to the ground being a thick
wood : theſe and others, who ſoon make a
conſiderable product, are ſuch as get a tract
of meadow, or rather up-land paſture in
their grant, which for profit they plough

O 4　　　　　　　up

up immediately and fow with corn. But at the fame time I fhould obferve, that in this province the expence of clearing, even the thickeft woods, is not great, it is more than repaid in good management, by the lumber which arifes on the land; but for this feveral hands are requifite, which cannot be procured by people who fettle with only fmall fums of money. It is much to be regretted, that the preceding account is not more complete, particularly in the common annual expence and produce: however, it is evident from it, that the profit of the plantation was very foon confiderable.

It is worthy of remark on thefe accounts, that the product feems to be made by the common hufbandry of the province, which is fo far from being perfect. May we not conclude, that the benefit would have been much greater, had a more correct agriculture been practifed? There is the greateft reafon to fuppofe, that a man well acquainted with the true principles of hufbandry fettling in this province, would be able to advance the profit of a plantation much beyond this account.

Having now laid before the reader, upon the beft authority I have been able to

gain,

gain, a ftate of the hufbandry of this province, it remains for me to compare it with
that of Great Britain ; which is one of the
moft important articles of this work, and
indeed of as great confequence as any intelligence that can be laid before the reader, concerning American affairs ; for, unlefs this comparifon is well underftood, it
is impoffible to know the principles upon
which America acts on the population of
Britain.   To find a man equally fkilled in
the hufbandry of both countries is hardly
to be expected ; but though I cannot give
accounts of which I have fuch certainty of
knowing to be accurate, in the cafe of Britain, as in that of Penfylvania, yet as there
are fome late writers concerning the Englifh agriculture, who are acknowledged to
be of undoubted authority, I fhall be able,
by means of their works, to draw up fuch
an account of the profit of hufbandry in
England, as fhall have no material errors
in it, in order to form the contraft to that
of Penfylvania.   Upon thefe authorities,
fuppofe a man, with a certain fum of money, to enter into hufbandry in England,
with a view to make the beft intereft he is
able of his money—I fhall fuppofe with
1200l.

1200l. as that sum has been calculated in the instance of this province. From the accounts we have of British husbandry, we are to suppose that the greatest profit is made by the culture of the best land.

Stock of a farm of 250 acres of rich land.

	l.	s.	d.
Rent, tythe, and parish taxes, of 250 acres at 27 s.	337	10	0
Housekeeping, &c. for one year, -	80	0	0
Eight horses for the culture of 150 acres arable land, at 15l.	120	0	0

Live stock for 100 acres of grass.

	l.	s.	d.
15 cows at 7l. - - - -	105	0	0
10 oxen at 5l. - - - -	50	0	0
20 young cattle at 30s. - - -	30	0	0
10 swine at 10s. - - - -	5	0	0
300 sheep at 10s. - - - -	150	0	0
Poultry, - - - - -	3	0	0
Two men, one maid, and a boy, wages,	27	0	0
Pay of four labourers a year, at 20l. -	80	0	0
Implements of husbandry and harness, -	130	0	0
Seed for the first crop, - - -	40	0	0
Contingent expences, and cash in hand, for advantage of markets, purchase of manure, &c. - - - -	42	10	0
Total £.	1200	0	0

The annual expences.

	l.	s.	d.
Rent, &c. - - - - -	337	10	0
Housekeeping, - - - -	60	0	0
Labour, - - - - -	107	0	0
Carried forward	504	10	0

	l.	s.	d.
Brought forward	504	10	0
Repair of implements, - - -	50	0	0
Ten oxen, - - - - -	50	0	0
Sundry expences, - - - -	30	0	0
	634	10	0
Interest of 1200l. at five per cent. -	60	0	0
Total £.	694	10	0

Annual produce.

	L	s.	d.
The system in which the arable fields are thrown is supposed to be, 1. Turneps, 2. Barley or oats, 3. Clover, 4. Wheat, which we are told is the best husbandry of Britain; upon this system the 37 acres of corn, sown in spring, is to be divided into 30 to sell of barley, and 7 for the teams of oats; 30 at 4 quarters an acre, 120 quarters at 24s. - - -	144	0	0
37 acres of wheat, 3½ quarters an acre, 129 quarters at 50s. - - -	322	10	0
Profit of 15 cows at 5l. - - -	75	0	0
Product of 10 oxen, - - -	100	0	0
Profit on young cattle, - - -	30	0	0
Do. on swine, - - -	35	0	0
Do. on sheep, - - -	130	0	0
Hay sold, - - - -	20	0	0
Profit by poultry, - - - -	10	0	0
Sale of wood, - - -	10	0	0
Total £.	876	10	0
Expences as above, - - -	694	10	0
Profit £.	182	0	0

This

This profit, with the interest before deducted, is 141 l. which from 1200 l. is 20 per cent. This calculation is upon the supposition of 100 acres out 250 being grass land; supposing the whole arable, which some writers esteem the most profitable, the account may then be stated as follows: though I should premise, that not many tracts in England are to be found without grass, and landlords are tenacious of having it ploughed up.

	l.	s.	d.
Rent, tythe, and parish taxes, of 250 acres at 27 s.	337	10	0
Housekeeping, &c. one year,	80	0	0
Twelve horses at 15 l.	180	0	0
Live stock for 60 acres of clover, and 10 of grass, and 60 of turneps (exclusive of maintaining the 12 horses)			
5 cows at 7 l.	35	0	0
5 young cattle at 30 s.	7	10	0
200 sheep at 10 s.	100	0	0
Swine,	10	0	0
10 oxen for turneps,	50	0	0
Poultry,	3	0	0
Four men, one maid, and two boys wages,	50	0	0
Pay of five labourers at 20 l.	100	0	0
Implements of culture of all sorts,	250	0	0
Seed,	55	0	0
Total £.	1258	0	0

The annual expence.

	l.	s.	d.
Rent, &c.	337	10	0
Housekeeping,	100	0	0
Carried forward	407	10	0

	l.	s.	d.
Brought forward	407	10	0
Wages and labour, - - -	150	0	0
Repairs of implements, - - -	80	0	0
Ten oxen, - - -	50	0	0
Contingent expences, - - -	40	0	0
Interest of 1258 l. - - -	62	18	0
£.	820	8	0

The annual produce.

	l.	s.	d.
The fystem of this farm, like that of the former, is suppofed to be,			
60 acres turneps,			
60 —— barley,			
60 —— clover,	525	0	0
60 —— wheat,			
10 —— grafs,			
60 acres wheat, 3½ qrs. per acre, 210 qrs. at 50s. - - - -			
48 acres of barley, 4 qrs. an acre, 192 qrs. at 24s. * - - -	230	8	0
Profit on 5 cows, - -	25	0	0
Do. on young cattle, - -	8	0	0
Do. on fheep, - -	90	0	0
Do. on fwine, - -	30	0	0
Do. on poultry, - -	15	0	0
Sale of wood, - -	10	0	0
Sale of 10 oxen, - -	100	0	0
Total, - - - £.	1033	8	0
Expence, - -	820	8	0
Profit £.	213	0	0

* The feed for the land in the next year, faved, befides thefe crops in both inftances.

Which,

Which, with 62 l. 18 s. interest, is 275 l. 18 s. and that on 1258 l. is about 21¼ per cent.

It appears from these accounts, that in England, on the best land, and with excellent husbandry, about 20 per cent. is made by employing 1200 l. on 250 acres. The circumstance of the husbandry being excellent, is not to be forgotten; for not all parts of this kingdom practise so good a system as,

1. Turneps,
2. Barley,
3. Clover,
4. Wheat,

which the writers on husbandry justly enough reckon to be excellent: nor will perhaps half the kingdom admit of such a system, from being too heavy and wet to yield turneps; in which case, the profit is not to be supposed nearly to equal the turnep culture, which excludes the barren expence of a fallow: but the number of farmers, even in this enlightened age and country, that practise the above culture is very small; on the contrary they, like the planters of America, are too apt to take several crops of corn running, instead of introducing turneps and clover.

It

It appeared above, that the profit on 1200 l. employed on a plantation of 5000 acres in Penfylvania, in a few years after fettling it, was 15 per cent. whereas in England, that fum yields 20 or 21 per cent. But then there are other circumftances to be confidered, which I am afraid will more than ballance this difference. The produce from the American farm was gained by the common management of the province, which is as bad and unprofitable a fyftem as can well be imagined; confequently it would admit of great improvements, without introducing any other crops: but the 20 per cent. in England is gained from the moft capital management which common crops will admit, and on the moft favourable foil that is to be found plentifully in Britain. In one cafe you are open to an immenfe improvement, in the other none can be imagined without deviating from common hufbandry. *Secondly,* The American has the fee fimple of 5000 acres into his bargain, with all the timber on it; this, however plentiful land may be, is a very different affair from *renting* 250. Of the fame fuperiority, is the houfe and offices, orchards and gardens, made and to be enjoyed for ever, with nothing in the
op-

opposite scale to balance them. The American lives upon his own freehold; if the Englishman would do the same, he must buy it, in which case his 250 l. a year would, at 28 years purchase, cost 7000 l. in which case his capital must be 8200 l. and upon 7000 l. of it he would make perhaps 2¼ per cent. *Thirdly*, and which is the most important of all, the Pensylvanian can by an annual increase of culture, expend all his savings at the same advantage of 15 per cent. or rather at 20 or 25; for when the buildings are raised, the estate bought and stocked, additions to culture will certainly pay better interest than the original sum, out of which were such expences, together with freight, &c. all which may, in respect of the profit, be called barren. On the contrary, the English farmer can do nothing better than put out his profits at the common interest of five per cent. or perhaps only four; for he can very rarely increase his land as he grows rich, without leaving one farm, and moving into a larger, which is quite another affair from the gradual increase of the American. *Fourthly*, Both the farmers are supposed to live partly off their farms, a sum of money being allowed in either case

cafe for buying fuch articles as their lands
do not produce. But what an amazing
difference is there between them in this
refpect. With the fum charged to the
Englifh farmer, he will not be able to live
much better than a day-labourer—and not
to live at all if he is not faving to a degree.
But on the other hand, the Penfylvanian
lives, in point of table and fports, to the
full equal with a country gentleman in
England of four or five hundred pounds
a year; and, in feveral inftances, far fuperior to one of 1000l. a year.

In all thefe articles, the freeholder in
Penfylvania is fo much fuperior, that the
comparifon will fcarcely bear mentioning;
nor is it lefs in all thofe circumftances of
convenience and agreeablenefs, which refult from living upon your own land—your
own manor: the farmer gets a long leafe
with difficulty, and at the end of it muft
pay perhaps more than the land is worth,
or quit his farm: and during the whole
leafe plagued poffibly either by his land-
land or fteward; he muft not kill a hare
or a partridge without being liable to a
profecution—he muft not —— but the
comparifon in all thefe refpects will not
bear an idea of equality.

But here it should be observed, that to gentlemen or any persons of enlarged ideas, agriculture in Britain is probably far more profitable than in the preceding sketch; for if plants not commonly cultivated are introduced on the farm, the advantage will be far more than 20 per cent. of this, carrots, potatoes, cabbages, hops, madder, &c. are instances. To give some idea of this, it will be proper to lay before the reader a calculation of this point, upon the data given by writers of husbandry that can be depended upon. I shall begin with carrots.

Expences per acre.	l.	s.	d.
Ploughing and other tillage,	0	15	3
Manuring, - - -	1	0	3
Seed and sowing, - -	0	5	.9
Hand hoeing, - -	1	9	0
Digging up, - -	1	10	0
Carting, clearing, &c. - -	1	7	0
Rent, tythe, &c. - -	0	17	0
£.	7	4	3

Produce.

	l.	s.	d.
560 bushels at 1s. 1d. -	30	6	8
Expences, - - -	7	4	3
Profit £.	23	2	5

This

This a single crop; but the average of several expence per acre, 6l. 4s. 5d.

				l.	s.	d.
Product,	-	-	-	27	14	1
Profit,	-	-	-	21	3	5*

This is 350 per cent. but then we are sensible that deductions muſt be made for general expences on the farm, which have no place here, as some labour, fences, houſekeeping, &c. &c.

In madder a gentleman has expended 206l. 14s. on 10 acres, the produce was 540l. and the profit 333l. 6s. † This is 161 per cent. With cabbages another person has made the following advantage upon an average.

Expences.

				l.	s.	d.
Rent,	-	-	-	1	10	0
Ploughing,	-	-	-	1	11	6
Planting,	-	-		0	4	6
Horſe hoeing and weeding,				0	9	6
			£.	3	15	6

---

* *Courſe of Experimental Agriculture,* Vol. II. p. 190.

† *Farmer's Tour through England,* Vol. II. p. 299.

Produce.

Produce.

	l.	s.	d.
By feeding cattle, -	16	16	4
Expences, - -	3	15	6

Profit £. *13 0 10

This is 347 per cent. In all thefe cafes, we know upon a whole farm, fuch crops are not in general to be gained : and that expences fo reckoned would run much higher ; but it is evident that the intro-duction of fuch crops would be far more profitable than common ones. Hops are found, in trials, to yield above 100 per cent. but potatoes exceed them all, yielding fome-times crops from 50 l. to 100 l. an acre, from an expenditure of from 20 l. to 30 l.

If a farm was to be cultivated in England upon the principle of cultivating crops only, which would yield fuch large products, in that cafe, the profit of hufbandry would turn out over a whole farm much more than 20 per cent. probably 40 or 50 per cent. Whether Penfylvania by adopting the fame improvements would equal it, is not to be

---

* *Six Months Tour*, Vol. II. p. 121.

de-

decided here, the trial never having been made; but certainly a man that could make 40 per cent. by hufbandry in England, would act very imprudently to change his fituation without much ftronger proofs of fuperior advantages elfewhere, than he can have at prefent.

Settling upon a plantation in this colony feems to be of fuperior benefit to people who can pay their freight to America, and then have money enough left to buy a fmall plantation, build a houfe, &c.—Alfo to thofe who with a fum of money from 500 l. to 2000 l. would *in common hufbandry* apply it to the greateft advantage.—Alfo to country gentlemen of fmall fortunes, to whom the extreme dearnefs of Britain is very burthenfome—but to men who will adopt the profitable modern improvements of hufbandry, Britain is more beneficial than America.—And to fuch whofe fortunes bear a proportion to the luxury of the age, England certainly is the firft country in the univerfe. Thefe diftinctions are never to be forgotten; general affertions for or againft any country are always erroneous : nothing can be plainer than the fact, that thofe whofe incomes are too fmall to maintain them in England, may live in a far fupe-

rior

rior ſtile in Penſylvania, but with other claſſes the contrary is the caſe : every one muſt know that in order to reap advantage from this circumſtance they muſt quit all connections in their native country ; they muſt give up both friends and relations, and all thoſe endearing circumſtances which renders a native country ſo agreeable.—— They muſt croſs an immenſe ocean, and fix in a new hemiſphere, where the people and the climate are equally new : they muſt ſubmit to a much hotter ſun than that of England, and alſo to greater cold ; and they muſt run the hazard of being deſtroyed or wounded by poiſonous ſerpents that abound far more than in Britain : in return for theſe circumſtances, they will enjoy the advantages ſpecified above ; great moſt certainly, but of value only to thoſe whoſe fortunes are ſo ſmall that they cannot live like their forefathers, whoſe money in cheaper times went ſo much farther. When a man lives the ridicule and contempt of his neighbours, becauſe his mean circumſtances force him to ſtrict frugality, he had better fly to vipers and rattle-ſnakes than into the company of his neighbours : and when even his penury will ſcarce keep him from ſtarving, it is of little conſequence to know that the
in-

inhofpitable clime he lives in is his native one: there are a thoufand comforts in a competency which may make amends for the lofs of fuch friends as poverty brings. And as to croffing an ocean, and living in another hemifphere, they are what are done by others even in wealthy fituations at home; there is nothing terrible in it to people of fenfe.

CHAP. XIV.

VIRGINIA and MARYLAND.

Climate of Virginia and Maryland—Soil—Productions—Face of the Country.

THESE two provinces lie between latitude 31½° and 40°, being in extent about 250 miles from north to south, and the same breadth from east to west, that is from the sea to the Alligany mountains. The parallel is the same as Morocco, Fez, the coast of Barbary, Syria, Lesser Asia, Greece, Sicily, Naples, and the southern provinces of Spain, that is perhaps, without exception, the countries of all the world that enjoy the finest climate.

That of Virginia and Maryland has its objections, but is notwithstanding fine: in summer the heats would be insupportable on the coast, were it not for the sea breezes which refresh them greatly. In the back country, among the mountains, this heat is much less violent than in the low country; for there they enjoy one of the most temperate climates in the world:

the

the weather is changeable, and the changes are sudden : in winter, frosts come on with very little warning, and after a warm day ; and in summer the tempests of thunder and lightning are extremely violent and sudden, but do no more harm than in much more temperate climates. Their rains at certain seasons of the year are very heavy, but not of long duration, and the frosts of winter are sooner : in general, throughout the year the sky is clear, and the air is pure and wholesome.

The soil of the country varies much ; all the sea coast, for above one hundred miles, is a low, flat, sandy beach, so low, that the country is not descried from on ship-board till you are in the rivers, out of which the trees seem to rise : the low lands on the banks of them are a rich, black mould, more than a foot deep, of a fertility exceeding every thing in Pensylvania or to the northward : the higher lands are sandy, but not therefore barren or of little value ; there is a moisture in it that is sufficient even for tobacco, which will do on the most luxuriant soils in the world. When you get from one hundred to one hundred and fifty miles from the coast, the country rises, and increases in inequality for another
hundred

hundred miles, till you come to the Alligany mountains. This line of country is
far superior to the coaſt in climate, healthi-
neſs, and agreeableneſs, and in general the
ſoil much exceeds it *.

The products of Virginia and Maryland
differ conſiderably from thoſe of Penſylvania, from their nearer neighbourhood to
the ſun. As to timber and wood, they
have all the ſorts that are found upon the
continent : many ſorts of oaks, cedars,
firs, cyprus, elm, aſh, and wallnut ; ſome

* " The whole ſea coaſt of North America, ſays Dr.
Mitchell, from the bay of New York to the gulph of
Mexico is a low, flat, ſandy beach ; the ſoil for a great
diſtance from it is ſandy and barren, the climate is very
rainy, and as theſe rains have no drains from the land,
but ſtagnate all over a low flat country, they form in-
numerable ſwamps and marſhes, which render it very
unhealthful. It is a common opinion, that all this part
of the continent, which ſtretches into the ocean at a
conſiderable diſtance from the reſt, has been recovered
from the ſea, and that it is nothing but a drained marſh
or ſand bank, which indeed it very much reſembles,
and in nothing more than its pernicious influence on
mankind. Accordingly in all this ſpace nothing is to
be found either on the ſurface or in the bowels of the
earth, but beds of ſea ſhells, in place of ſtones, metals,
and other minerals, and the earth is as barren in theſe
as in other productions." *Preſent State*, p. 184. This
is in general true of the coaſt, but the ſame writer acknowledges all the merit of the back country.

of

of their oaks are faid to meafure two feet fquare and fixty feet in height. They have alfo beech, poplar, hazel, befides faffafras, farfaparilla, and other dying woods. The unfettled country is all a foreft of thefe trees, without underwood, and not ftanding fo clofe but they may any where be rode through. Near the coaft the low lands are all fwamps, from which grow cedars, pines, and cypreffes. This plenty of wood is of great advantage here, as in all the colonies more to the north, in affording lumber for the Weft Indies, which forms a confiderable article in the exports of the province.

As to fruit trees, they have all thofe which are known to us in Europe or Penfylvania; particularly apples, pears, cherries, quinces, plums, grapes, peaches, and nectarines, in the fame plenty as in Penfylvania, fo as to be applied to the fame ufe of feeding hogs as there. All other fruits are produced here, as may from the climate be fuppofed

Befides tobacco, which is the ftaple of thefe colonies, and of which I fhall fpeak more by-and-by, wheat and all our other kinds of grain and pulfe thrive here equally, if not in a fuperior degree, to any of

our

our other colonies; a circumftance in which the country refembles thofe in the fame parallel in Europe and Africa, Sicily, Spain, and Barbary, which produce the beft wheat that is known in the world; and in thefe articles of common hufbandry the planters have increafed much more than in tobacco, for reafons which I fhall explain hereafter.

No part of America, or indeed of the world, boafts more plentiful or more general production of all forts of garden vegetables; and in a ftate of excellence that is proportioned to the heat of the climate. The fame remark may alfo be made of their fifh and fowl, having every fort that is found in Penfylvania, with others that are peculiar to the country; being in all refpects of food as plentiful as any territory in the world.

The face of the country varies in different parts of the provinces: for about one hundred or one hundred and fifty miles from the fea it is generally low and flat, much fpread with marfhes and fwamps: thefe in Carolina are applied to the culture of rice, but Virginia and Maryland are not hot enough for that production, which by the way is a proof how much better their climate

mate

mate is. This part of the country is in-
terfected with immenfe rivers and bays of,
the fea, fo as to afford a greater inland navigation than is known in any other country in the world. As the land recedes
from the coaft it gradually rifes, until at
the diftance above-mentioned it begins to
grow hilly, which in as many miles more
ends in the Alligany mountains. In all
this part of the provinces, the face of the
country is as beautiful as can well be imagined : there are not many level tracts,
and thofe are rich meadows, not fwamps or
marfhes. In the vales ftreams of clear water are every where to be found, and even
navigable rivers enter among the mountains : the hills hang to the eye in a great
variety of forms, and fpread with forefts
that give an amazing magnificence to the
fcenery. Spots are here frequently found,
that poffefs every picturefque beauty which
in England our nobility are fo emulous to
create in their parks ; and all this back
country poffeffes a climate free from the
extreme heats which opprefs the inhabitants of the coaft. At the fame time that
it enjoys fo many advantages of health and
agreeablenefs, it is likewife fertile in an
high degree, and in moft parts of it capable

of

of producing fine crops of tobacco, to which it is in moſt parts applied, where navigation is at a convenient diſtance. From all theſe circumſtances it is evident, that no part of our American colonies is more deſirable in moſt reſpects.

C H A P. XV.

Deſcription of tobacco—The culture—Remarks—Full account of a plantation.

THIS plant is cultivated in all parts of North America, from Quebec to Carolina, and even the Weſt Indies; but, except in Maryland, Virginia, and North Carolina, they plant no more than for private uſe, making it an object of exportation only in theſe provinces, where it is of ſuch immenſe conſequence.

It was planted in large quantities by the Indians, when we firſt came to America, and its uſe from them brought into Europe; but what their method of culture was is now no longer known, as they plant none, but buy what they want of the Engliſh.

To-

Tobacco is raifed from the feed, which is fown in fpring upon a bed of rich mould; when about the height of four or five inches, the planter takes the opportunity of rainy weather to tranfplant them. The ground which is prepared to receive it, is, if it can be got, a rich black mould; frefh woodlands are beft: fometimes it is fo badly cleared from the ftumps of trees, that they cannot give it any ploughings; but in old cultivated lands they plough it feveral times, and fpread on it what manure they can raife. The negroes then hill it; that is, with hoes and fhovels they form hillocks, which lie in the manner of Indian corn, only they are larger, and more carefully raked up: the hills are made in fquares, from fix to nine feet diftance, according to the land; the richer it is the further they are put afunder, as the plants grow higher, and fpread proportionably. The plants in about a month are a foot high, when they prune and top them; operations, in which they feem to be very wild, and to execute them upon no rational principles; experiments are much wanting on thefe points, for the planters never go out of the beaten road, but do juft as

their

their fathers did, refembling therein the
Britifh farmers their brethren. They prune
off all the bottom leaves, leaving only feven
or eight on a ftalk, thinking that fuch as
they leave will be the larger, which is
contrary to nature in every inftance thro'-
out all vegetation. In fix weeks more the
tobacco is at its full growth, being then
from four and a half to feven feet high:
during all this time, the negroes are employed twice a week in pruning off the
fuckers, clearing the hillocks from weeds,
and attending to the worms, which are a
great enemy to the plant; when the tobacco changes its colour, turning brown, it
is ripe, and they than cut it down, and lay
it clofe in heaps in the field to fweat one
night : the next day they are carried in
bunches by the negroes to a building called
the *tobacco houfe*, where every plant is hung
up feparate to dry, which takes a month
or five weeks ; this houfe excludes the
rain, but is defigned for the admiffion of
as much air as poffible. They are then
laid clofe in heaps in the tobacco houfes
for a week or a fortnight to fweat again,
after which it is forted and packed up in
hogfheads ; all the operations, after the

7

plants

plants are dried, muſt be done in moiſt or wet weather, which prevents its crumbling to duſt.

There are among many inferior diſtinctions of ſorts two generally attended to, *Oroonoko*, and *ſweet ſcented*; the latter is of the fineſt flavour, and moſt valued, growing chiefly in the lower parts of Virginia, viż. on James river, and York river, and likewiſe on the Rappanhannock, and the ſouth ſide of the Potomack: the Oroonoko is principally in uſe on Cheſepeak bay, and the back ſettlements on all the rivers. It is ſtrong and hot; the principal markets for it are Germany and the North.

One of the greateſt advantages attending the culture of tobacco, is the quick, eaſy, and certain method of ſale. This was effected by the inſpection law, which took place in Virginia in the year 1730, but not in Maryland till 1748. The planter, by virtue of this, may go to any place and ſell his tobacco, without carrying a a ſample of it along with him, and the merchant may buy it, though lying a hundred miles, or at any diſtance from his ſtore, and yet be morally ſure both with reſpect to quantity and quality. For this purpofe, upon all the rivers and bays of both provinces, at the diftance of about twelve or fourteen miles from each other, are erected warehoufes, to which all the tobacco in the country muft be brought, and there lodged, before the planters can offer it to fale ; and infpectors are appointed to examine all the tobacco brought in, receive fuch as is good and merchantable, condemn and burn what appears damnified or infufficient. The greateft part of the tobacco is prized, or put up into hogfheads by the planters themfelves, before it is carried to the warehoufes. Each hogfhead, by an act of affembly, muft be 950lb. neat, or upwards ; fome of them weigh 14 cwt. and even 18 cwt. and the heavier they are the merchants like them the better ; becaufe four hogfheads, whatfoever their weight be, are efteemed a tun, and pay the fame freight. The infpectors give notes of receipt for the tobacco, and the merchants take them in payment for their goods, paffing current indeed over the whole colonies; a moft admirable invention, which operates fo greatly, that in Virginia they have no paper currency.*

---

* *Main's Book keeping*, p. 333.

The

The merchants generally purchafe the tobacco in the country, by fending perfons to open *ftores* for them; that is, ware-houfes in which they lay in a great affort-ment of Britifh commodities and manu-factures, to thefe, as to fhops, the planters refort, and fupply themfelves with what they want, paying, in infpection receipts, or taking on credit according to what will be given them; and as they are in general a very luxurious fet of people, they buy too much upon credit; the confequence of which is, their getting in debt to the Lon-don merchants, who take mortgages on their plantations, ruinous enough, with the ufury of eight per cent. But this is ap-parently the effect of their imprudence in living upon truft.

Refpecting the product of tobacco, they know very little of it themfelves by the acre; as they never calculate in that man-ner, and not many tobacco grounds were ever meafured: all their ideas run in the the proportion per working hand. Some are hired labourers, but in general they are negroe flaves; and the product, from the beft information I have gained, varies from an hogfhead and a half to three and an

Q 2   half

half per head. The hogshead used to be of the value of 5 l. but of late years it is 8 l. The variation is therefore from 12 l. to 28 l. per head, according to the goodness of the lands and other circumstances. But the planters, none of them depend on tobacco alone, and this is more and more the case since corn has yielded a high price, and since their grounds have begun to be worn out. They all raise corn and provisions enough to support the family and plantation, besides exporting considerable quantities; no wheat in the world exceeds in quality that of Virginia and Maryland. Lumber they also send largely to the West Indies. The whole culture of tobacco is over in the summer months; in the winter the negroes are employed in sawing and cutting timber, threshing corn, clearing new land, and preparing for tobacco: so that it is plain, they make a product per head, besides that of tobacco.

Suppose each negroe makes two hogsheads of tobacco, or 16 l. and 4 l. in corn, provisions, and lumber, besides supporting the plantation, this is a moderate supposition; and if true, the planter's profit may be easily calculated: the negroe costs him

50 l.

50 l. his cloathing, tools, and fundries, 3 l. in this cafe, the expence of the flave is only the intereſt of his coſt, 2 l. 10 s. and the total only makes 5 l. 10 s. a year. To this we muſt add the intereſt of the planter's capital, province taxes, &c. which will make fome addition, perhaps thirty or forty fhillings per head more, there will then remain 12 l. 10 s. a head profit to the planter ; which is more than cent. per cent. profit : but this being a point of confiderable importance, fhall be further examined.

There is no plant in the world that requires richer land, or more manure than tobacco ; it will grow on poorer foils, but not to yield crops that are fufficiently profitable to pay the expences of negroes, &c. The land they found to anfwer beſt is freſh woodlands, where many ages have formed a ſtratum of rich black mould. Such land will, after clearing, bear tobacco many years, without any change, prove more profitable to the planter than the power of dung can do on worfe lands : this makes the tobacco planters more folicitous for new land than any other people in America, they wanting it much more. Many of them have very handfome houfes, gardens,

Q 3

dens, and improvements about them, which fixes them to one spot; but others, when they have exhausted their grounds, will sell them to new settlers for corn-fields, and move backwards with their negroes, cattle, and tools, to take up fresh land for tobacco; this is common, and will continue so as long as good land is to be had upon navigable rivers: this is the system of business which made some, so long ago as 1750, move over the Allegany mountains, and settle not far from the Ohio, where their tobacco was to be carried by land some distance, which is a heavy burthen on so bulky a commodity, but answered by the superior crops they gained: the French encroachments drove these people all back again; but upon the peace, many more went, and the number increasing, became the occasion of the new colony which has been settled in that country.

A very considerable tract of land is necessary for a tobacco plantation; first, that the planter may have a sure prospect of increasing his culture on fresh land; secondly, that the lumber may be a winter employment for his slaves, and afford casks for

his

his crops. Thirdly, that he may be able
to keep vaſt ſtocks of cattle for raiſing proviſions in plenty, by ranging in the woods ;
and where the lands are not freſh, the neceſſity is yet greater, as they muſt yield
much manure for repleniſhing the worn-
out fields. This want of land is ſuch, that
they reckon a planter ſhould have 50 acres
of land for every working hand ; with leſs
than this they will find themſelves diſ-
treſſed for want of room.

But I muſt obſerve, that great improvements might be made in the culture of this
crop : the attention of the planters is to
keep their negroes employed on the plants
and the ſmall ſpace that the hillocks occupy, being very apt to neglect the intervals ; the expence of hoeing them is conſiderable, and conſequently they are apt to
be remiſs in this work. Here they ought
to ſubſtitute the horſe-hoeing management,
which would coſt much leſs, and be an
hundred times more effectual. The roots
of the tobacco are powerful ; they ſpread
far beyond the hillocks, which ought to
convince the planters that they ſhould feed
them there by good culture, but this is
little conſidered. A few men once got

into

into the ufe of a plough, they invented in the back parts of Virginia, for opening a trench in the intervals, to kill weeds, loofen the earth, and carry the water of hafty rains off; but, from the carelefnefs of fervants, the fcheme came to nothing, though it promifed better ideas in future.

I would propofe to them the ufe of fuch a machine as in Kent is applied to cultivating the intervals of the hop-grounds, which confifts of feveral flat triangular fhares, which work near each other, being let into a beam from which it is drawn; they call it, if I miftake not, a nidget; this would keep the tobacco intervals in a fine pulverized flate, and prepare them to be thrown againft the hillock, for the nourifhment of the roots, by a machine made upon the principles of that I have juft mentioned, but upon an improved conftruction. In one of the *Tours through England,* there is a draft of one, which, with a little alteration for breadth, would do admirably for this purpofe. Would the planters enter into thefe ideas, they would foon find their expences leffen, at the fame time that their products increafed. This culture, upon the Tullian fyftem, would fo improve the in-

intervals, as to prepare them for the plants in the following year, and they would not so soon come to the complaint of their lands being exhausted.

Let us calculate what the culture of tobacco would cost per acre, if labour was the same price as in England; this is not difficult to do.

	L.	s.	d.
Seed, sowing, and preparation of a seed bed, the share of an acre, -	0	1	6
Three ploughings of the plantation, -	0	3	6
Harrowing, - - -	0	0	6
Measuring out the spaces for the hillocks, and marking them by setting up sticks,	0	1	2
Hilling with hoes and shovels, - -	0	2	6
Planting, - - - - -	0	1	2
Topping and pruning the plants at ½ a plant, at six feet asunder, there are 1210 upon an acre,	1	5	0
Pruning ten times more. at 3s. 6d. an acre,	1	15	0
Worming ten times, at 2s.	1	0	0
Hoeing the hillocks four times during the season, at 1s 6d. - -	0	6	0
Hoeing the intervals, suppose once, -	0	5	0
Cutting down, and laying into heaps, -	0	2	0
Carrying to tobacco-house, and hanging up,	0	8	10
Taking down, and laying in heaps, -	0	3	6
Sorting, - - - - -	0	2	6
Packing in hogsheads, - -	0	3	6
£.	6	1	8

Suppose a man earns, on an average 1s. 4d. a day, the year round, it amounts in a year to 20l. 16s. At 6l. 1s. 8d. an acre, therefore he would be able to cultivate something

thing better than 3½. The fame proportion probably holds for the negroes, for as
their annual expence is only 7 or 8l. a
year, the feparate charges per acre would
be proportioned, and the quantity of land
to be managed by one hand the fame: this
calculation is upon fuppofition that the
ground is frefh, and requires no manure;
if that is to be carried on, the account
would be different; and perhaps three
acres would prove the quantity. The product we found, was from one hogfhead and
half to three, and an half per working
hand, or from 12 to 28l. The average is
about two hhds. or 16l. which divided by
three, the number of acres, gives the produce per acre of 5l. 6s. 8d. when tobacco
is at 8l. a hhd. according to the rate of labour in the dear parts of England, it cofts
more than this in mere labour to cultivate,
which fhews, if any thing can fhew it, how
much cheaper the labour of negroes is,
being certainly as about three to one.

Having afcertained thefe points as nearly
as I am able, I fhall in the next place calculate the fettling a tobacco plantation. I
am forry I cannot give a real account, but
though I applied to many for it, it is what
I could not procure; from the fimilar accounts

counts before given in other colonies, I shall be able to come near the truth. I shall suppose the planter to go from England as in former cases.

	£. 50
Freight and expences of two persons from London - - -	£. 50
Ditto of two others - - - -	25
20 negroes at 50 l. - - - -	1000
Two ditto women - - -	100
An overseer - - - - -	40
Patent fees and expences on taking up 2000 acres,	40
House, - - - - -	100
Offices and tobacco-house, - -	100
Furniture, - - - -	100
Implements of culture, - -	50
A sloop and canoe, - - - -	50
Arms, ammunition, and sundries, - -	10
Expences of negroes, - - -	60
Extra expences * on ditto. - - -	10
House-keeping and family expences, - -	100
House servants wages, - - -	20
Live stock, 10 horses, at 4 l. - £. 40	
40 cows, at 3 l. - 120	
50 young cattle, - - 50	
100 swine - - 25	
100 sheep, - - 25	
Poultry, - - 5	
————265	265
Expences on orchard and garden, - - .	20
Incidental expences, - - - .	80
	£. 2210

* Their first year's work is clearing some ground and the garden and orchard: after that the getting lumber and the negroes spare time from the crop, will clear land as fast as it is wanted.

The

The annual expence.

	l.	s.	d.
Province taxes, - - -	20	0	0
Expence of negroes, - -	60	0	0
Repairs of implements, - -	15	0	0
House-keeping, &c. - -	60	0	0
Building and furniture - -	20	0	0
Overseer, - - -	30	0	0
House servants wages, - -	20	0	0
Incidents, - - - -	20	0	0
	245	0	0
Interest of 2200l. - -	110	0	0
	£. 355	0	0

Annual produce.

	l.	s.	d.
44 hogsheads of tobacco, at 8l. -	352	0	0
4l. a head in corn, provisions, and lumber,	88	0	0
Product of cattle, - - -	80	0	0
Fruit and cyder, - - -	10	0	0
	530	0	0
Expences, - -	355	0	0
	175	0	0
Add the interest before charged, . -	110	0	0
	£. 285	0	0

which from 188 5l. is 13 per cent. but house-keeping 60 l. might be added, as it is expended in products extra from the plantation. The receipt would then be 345 l. and the interest 15 per cent. The 175 l. is the sum the planter might an-

I   nually

nually lay out in negroes and other labour : here lies his great advantages, if he
chooses to make use of them; for having
land plenty, and able at any time to get
more, the money he lays out in labour and
the small additions of tools, &c. is expended at compound interest, at the rate he
makes per cent. by his negroes. Suppose
the negro (which is much more than truth
with good management) and attendant
charges costs him 8 l. a year, the produce
is 20 l. and all other contingent charges
would not reduce it so far but the profit
would be immense, and soon accumulate
into considerable fortune.

On the other hand it is said, fortunes
are rarely made by tobacco planters, and
that it is much more common to see their
estates eat out by mortgages; but this
proves nothing; it deserves, however, a
due examination.

The tobacco planters live more like
country gentlemen of fortune than any o-
ther settlers in America; all of them are
spread about the country, their labour being mostly by slaves, who are left to over-
seers; and the masters live in a state of emulation with one another in buildings, (many
of their houses would make no slight figure
in

in the Englifh counties) furniture, wines, drefs, diverfions, &c. and this to fuch a degree, that it is rather amazing they fhould be able to go on with their plantations at all, than they fhould not make additions to them : fuch a country life as they lead, in the midft of a profufion of rural fports and diverfions, with little to do themfelves, and in a climate that feems to create rather than check pleafure, muft almoft naturally have a ftrong effect in bringing them to be juft fuch planters, as foxbunters in England make farmers. To live within compafs, and to lay out their favings in an annual addition to their culture, requires in the conduct a fixed and fettled œconomy, and a firm determination not to depart from it, at leaft till a handfome fortune was made. This would not be long, as a flight calculation will fhew.

First year of increafe.

	l.	s.	d.
Saving of the laft, - - -	175	0	0
Four negroes at 50l. - - -	200	0	0
Implements, - - - -	10	0	0
Expences on negroes, - - -	12	0	0
Addition to buildings, - - -	20	0	0
Sundries, - - - -	8	0	0
£.	250	0	0

Pro-

	l.	s.	d.
Produce 20 l. a head,	80	0	0
Annual faving,	175	0	0
	£. 255	0	0

Second year.

	l.	s.	d.
Six negroes at 50 l.	300	0	0
Implements,	20	0	0
Negroe expences,	30	0	0
Sundries,	10	0	0
	£. 360	0	0
Produce 10 at 20 l.	200	0	0
Annual faving,	175	0	0
	£. 375	0	0

Third year.

	l.	s.	d.
Eight negroes at 50 l.	400	0	0
Expences on 18, at 3 l.	54	0	0
Implements bought, and additional repairs,	30	0	0
Sundries,	16	0	0
Building,	10	0	0
	£. 510	0	0
Produce 18 at 20 l.	360	0	0
Annual faving,	175	0	0
	£. 535	0	0

Fourth year.

	l.	s.	d.
Ten negroes at 50 l.	500	0	0
Expences, &c. 28 at 3 l.	84	0	0
	Carried over 584	0	0

		l.	s.	d.
Brought over	584	0	0
Implements,	- - -	40	0	0
Building,	- - - - -	30	0	0
Sundries,	- - - -	20	0	0
Clearing land,	- - -	26	0	0
	£.	600	0	0

Produce 28 at 20l.	- - -	560	0	0
Annual faving,	- -	175	0	0
	£.	735	0	0

Fifth year.

2000 acres more land patent fees,	-	40	0	0
Another overfeer,	- -	40	0	0
Buildings,	- - -	50	0	0
Clearing land,	- -	100	0	0
Implements,	- -	50	0	0
Sundries,	- - -	30	0	0
8 negroes at 50l.	- -	400	0	0
Expences on them,	- -	102	0	0
Allow the planter,	- -	48	0	0
	£.	860	0	0

Produce 34 at 20l.	- -	680	0	0
Annual faving,	- , -	175	0	0
	£.	855	0	0

Sixth year.

Overfeer,	- - -	40	0	0
Clearing land,	- - -	50	0	0
Implements,	- - -	50	0	0
Carried forward	140	0	0

	l.	s.	d.
Carried forward	140	0	0
Sundries, - - - -	40	0	0
15 negroes at 50l. - -	750	0	0
Expences, &c. 49, at 3l. - -	147	0	0
Allow the planter, - -	28	0	0
£.	1095	0	0
Produce 49 at 20l. - - -	980	0	0
Annual faving, - - - -	190	0	0
£.	1170	0	0

Seventh year.
Account of the whole plantation.

	l.	s.	d.
Province taxes, - - -	40	0	0
Expences on 72 negroes at 3l. -	216	0	0
Repairs of implements, - - -	50	0	0
Housekeeping, - - -	300	0	0
Building and furniture, - - -	50	0	0
Overseers, - - - -	80	0	0
House servants, - - - -	30	0	0
Incidents, - - - -	50	0	0
Interest, - - - -	94	5	0
£.	910	5	0

Produce.

	l.	s.	d.
72 negroes at 20 l. - - -	1440	0	0
Cattle, - - - -	150	0	0
Fruit and fundries, - -	50	0	0
	1640	0	0
Expences, - - -	910	5	0
Remains, - - -	£. 729	15	0

Hence it appears, that he can either continue the increafe of culture, with a view

to grow rich as soon as possible ; or he may stop, and at the same time that he spends 300l. a year in manufactures, and foreign luxuries, may lay up 729 l. 15s. a year: or else he may here begin a a second system of increase ; taking the annual sum of 729l. for the foundation in the manner before explained, which would soon accumulate into a great income.

To all accounts of that sort, there may be many objections made, in all countries, and in all branches of culture — and it would be the same if the account had been actually realized by a planter ; but slight variations should not be attended to : and the greatness of this profit will admit of deductions, according to more accurate ideas, and yet the remainder be far more than sufficient to prove that the poverty of the planters is not necessary to their condition, but merely owing to their extravagant way of living. In most articles of life, a great Virginia planter makes a greater show, and lives more luxuriously than a country gentleman in England, on an estate of three or four thousand pounds a year. The great object I labour to prove, is, that this branch of agriculture, under its present circumstances, of price of negroes, and

and price of product, is such as will admit
of great profit—to the capability of making
a considerable fortune; and this advantage
to be gained while the planter shall live in
the midst of all the conveniencies of life,
and most of its agreeableness!

I must own I am very solicitous to have
this point well understood, for upon it
much of this country's interest depends.
Tobacco is one of the most valuable commodities that is produced by our colonies,
perhaps the most so; and therefore the great
advantages of selling in these parts should
be well known. Settlers are always going
to America, but those who go to the north
of these provinces can raise no commodities that are of consequence to Britain : all
the corn and provisions that the West Indies wants, can be more than raised in the
tracts from New York to Florida; and
lumber is had in plenty in the southern
ones, as well as in the northern; new settlers, therefore, going to colonies that
have not a staple, is going where they can
be of little use to Britain, and their making
a choice so disadvantageous to the mother-
country, can only arise from a want of
knowledge of the real state and improvements of the tobacco colonies; since in the

back

back parts of thefe they will find that
healthy and agreeable country which at-
tracts them in Penfylvania ; as to the more
fouthern colonies we are not to expect
many to go to them, becaufe the heat is
too great to be agreeable to Britifh conftitutions. Since, therefore, tobacco culture
is that which fuits the central country,
which is free from the intenfe cold of the
northern colonies, and the oppreffive heats
of the fouthern ones, and at the fame time
is in poffeffion of a ftaple highly valuable
to Britain, and profitable to cultivate, they
are neceffarily the country which fhould be
fo well known as to induce fettlers to make
it their choice. The poverty of the planters here, many of them at leaft, is much
talked off, and from thence there has arifen
a notion that their hufbandry is not profitable : this falfe idea I have endeavoured
to obviate, and to fhew that the caufe of
it has little or no reference to their culture, but to the general luxury, and extravagant way of living which obtains a-
mong the planters—a circumftance which
ought rather to occafion a contrary conclufion ;—a fuppofition that their agriculture was very valuable ; for men without
fome rich article of product cannot afford,

even

even with the affiftance of credit, to live in fuch a manner: it muft be upon the face of it a profitable culture, that will fupport fuch luxury, and pay eight per cent. intereft on their debts. What common culture in Europe will do this?

The obfervation I made on fettlements in Penfylvania, are applicable in the prefent inftance. It is not fo much the profit which the farmer makes on his land, as the ability he has of extending his culture, in proportion to the money he makes. This cannot be done in Britain, nor in any cultivated country, but is the glory of America. If a man makes twenty per cent. on his agriculture in England, and lays by 500 l. a year; he can get only four or five per cent. for that faving of 500 l. he cannot lay it out in an increafe of culture. But let him do the fame in America, and he is able every year to increafe his hufbandry in whatever proportion his money will allow: this is making compound intereft of his favings, and will, under a thoufand difadvantages, accumulate prefently into a confiderable fortune, in comparifon with the fum the planter firft began with. This is a point which fhould never be forgotten, and in which confifts the great fuperiority

R 3   of

of America. It is not sufficiently considered by those who decry the profit of the Virginia planters, because they are not rich. They enjoy advantages which would make any set of men rich; but if instead of applying their money to making use of those advantages, he spends it in temporal enjoyments of living, dress, and equipage, he, nor the by-stander cannot, with any degree of propriety, charge that to the agriculture of the province, which is in fact owing to the private expences of individuals.

Before I quit these observations on this part of the husbandry of Virginia and Maryland, I should remark, that to make a due profit on tobacco, a man should be able to begin with twenty slaves at least; because so many will pay for an overseer: none, or at least very few, can be kept without an overseer, and if fewer than twenty be the number, the expence of the overseer will be too high; for they are seldom to be gained under 25 l. a year, and generally from 30 to 50 l. But it does not follow from hence, that settlers are precluded from these colonies, who cannot buy twenty negroes; every day's experience tells us the contrary of this; the only
differ-

difference is, that they begin in small; and either have no slaves at all, or no more than what they will submit to take care of themselves; in this case, they may begin with only one or two, and make a profit proportioned to that of the greater number, without the expence of an overseer. This is exactly similar to the conduct of English husbandry; a great farmer will employ a bailiff at the expence of 40 or 60l. a year; but this is far enough from preventing others from farming, who occupy no more than they can cultivate with their own hands, or with the assistance of only one man. Settlers of all kinds fix in these colonies, with advantages as great, if not greater, than any others. The culture of corn and other provisions, is as profitable here as any where else; and plantations are every day left by tobacco-planters, who quit and sell them at low prices, in order to retire backwards for fresh land, to cultivate tobacco to advantage; besides which, the new country is to be had here, equally with any other province, and upon terms as advantageous.

It is no slight benefit to be able to mix tobacco-planting with common husbandry's

this

this is as eafily done as can be wifhed, and is indeed the practice of the greateft planters. A man may be a farmer for corn and provifions, and yet employ a few hands on tobacco, according as his land or manure will allow him. This makes a fmall bufinefs very profitable, and at the fame time eafy to be attained, nor is any thing more common throughout both Maryland and Virginia.

CHAP.

CHAP. XVI.

Observations on the waste lands of Great Britain—Not applicable to the same profit as those of Virginia—Reasons—Are superior in the hands of their owners—Remarks.

I AM sensible that an objection may be made to the preceding recommendations of settling in Virginia, &c. upon the principles of the superior, or at least equal advantages of settling on the waste lands of Britain; the great benefit of the American wastes is the capability of enlarging the husbandry at pleasure proportioned to the money which the farmer has annually to lay out: agriculture in the cultivated parts of Britain has nothing equal to this advantage, but the identical circumstance is to be found in the moors and other wastes of Britain; this therefore is a case in direct opposition to that of the colonies, and consequently deserves examination here.

In the plantations every man, however low his condition and rank in life, can obtain on demand, and paying the settled

fees,

fees, whatever land he pleases, provided he engages to settle on it in ten years a certain number of white persons; and when he has got his grant, it is a freehold io him and his posterity for ever. In this circumstance nothing can be more different, or in more direct opposition than the two cases. The wastes in Britain are all private property, generally belonging to men of fortune, who, so far from being ready to make presents of them to whoever demands them, will scarce be prevailed on to let them on long leases: but suppose they gave leases at a trifling rent, they would not build and enclose them, and that is too great an expence here for a new settler, who could build a handsome house in Virginia for less than a beggarly cottage would cost in England: Thus therefore there are many essential reasons for mens preferring the wilds of America to the wastes of Britain, in relation to the state of the land; and the ease and plenty of living makes another object highly advantageous in Virginia, but by no means so in Britain.

The pleasures of being a land owner are so great, and in America the real advantages so numerous, that it is not to be

wondered

wondered at, that men are so eager to enjoy, that they cross the Atlantic ocean in
order to possess them; nor is it judicious to
draw comparisons between our British
wastes and these, between which there is
no analogy in those essential circumstances
that are the foundation of the great population of America; and at the same time
that this is the case with our waste lands,
it is the same with our cultivated ones
which are equally different.

It is true that many of the good farmers
in Britain will make more per cent. for
their money than is done in America; but
this singly is not the enquiry: in all the
articles of living while the money is made,
the state of the farmer and planter is very
different: the one lives penuriously and
with difficulty, the other on comparison
riots in plenty; the poorest villager in
some of our colonies lives better than a
farmer of 200 l. a year in Britain, that is
frugal enough to save money. Besides this
what a difference there is between living
in one case on their own freehold, and in
the other on the grounds of a landlord!
But the great point is the advantageous
disposition of the savings or other money
which a Virginia planter can apply annually

ally to an increafe of culture ; this is a
point deferving the higheft attention.

At the fame time that I have been fo
clear in ftating the fuperiority of Virginia
in thefe cafes, I muft form an exception
which is that of the landlords farming their
own waftes in Britain : in this cafe they
enter at once into moft of the advantages
of America, and with a power of making
yet greater profit ; for they may improve
them in any quantities, and by building
farm-houfes, let them in farms very foon
after the breaking up, in which rotation
they will make a profit of many more per
cent. than is commonly made any where in
America ; efpecially if he proceeds in the
work of improvement upon the plan of
taking in land enough to form a farm e-
very year, and to let one every year.   In
this manner from 3147l. capital, 62,066l.
may be made in eleven years on moors *.
From 9558l. capital, 142,294l. may be
made in eight years +.   From 1781l. the
loweft fum that can be thus employed,
12,000l. may be made in fifteen years ‡.
This writer feems to think fuch a work
might be as well executed by a renter as

* So ftated in the *Farm. Lett.* Vol. II. p. 189.
† P. 224.   ‡ P. 263.

by

by a landlord: but this does not by any means appear; for the latter I think the reasoning clear, but not for the former, since difficulties may be found at setting out, in procuring the land; it is not every landlord would let his wastes on *long* leases, at rents *low* enough. Other sorts of wastes are calculated in the same book to yield an equal and superior profit.

This immense profit to be made by improving British wastes turns on the very circumstance which makes husbandry so advantageous in America; the plenty of land enabling the farmer to extend himself annually: this is the great object that will be found uniformly profitable through every part of the world; and as wastes in Britain are plentiful enough, there is no reason for general assertions, that land is plentiful in America but dear in Britain, since it is plain this is applicable only to those who want to buy or hire, but to those who are already the possessors, many have in Britain as much as they could have in America, and far more than they know what to do with.

Before I conclude this chapter I shall remark, that the quick population of the American wastes, and the desolate state of

the

the Britifh ones, form a contraft which deferve attention in the legiflature of this ifland : I have fhewn that the reafon of one country peopling and improving fo quick, and the other being quite at a ftand, is lands being given away in America, or next to it, and not to be had at all in Britain ; for very few will be induced to fell land abfolutely wafte, the price it brings being too fmall, and vanity of poffeffing many acres (however wild) great in every one. Thus there being plenty of land in Britain as wafte as that of America, is no object, unlefs thofe who are defirous of poffeffing it in the latter country could get it equally eafily in the former one.

But as the improvement of the waftes of a kingdom is ever an object of the higheft confequence, particularly to population, the legiflature might eafily devife a method if not to cure the whole evil, at leaft to do much good : and this would be to appoint an office to buy up all the wafte land that accidentally came to market in the three kingdoms, and to fettle large families on little farms in them, giving them as freeholds for ever, with a refervation of a quitrent ; not fufficient to pay the intereft of

the

the purchafe, but to leffen the expence if it was too great—but as long as it was kept moderate, no quit-rent at all fhould be taken, fince the object of peopling great tracts of wafte land, in the heart of a country, is of much more confequence than any moderate fum would be. Without fome plan of this fort being executed, we may be certain the moors and waftes will never be improved, and confequently our political writers fhould ceafe declaiming on the impropriety of peopling American waftes, inftead of Britifh ones; the one can be done, the other cannot; and therefore if the peopling America is an advantage to this kingdom, as it certainly is, it ought, beyond a doubt, to be promoted, notwithftrnding the inability of peopling our own waftes.

CHAP.

C H A P. XVII.

*Exports of Virginia and Maryland—Obfer-
vations—General bufbandry—Defects—
Improvements propofed.*

TO fhew the vaft importance of thefe
colonies to Great Britain, it will be
neceffary to lay before the reader the laft
accounts of their exports, from which we
fhall alfo fee what proportion their common hufbandry bears to their tobacco.

Tobacco, 96,000 hogfheads, at 8l.	*L.* 768,000
Indian corn, beans, peafe, &c. - -	30,000
Wheat, 40,000 quarters, at 20s. - -	40,000
Deer and other-fkins, - -	25,000
Iron in bars and pigs, - -	35,000
Saffafras, fnake-root, ginfeng, &c. -	7,000
Mafts, plank, ftaves, turpentine, and tar, -	55,000
Flax-feed, 7000 hogfheads, at 40s. -	14,000
Pickled pork, beef, hams, and bacon,	15,000
Ships built for fale, 30 at 1000l. -	30,000
Hemp 1000 tons at 21l. (befides 4000 tons more and 2000 of flax worked up for their own ufe, - -	21,000
Total	1,040,000

Upon this table I muft obferve once
more, how extremely important thefe colonies

lonies are to the mother country. To raise above a million sterling, the greatest part of which are true staples, and the rest necessary for the West Indies, with no fish, whalebone, oil, &c. commodities which some of the colonies have run away with from Britain, by rivalling her in her fishery—possessing no manufactures, even to such a degree that all attempts to bring the people into towns have proved vain. By manufactures, I mean those for sale; for as to private families working wool, hemp, and flax for their own use, it is what many do all over America, and are necessitated to do, for want of money and commodities to buy them. A colony so truly important, I say, deserves every attention from the mother country, and every encouragement to induce settlers to fix in it.

But in this list of exports one article appears which demands particular attention, I mean hemp. To the north of these colonies, none is exported; on the contrary, they import from Britain the hemp which we import from Russia, which is brought from the Ukraine, paying this immense freight; a proof strong enough that they cannot raise it. In Virginia and Maryland

the foil is much better than to the northward, and will yield it, which we find it
does in large quantities, even to the amount
of 100,000l. an amount that is near a feventh of their tobacco, befides flax. This
is the commodity of all others which we
moft want from our colonies, for it is
fo neceffary for our navy, that we ought
certainly to have it more within our own
command than it is at prefent; and the
purchafe carries away immenfe fums of
money annually: to raife it therefore in
America, and purchafe it with our manufactures, is an object of the greateft importance. It is evident that if we are to
expect hemp, it muft be from this part of
that continent; and confequently here we
fhould give our great attention. It is alfo
a matter of great importance to fettlers,
to know that the climate and foil of the
country will do for fo valuable a product
as hemp as well as tobacco; and their
management is fuch, that both may be cultivated to advantage on the fame plantation ; and it is well known, that in America the profit on hemp, when land is found
that will produce it, is as great as that on
tobacco.

The

The latter plant thrives beſt on a rich, deep, black mould that is dry, and upland ı but hemp loves the ſame ſoil in low lands, that have a good degree of moiſture in them. Very many tracts of land are yet to be had in the back parts of Virginia, which contain both ſorts in plenty, and would conſequently do well for the cultivation of both theſe products. A ſituation for hemp requires water-carriage as well as tobacco, being a bulky commodity.

	l.	s.	d.
Hemp per ton,	21	0	0
Tobacco,	16	0	0
Wheat, at 30s. a quarter,	7	10	0
Indian corn, barley, peaſe, beans, &c. at 16s. a quarter,	4	8	0
Indigo, at 2s. 6d. a lb.	280	0	0
Ditto at 5s.	560	0	0
Silk, at 20s. a lb.	2240	0	0
Wine,	20	0	0

Such a ſcale of value per ton ſhould always be attended to by new ſettlers: from hence it is apparent, that indigo may be cultivated without water-carriage; or at leaſt will bear a conſiderable land-carriage. to get at water, becauſe the expence of moving it will bear very little proportion to the value: but the Indian corn, peaſe, &c. being worth but 4l. 8s. a ton, the carriage muſt neceſſarily be that of water alone, as the value is too ſmall to bear an expenſive

S 2

car-

carriage: even wheat is in the same pre-
dicament; at 30s. a quarter I should not
suppose it would ever bear a land-carriage
of above ten or twelve miles in order to get
at water. Hemp and tobacco will pay it
much better, and will allow of being
brought much farther by land. The
writers on American affairs have, respecting navigations, confined themselves to the
circumstance of the bulkiness of hemp and
tobacco; but the value per ton is the only
object that deserves attention; and we
find that upon comparison with any sort
of corn, hemp and tobacco is of a value that
will bear some carriage, though not a very
long one. In Virginia the planters are
many of them able to ship their tobacco at
their doors: this great advantage, which
is of equal importance in all other productions as well as tobacco,—in silk, indigo,
&c. it is the same; this advantage has
made it supposed a necessity; but there are
many plantations in which they think a
navigable river for sloops and boats, of great
importance to them; and not a few have
not even this.

The culture of hemp in several circumstances of expence and produce has a resemblance with tobacco. In the richest

soils

foils of England it takes from three and a
half to four acres and a half to produce a
ton, which is worth from 28l. to 35l.
And the labour upon an acre amounts to
from 3l. 10s. to 5l.   This is lefs than
what I fuppofed tobacco would coft in England ; confequently we may determine that
hemp is cultivated in Virginia by negroes
at an expence fomething lefs per acre than
tobacco.   One negroe manages three acres
of tobacco, and would therefore do the
fame or better in hemp, which, to produce
the fame as in England, would be near a ton,
or 21l. the price in America ; this exceeds
tobacco.   That this calculation does not
exceed the truth we may find by an ex-
preffion of Dr. Mitchell's, fpeaking of the
lands on the Ohio and Miffiffippi, "Every
labourer," fays he, " might cultivate TWO
ACRES or more in hemp, and ONE OR TWO
in indigo, the produce of which would be
worth from 30 to 40l. a year *.   Now if
they could manage two in hemp, and one
or two in indigo, we may fairly conclude
they might cultivate three in hemp : and
this makes hemp more profitable to the

---

* *Prefent State*, p. 248.

S 3   planter.

planter than tobacco: but supposing them only on a par, it is an object of no slight importance to know, that those lands which are not perfectly adapted to tobacco, may be made equally profitable under hemp.

The wheat and other corn which is a-mong these exports, are raised principally on old tobacco plantations that are worn out for that plant without the assistance of much manure. This is a point which deserves attention: exhaust the lands in these colonies as much as you will with tobacco, you will leave it in order for grain, which is a matter of great consequence to the settlers; since corn is there a very profitable article of culture, and upon the rich lands of this country will (even after tobacco) yield large crops, with very little assistance from manure.

The usual course of the business has been the planters exhausting the land first with tobacco, and then retiring backwards with their negroes in quest of fresh land for tobacco, sell their old plantations to new comers, who have not money enough to go largely into tobacco with negroes, and therefore confine themselves to common husbandry: and this is upon the whole very advantageous. Planters who meet
with

with very rich frefh woodland, employ themfelves fo eagerly on tobacco, as fcarcely to raife corn enough for their families, in which cafe their little neighbours are very ufeful to them in felling it. This does not however feem to be good management, as tobacco employs the negroes only in fummer: indeed they may occupy the winter entirely in clearing frefh land.

Tobacco and hemp, I have already given as good an account of as my intelligence will allow: but the common hufbandry of thefe provinces demands the fame attention. Wheat they fow as we do in England in October; about two bufhels to an acre, which produces feldom lefs than twenty-five; fometimes thirty-five and forty. Rye they do not cultivate much, as their lands are in general good enough to give them great crops of wheat. Barley produces from twenty-five to forty bufhels: oats from 30 to 60: peafe from 10 to 60: Indian corn feldom lefs than 50, and fometimes 80. Turneps and cabbages thrive in the greateft luxuriance, and produce crops far beyond any thing we know in Britain. Potatoes alfo, with good management, yield without any dung, crops much greater than can in thefe iflands be

gained

gained by the force of manuring: yet are
the farmers of these colonies most inex-
cusably negligent in not giving these crops
due justice, in properly preparing their
land, and keeping them during their growth
free from weeds. If the fertility of the
soil and climate was well seconded by the
knowledge and industry of the planters,
the crops would be much greater than they
are, and husbandry would prove the most
profitable business in the known world.
But the planters, who have the power of
being good cultivators of their fields, aban-
don them to the overseers of their negroes,
and pursue only their own pleasures—and
others, who may have more knowledge, have
not the substance to make improvements :
it is the same in Britain, and probably in
every other part of the world. The fore-
going account of the products of the crops
of common husbandry, is sufficient to shew
the immense profit which might be made
by agriculture in this country, if it was
followed with understanding and spirit: for want of these necessary ingredi-
ents, twice the land is run over to produce
that which half of it would be more than
sufficient for, under scientific management.

In

In the fyftems of crops generally purfued here, the farmers go upon the bad
ideas of their brethren to the northwards;
they take fucceffive crops of corn, till the
land will produce no more, then they leave
it fallow for fome years, and ferve frefh
ground in the fame manner: all the inconveniences which I have mentioned in
preceding articles refult from this, but the
plenty of land feduces the planters to act
thus contrary to their own interefts. The
fummers in Virginia and Maryland being
hotter than in Penfylvania, this method
muft be ftill worfe than there, becaufe the
land they leave in this manner fallow muft
be the longer before it acquires a turf to
fupport cattle: this fhews the neceffity, if
the farmer would make the moft of his
grounds, of leaving the land in tolerable
heart; and with the laft crop of corn fowing grafs feeds that are adapted to the climate. Good meadows are very fcarce, except where water can be thrown over them,
a hufbandry not practifed near fo much as
it ought.

In the management of their woods, they
have fhewn the fame inattention to futurity with their neighbours; fo that in the
old fettled parts of the provinces, they begin

gin to fear a want of that useful commodity, and would have felt it long ago, had
they not such an immense inland navigation to supply them. The woods, upon a
tobacco plantation, must be in great plenty,
for the winter employment of the slaves,
or else the planter's profit will not equal
that of his neighbours.

Their fences are extremely incomplete,
and kept in very bad order: all their attention is to secure the tobacco-field, but
the rest of the plantation is never in this
respect kept in the order that it ought to
be: this is another evil occasioned by plenty of land; they will grasp at more than
they have money to cultivate, even upon
the tobacco system, which requires plenty;
and then they are forced to manage it in a
slovenly manner.

Cattle might be made an article of great
profit in these provinces: the planters are
obliged, on account of manure, to keep
great stock; but they are little attentive to
make the most advantage of them, either
in the raising manure, or in the management of the beasts themselves. The breed
they think little of improving; and their
treatment of their horses and oxen, for
draft, is such as would move the ridicule
of

of the fmalleft farmers in England. Thefe
are points which they miflakenly think of
little importance, giving all their attention to the tobacco; but with better management thefe objeds would prove fo profitable as to fhew that they demanded no
lefs conduct than their principal crop. In
the article of raifing manure, particularly,
they might make five times their prefent
quantity, which would be attended with
a correfponding increafe of their ftaple in
fome of their fields; but for want of knowledge in this effential part of their bufinefs
they lofe much.

There are fome improvements in the
rural œconomy of thefe provinces, which
demand particular attention, for they would
admit of more and greater, than any of our
other plantations. Under the article tobacco, I remarked feveral alterations which
would render that culture much more beneficial; of which the effect of general
good management, enabling them to keep
more land under that ftaple, is an effential
article, which would make a vaft difference in the intereft of Britain. No objed
in the American department is of fuch confequence; and this fhould induce the adminiftration to take whatever meafures that
could

could be defired, in order to improve the agriculture of thefe provinces. Means might be invented which would introduce by degrees better ideas.

Among the articles of improvement, which are the moft obvious, there is nothing which demands greater attention than the culture of filk. None of our colonies enjoy a climate fo well adapted to the purpofe.: mulberry trees are found every where in profufion, and the work of winding the filk, and attending the worms, might be carried on without any material interruption of their tobacco culture; but the advantage of making filk, is its being in a great meafure proper for uniting with almoft any bufinefs, fince women, old, infirm, perfons, and even children, make as good a figure in it as the moft robuft men, a point of vaft confequence. The common objection is, the want of hands; but that feems to be made by perfons who are not acquainted with the bufinefs: five or fix weeks in a year would be fufficient for the work, and a family of a moderate number might, it is very well known, make 40 or 50 l. a year, which would at once be 40 or 50 l. fterling a year to them, an object of equal confequence with any that could be found. It

is

is fuppofed that the number of people in the tobacco colonies does not fall fhort of 800,000; if filk was well underftood among them, it would be no difficult matter to have from them as many pounds of filk, without any deduction from their tobacco; but if only 500,000l. were made, it would add exceedingly to the wealth both of Britain and the colony.

In a country newly fettling, or fettled, people really cannot fpare either the time or attention, fmall as it is, for making filk; but the cafe is very different in Maryland and Virginia, which are in a great meafure well peopled countries, compared to feveral of our colonies. The people are numerous enough to make it an object of confequence, and are in general fufficiently at their eafe to render the undertaking as profitable as it is in Italy or China. I cannot but attribute the remiffnefs fhewn in this article, to a want of people, or of time, but merely to that of attention and knowledge. They are unacquainted with the conduct of the worms, and the winding of the filk, and probably think it a more troublefome bufinefs than it is, and one which is of much longer duration. But this ignorance might foon be banifhed,

7

if

if persons skilled in the culture were sent from Europe to instruct them; a few, moving through these provinces, and shewing the women the management (which is a matter of entertainment rather than of labour) would in a few years make it familiar to abundance of families. The importance of silk from our colonies, is an object that well deserves some expence, it will pay excellently for it; since there is great difference between paying for our raw silk with money, and buying it with our manufactures.

Another article to be mentioned here, is the culture of vines, for which the back parts of Virginia are as well if not better adapted to than those of Pensylvania : wine is another commodity which the nation is in as great want of from the colonies as any other, for the sums paid by this kingdom to France, Spain, and Portugal, for this production of their lands, are immense. There is the greatest reason to suppose, that vineyards would thrive here advantageously, from the uncommon plenty of wild vines found in the woods thro' all the back country. The planters know not what would be the effect of culture on these vines, though the grapes at present

will

will not make good wine, yet is there no
reafon to think that cultivation, upon approved principles, would not render them
of a quality fufficiently excellent? The
richeft vineyards of Champagne and Burgundy, left wild, would, it is well known,
produce a wine far enough from the flavour
of thofe celebrated ones: it is ploughing
between the rows, dreffing, and pruning,
that gives the flavour to the grapes; and
why fhould not the fame caufes have the
fame effect in America? But the trial upon a large fcale, and executed with the
requifite fkill and fpirit, would prove this:
for attaining fo excellent a purpofe, it
would be neceffary to plant a large vine-
yatd, in a proper fituation, refpecting afpect and foil, and to cultivate it by hands
brought from the vine-countries of Europe.
At the fame time, divifions fhould be al-
lotted to fets of European and Madeira
vines, of various forts; by which means it
would be found with certainty what the
foil and climate would yield in this article
of hufbandry. Probably the native wine
would, with culture, produce the beft
wine, from its agreeing with the peculiar
climate of North America.

In

In all colonies, government ſhould be at the expence of a large plantation, for the valuable purpoſe of making experiments on thoſe products, which are deſired to be produced. Thus in the back parts of Virginia, in ſuch a plantation, ſhould be cultivated vines among other articles : by ſuch a conduct, that certainty would be gained which we want at preſent. The Society for the Encouragement of Arts Manufactures and Commerce, have offered ſome very ſenſible and patriotic premiums for planting the largeſt quantity of ſetts in various diſtricts : ſuch endeavours can never be too much commended ; but at the ſame time it wants not much ſagacity to foreſee that the effect muſt be very trifling : ſuch premiums may be eaſily gained, without the knowledge that is deſired ; for ſuppoſe a certain number of ſetts planted (not amounting to any thing like a ſufficiency for one tenth of a vineyard) this is but of little conſequence, if the ſucceeding management is not duly and ſpiritedly performed, and by perſons ſkilled in the vineyard culture ; points which it is not to be ſuppoſed will be attended to by the accidental perſons that may be candidates for
ſuch

fuch premiums. And how is the fociety, or any perfons in England to know, whether the perfon who plants the greateft number of fetts, is fituated in the moft favourable fpots—or poffeffes a foil equally proper with many other tracts in the province? All fuch experiments fhould certainly be encouraged, but there is very little reafon to believe that they can be attended with any great effect.

The want of people is urged in this cafe, as well in that of filk; and I own with much more reafon, fince population is more neceffary for the management of vineyards, than for that of filk-worms; but in anfwer to this, I fhould propofe the employment of negroes. Why fhould not they be inftructed in pruning and dreffing vines, as well as pruning and picking tobacco, or the operofe performances they execute in the culture of fugar, in the manufacture of which there is very great dexterity requifite, fo that negroe boilers, &c. have been fold for above three hundred pounds a-piece, when experienced in the work. There can be no doubt but they might be employed in the culture of vines equally well, and perhaps to great advantage; this is a point of importance which fhould be well attended to, for the vineyard culture requires many hands, of some kind or other; and as the colonies have not the common population (except in certain districts) sufficient for the purpose, vine planters would be under a necessity of depending for at least much of the work on slaves, the number of which can be multiplied at pleasure to any amount. In the article of cooperage, the Virginians would have great advantage over the vine countries of Europe; their woods would yield them staves, hoops, and heading upon the spot, instead of sending those articles to the West Indies. The length of freight from America to England might easily be remedied, by favouring the import at the custom-house; perhaps it would be proper to exempt them for some time from all duties.

I have in several parts of this work mentioned the great importance of raising hemp in our colonies, and at the same shewn the the difficulties which have prevented any export of it, except the tobacco colonies; these are principally the want of good land, or plenty of manure. But they have a native hemp in Virginia, which they call silk-grass, which might probably be made to answer many purposes of the high-

est

eft ufe, if not exceed the common hemp, fince the threads of it are ftronger; fome moft excellent fabrics have been made in private families of this grafs, which fhew it to be perfectly well adapted to a manufacture, yet has it been quite neglected: befides this filk-grafs, they have three or four forts of native hemp, which thrive well on their pooreft lands, and which have been found to anfwer well in culture on a fmall fcale *.

It is impoffible to know what the merit of the plants indigenous in thefe colonies, is, unlefs there was a plantation eftablifhed at the public expence, under the direction of a fkilful botanift, and one perfectly well acquainted with the practice, as well as the theory of agriculture. In fuch a plantation, improvements might be made in the culture of tobacco: vineyards might be planted and cultivated, both of the native vines, and alfo of foreign ones. Experiments might be made on the culture of filk. All the native plants, like thofe I have juft mentioned, which promifed any thing of utility, might be brought into culture, and trials made of

_____

* Mitchel's *Prefent State*, p. 261.

their

their worth, as materials for manufacture. Such a plantation well supported, would be attended with some, if not all those excellent consequences which flowed from the gardens of the Dutch East India Company, at the Cape of Good Hope. Such objections may be made to the proposal I have now offered, as were doubtless made to the establishment of those famous gardens; but the company wisely rejected objections, when they did not amount to a proof that the measure was wrong; and it has accordingly turned out one of the finest monuments of the spirit of that celebrated body of merchants. Objections may certainly be made to the proposal, and the expence mentioned as a reason for not adopting a design which could not fail of being most highly beneficial; but the expence is a very poor reason against measures of this nature, unless it was urged by ministers who shewed, in all their other actions, the same spirit of œconomy which seemed to dictate such a refusal.

On another occasion I remarked, that the heat of the climate of Pensylvania burnt up the grasses of the pastures, except the low tracts over which water was thrown; this is yet stronger with Virginia and Mary-

land,

land, which are hotter than Penfylvania ; for this reafon the culture of lucerne would, in thefe provinces, be attended with yet greater advantages : their tobacco and hemp demand far more manure than they can at prefent raife, no objeft therefore can be of greater importance than an increafe of it.   This is only to be brought about by keeping their cattle confined; if they were folded in yards, fed in the foiling . way, on lucerne, they would raife greater quantities of dung than in any other method could be effected.   This obfervation is alfo applicable to the winter food of cattle ; the climate of thefe colonies is fo mild, that the cattle run out all winter; which, though an amazing advantage to the planter in many refpects, is yet a preventive of raifing manure, for it is the confinement alone of cattle which affords that. Upon this principle the planters here ought to attend to cabbages, turneps, potatoes, &c. as well as their brethren in the more northern fettlements.

CHAP.

CHAP. XVIII.

THE OHIO.

Defcription of the Countries adjacent to the Ohio—Staples—New colony—Principles on which it is founded—Remarks.

THIS immenfe country, which in our maps is laid down as a part of Virginia, reaches from the eaftward of lake Erie, on the frontiers of New York, in latitude 43°, to its junction with the Miffifippi, in latitude 36½°; the length of this tract, in a ftrait line, is not lefs than 800 miles. For 300 miles it bounds on the mountains, which are the limits of Penfylvania, from which to lake Erie is an oblong of 200 miles long, by about 100 broad, which fpace is one of the fineft parts of North America. But the territory which is here principally to be confidered, is to the fouth of this, from the neighbourhood of Fort Pitt, to the Cherokee river, which falls into the Ohio, near the Miffiffippi, to the fouth of the former river, moft of the country to the north of it belonging to the Six Nations, partly inhabited by them, and part their hunting ground.

The

The want of fresh land in Virginia, for the tobacco planters to spread themselves over, occasioned many settlers to pass the Alligany mountains, and fix themselves on the rivers that fall into the Ohio; this was so early as from 1750 to 1755. the French had in 1748 and 1749 partly usurped and secured all this tract of back country, by their forts; a plan which they afterwards brought fully into execution; and when they were informed of the step taken by the British settlers, they warned them from what they called their master's territories, and soon after by force drove them back. This was the origin of the late war; the events of which relating to this country need no recapitulation here.

Upon the conquest of Fort du Quesne, the back settlers of Virginia and Pensylvania, renewed their emigration, and in great numbers once more passed the mountains, and settled themselves on the Ohio and its branches. Here they cleared grounds, and began their plantations; but in the latter end of 1763, a proclamation appeared, which forbid all settlements beyond the rivers, which fall into the Atlantic Ocean. But the people who had

fixed

fixed themfelves on the fertile lands of the Ohio, were too well pleafed with their fituation to obey this proclamation, while others continued daily to join them.

The territory in which they planted themfelves being without the bounds of the provinces of Virginia and Penfylvania, the people who had fettled there became foon a lawlefs fet, among whom a licentious fpirit prevailed ; living without government, they had continued quarrels with the Indians, and the whole afpect of their affairs foreboded no good. The country in which they fettled belonged to the Six Nations, who complained repeatedly of this invafion of their property, offering to the governor of Virginia to fell their right in all the country to the fouth of the river Ohio.

. Their remonftrances were too much flig⅃ ted, for it was feveral years before any meafures were taken to give them fatisfaction ; from remonftrating they proceeded to threaten in terms fevere, though not departing from refpect. Then it was that a conference was held with the chiefs of thefe nations, and a bargain was ftruck : for the fum of fomething more than ten thoufand pounds paid by government to the Six Nations, they made over all their
right

right to the tracts of country to the south of the Ohio.

This purchase was made, not with a view to encourage any settlements beyond the mountains, but only to satisfy the Indians; the tenor of the proclamation of 1763 was adhered to, and the governor of Virginia ordered to admit of no colonization within the specified limits. But such orders could not be obeyed; for the country was found so fertile and pleasant, that fresh numbers every day thronged thither; and the expediency of establishing a government over them, was found daily greater.

In this situation of affairs it was, that an association of gentlemen, principally of America, formed the plan of establishing a new colony in the lands thus purchased of the Indians; they brought into the idea some respectable merchants of London, at the head of whom was a member of the House of Commons, Mr. Walpole. They petitioned the treasury for leave to execute their plan, offering to pay to government the ten thousand pounds the whole country had cost, for the property of only a part of it, and to be at the whole expence of the civil government of the new province.

This

This petition was referred from the treasury to the board of trade, which board made a report upon the petition, in which they strongly condemned the project, offering the reasons on which they founded their opinion; reasons which were by no means satisfactory to the understanding of those who were well acquainted with the state of the colonies.

The affair then came before the privy council, in which it was debated, and a difference of opinion found, which occasioned a debate; it ended in the petition being granted; after which Mr. Walpole and his associates took such measures as they thought necessary for the establishment of their new colony.

This is the history of the transaction brought down to the present time *; the latter part is too recent to know upon what terms the proprietors portion out the lands, nor yet are the exact limits known: but the accounts we have had of the country before it was thought of establishing a colony in it, are such as will enable us to form a pretty clear idea of it. In the ob-

* Since this was written, it has been reported that some interruption has happened in the grant.

servafervations on the report of the board of trade on the petition of Mr. Walpole and his affociates, the following circumftances are drawn up.

Firft, The lands in queftion are excellent, the climate temperate, the native grapes, filk worms, and mulberry-trees are every where; hemp grows fpontaneoufly in the vallies and low grounds; iron ore is plenty in the hills, and no foil is better adapted for the culture of tobacco, flax, and cotton, than that of the Ohio.

Second, The country is well watered by feveral navigable rivers, communicating with each other; and by which and a fhort land-carriage of *only forty miles*, the produce of the lands of the Ohio can, even *now*, be fent cheaper to the fea-port town of Alexandria, on the river Potomack, (where general Braddock's tranfports landed his troops) than any kind of merchandize is at this time fent *from Northampton to London*.

Third, The river Ohio is, at *all* feafons of the year navigable for large boats like the weft country barges, rowed only by four or five men; and from the month of January to the month of April large fhips may be built on the Ohio, and fent laden

with

with *hemp*, *flax*, *filk*, &c. to this king-dom.

Fourth, Flour, corn, beef, fhip-plank, and other neceffaries can be fent down the ftream of the Ohio to Weft Florida, and from thence to the iflands, much cheaper and in better order, than from New York or Philadelphia.

Fifth, Hemp, tobacco, iron, and fuch bulky articles, can alfo be fent *down* the *ftream* of the Ohio to the *fea*, at leaft 50 per cent. cheaper than thefe articles were ever carried by a land-carriage of only fixty miles in Penfylvania ;—where *waggonage* is cheaper than in any other part of North America.

Sixth, The expence of tranfporting Bri-tifh manufactures from the fea to the Ohio colony will *not* be fo much as is now paid, and muft ever be paid to a great part of the countries of Penfylvania, Virginia, and Maryland.

That we may more particularly eluci-date this important point, we fhall take the freedom of obferving—that it is *not* dif-puted, but even acknowledged, by the very report now under confideration, that the climate and foil of the Ohio are as favour-able as we have defcribed them ; and as to

the

the native filk-worms—it is a truth, that above 10,000 weight of cocoons was, in Auguſt 1771, fold at the public filature in Philadelphia, and that the filk produced from the *native* worm is of a good quality, and has been much approved of in this city. As to hemp, we are ready to make it appear that it grows, as we have reprefented, fpontaneoufly, and of a good texture on the Ohio." In the report itfelf it is urged—" every advantage derived from an eſtabliſhed government would naturally tend to draw the ſtream of population ; fertility of foil, and temperature of climate, offering fuperior incitements to fettlers, who, expofed to few hardſhips, and ſtruggling with few difficulties, could with little labour earn an abundance for their own wants." This is the ſtate of the intelligence which is to be gained from the parties concerned ; from thofe who petitioned, and from thofe who wanted the petition to be rejected, both agree as to the fertility and healthinefs of the territory. But I remarked. before, that the fame accounts were current before a colony was thought of.

Upon occafion of the laſt war Dr. Mitchel was employed by the miniſtry to

take

take an accurate furvey of all the back
countries of North America, moſt of them
being then but little known, except to the
French, who were in poſſeſſion of a line
of forts through all North America. No
perſon could have been more properly appointed, for he was not only able to lay
down the country with exactneſs, but being well acquainted with practical agriculture in Virginia and Penſylvania, he was
able to underſtand the nature and value of
thoſe countries he ſhould traverſe. This
was the origin of his map of North America, the beſt general one we have had : at
the time it was publiſhed, it was accom-
panied by a bulky pamphlet, written by
the Doctor, and entitled, *The Conteſt in
America*, in which he enters into a full
elucidation of the importance of the back
countries, and of the fatal effects which
muſt flow from leaving the French in poſſeſſion of their encroachments. Among
others he conſiders particularly the territory of the Ohio, and ſhews of how much
importance it is to the planters of Virginia ; he there mentions the want of freſh
lands for planting tobacco, and the necef-
ſity of their being able to extend themſelves for that purpoſe beyond the mountains.

tains. The country is deſcribed as one of the fineſt and moſt fruitful in all America, and abounding greatly in deer, wild cows, and wild oxen; and at the ſame time ſituated in one of the fineſt and moſt healthy climates in all that country.

This account agrees alſo with another which was given near an hundred years ago by La Honton, who, ſpeaking of the country to the ſouth of lake Erie, mentions its being one of the fineſt on the globe, both in reſpect of climate and ſoil; it is a tract, he obſerves, of vaſt meadows, full of wild bees and deer, and the woods of vines and wild turkies.

Dr. Mitchel, in another work publiſhed in 1767, *(The Preſent State)* gives other particulars concerning this territory, which deſerve attention; and eſpecially in the point of affording that freſh land which is ſo much wanted in the tobacco colonies, where their plantations (as was ſhewn in the article of Virginia) are exhauſted by continual crops of that product: " they will," ſays he, " be in a ſhort time worn out, and when that happens, there muſt be an end of the tobacco trade, without a ſupply of freſh lands, fit to produce that exhauſting weed, as well as to maintain cattle

tle to manure them, with convenient ports
and an inland navigation to ſhip off ſuch a
groſs and bulky commodity; of which
there are none in all the Britiſh dominions
in North America, but the rich landȿ on
the Miſſiſſippi and the Ohio: whoever
are poſſeſſed of theſe muſt ſoon command
the tobacco trade, the only conſiderable
branch of trade in all North America, and
the only one that this nation has left" In
other paſſages the ſame writer deſcribes
theſe lands as being of conſiderable depth
and fertility, having a natural moiſture in
them, and being excellently adapted for
hemp, flax, and tobacco; alſo that no
country can promiſe better for ſilk, wine,
and oil, the climate being dry, which is
the contrary of the maritime parts of A-
merica, where the rains are almoſt continual. And from the natural plenty of
graſs in meadows of great extent, with the
general fertility of the ſoil, the maintenance
of all ſorts of cattle would be perfectly
eaſy, and conſequently proviſions would
be raiſed with ſcarcely any trouble; a point
of great importance when a ſtaple commodity is cultivated; for the planter ought to
be able to give all his attention to the principal article: but if he is forced to divide
his

his ſtrength for providing food for cattle, &c. he cannot raiſe ſuch a quantity of his ſtaple as if more favourably circumſtanced.

In a word, this territory of the Ohio enjoys every advantage of climate and ſoil which is to be found in the back parts of Virginia, but in a much higher degree, the ſoil being far more fertile, and the climate more pleaſant and more wholeſome. The aſſertions in the obſervations on the report of the board of trade are ſtrong to this point, and may be depended on, as ſeveral of the gentlemen in the aſſociation for eſtabliſhing this colony have lived long in Virginia and Penſylvania, and appointed perſons to gain intelligence of all the material circumſtances concerning it. From theſe, and the other authorities I have mentioned, it is plain, that this new colony will probably be found of the higheſt conſequence in the production of the following commodities.

TOBACCO.

This valuable ſtaple is cultivated in Virginia upon the freſheſt and moſt fertile lands ; none can be too rich for it : a newly broken up woodland is what it moſt affects,

sects, and is what the planters choose for
it, whenever it is in their power. I before observed, that such new land was no
longer in plenty in the tobacco colonies,
which makes this acquisition of country of
the more importance : here are immense
forests upon a soil the most fertile that can
be imagined, and consequently such a field
for enlarging our tobacco plantations as the
nation has long wanted. Such a soil may
well prove an inducement to many to purchase great numbers of negroes, in order
to employ them on staple productions,
which in such fresh and fertile lands may
safely be expected to pay them better than
in the old colonies, where the good land
has been for some time scarce ; that is private property : there is in several of our
colonies great tracts that are excellent, but
this is like the wastes in Britain ; plenty of
land is of no effect, if it is not to be had by
the new settlers without paying a large price
for it. But the value of the lands on the Ohio
is not disputed, the great point for tobacco
is that of carriage ; for it is so bulky, that
if carriage is expensive, it cannot be brought
cheap enough to market. The proprietors
give the following account of the communication with the Atlantic. " During the
last

laſt French war, when there was no back carriage from the Ohio to Alexandria, the expence of carriage was only about a *half-penny* a pound, as will appear from the following account, the truth of which we ſhall fully aſcertain, viz.

	l.	s.	d.
From Alexandria to Port Cumberland by water	0	1	7 per cwt.
From Port Cumberland to Red Stone Creek, at fourteen dollars per waggon load, each waggon carrying fifteen cwt.	0	4	2
	0	5	9

Note, The diſtance was *then* ſeventy miles, but by a *new* waggon road *lately* made, it is *now* but forty miles—a ſaving, of courſe, of above one half of the 5s. 9d. is *at preſent* experienced. If it is conſidered that this rate of carriage was *in time of war*, and *when* there were no inhabitants on the Ohio, we cannot doubt but every intelligent mind will be ſatisfied that it is now *leſs* than is daily paid in London for the carriage of *coarſe woollens, cutlery, iron ware,* &c. from ſeveral counties in England." And in the enumeration of advantages quoted above, it is aſſerted, that *large ſhips* may be built on the Ohio, and ſent loaded, from January to April, to Bri-

U 2   tain ;

tain ; alſo that proviſions and lumber may be ſent from thence cheaper to the Weſt Indies, than from New York or Philadelphia.

Theſe accounts call for ſeveral material obſervations : as to the truth of them, they are advanced in ſuch a manner, and by ſuch perſons, that we have no reaſon to doubt it ; nor ſhould I omit to remark, that the account coincides with others, particularly with the exportation which the French are well known to have carried on from the Illionois, and do at preſent carry on from thence. But it was never known that the mouth of the Miſſiſſippi was navigable for *large* ſhips ; Captain Pittman, who ſurveyed the river, ſays, a thirty-ſix gun frigate has gone over with her guns *out* ; but after you are over the bar, he acknowledges there is depth of water, all the way up, for *any ſhip whatever*. The proprietors remark, that half the 5s. 9d. is ſaved ; but that does not appear, as the price from Alexandria to Fort Cumberland is not changed ; but ſuppoſing inſtead of 4s. 2d. from Fort Cumberland to Redſtone Creek, that it ſhould be only 2s. then the total price per cwt. would be 3s. 7d. or per ton 3l. 11s. 8d. Now two hogſ-
heads

heads of tobacco make a ton, which at 8l.
are 16l. from which price the deduction of
3 l. 11 s. 8 d. more than is paid by the
planters near Alexandria, is too high to
be submitted to, if any cheaper method
can be found of conveying that product to
shipping; and this cheaper method must
surely be by the Mississippi, to the gulph
of Florida; for if lumber and provisions
can be sent by that channel cheaper than
from New York or Philadelphia, as the
proprietors assert, it must plainly be a
cheaper way than a carriage which comes
to 3l. 11 s. 8 d. per ton, which can
never be supported by a commodity,
the value of which at shipping is only
16 l. a ton. The reason of this carriage being so dear, must be the number
of falls above Alexandria. As to wheat
and other provisions, they could never be
sent by such a conveyance, five quarters of
wheat are a ton, which at 20s. a quarter
come only to 5l. a sum that will never
bear 3l. 11s. 8d. carriage before it gets to
the shipping; and if it is reckoned at 30s.
or 7l. 10s. still 3l. 11s. 8d. is far more than
it would bear.

Relative to the mother country, it is of
very little consequence whether wheat and

pro-

provisions can be exported from a colony
or not, becaufe ftaple commodities alone
are valuable to Britain ; but to fettlers it is
an object to know if all the furplus of their
products can be exported to advantage.
What they may be by the Miffiffippi is not
the point at prefent, but certainly they
cannot be to the Atlantic. By the accounts
of the proprietors it is clear, that no commodity fcarcely 'can be raifed, but what
may be fent from the Ohio to the Weft
Indies. This concern of navigation is of
great confequence to the tobacco planter,
whofe product is one of the moft bulky
ftaples of America ; and in Virginia and
Maryland the convenience of water-carriage is fo great, that many planters load
fhips at their own doors ; but this is not
in common to be expected, though it
feems that it might be the cafe along the
Ohio, if once the navigation of the Miffiffippi be well underftood from practice.

In refpect of the advantages for tobacco
planting, that refult from a great plenty of
land, enabling the planter to keep whatever ftocks of cattle he wants, and to raife
provifion for the plantation, no country in
America is comparable to the territory in
queftion, where a country is now fettling
more

more than 500 miles long, by from 2 to 300 broad, poſſeſſing, in the utmoſt luxuriance of plenty, every neceſſary of life.

H E M P.

As tobacco requires for yielding great crops a rich woodland that is rather dry ; hemp on the contrary, loves a large degree of moiſture, in rich low lands. Such are found in great plenty in all the valleys, between the hills, in the new colony, where the ſoil is natural to this production, as we may judge from the circumſtance of ſuch quantities of wild hemp being found in almoſt all the low lands. This circumſtance ſhews alſo how well the climate may be expected to agree with it. There is all the reaſon in the world to think that the nation's expectations of having hemp from the colonies will at leaſt, after ſo many diſappointments, be anſwered by the lands on the Ohio. They are, it is univerſally agreed, of that nature which is peculiarly adapted to the production ; the vales are rich, deep, moiſt, and ſo fertile that it will be many years before they are exhauſted. This is preciſely what has been ſo long wanted ; for if hemp will not pay for the employment of negroes, it will never be

made

made an article of culture in large : fecondary objects are always neglected ; it is
only thofe of the firft importance which
enjoy that degree of attention neceffary to
make any thing fucceed. The only thing
to be feared, upon this principle, is the
neglect of the planter, who, ufed to tobacco, may be fo eager in raifing that
ftaple as to neglect every other. Neglect
of this fort fometimes gives rife to ideas
of incapacity in a country, when the fault
is only in the cultivator : for this reafon I
cannot but regret, that the proprietors offer of ten thoufand pounds fhould have
been accepted ; they ought to have been
bound to fupply the navy with a given
quantity of hemp, *the growth of the colony,*
annually : this would have forced them to
give a degree of attention to this important
article, which in the prefent cafe may not
be thought of. Nothing is more common
in the eftablifhment of colonies, than proprietors to make large promifes at firft, and
afterwards to forget that ever fuch things
were thought of. The territory of the Ohio
is in no want of *encouragement* from the
proprietors ; but people are fo apt to move
only in their accuftomed line, and fo averfe
from all ufeful trials and experiments, that
they

they fhould in fome cafes be driven to do that which is equally for the intereft of their country and themfelves.

VINES.

Of all North America, this is the tract which bids faireft for yielding wine: the native vines are in greater plenty and variety, than in any other part; the country at fome diftance from the Ohio is hilly and very dry, and in fome places even rocky; but thefe plants do not require the rocky foil near fo much as European ones; for they thrive and bear well on rich deep foils. " We have feen, fays Dr. Mitchel, fifteen different forts of native grapes there, the like of which growing wild are certainly not to be found in any part of the world. The ordinary forts of thefe in Virginia, yield a wine fo like the common Bourdeaux wine, that it is difficult to diftinguifh the one from the other; and from another fort, fome wine has been made which was compared by good judges, both here and there, to the beft that is drank. Other forts yield wine exactly like the Lifbon. But inftead of thefe, they have tranfplanted grapes from the hills of Normandy to the maritime parts of Virginia

and

and Carolina, where no one could expect them to thrive nigh so well as they do. They ripen there in the beginning and middle of August, when no one can expect to make good wine; although they yield a very good wine for present drinking. But this is the most improper for their climate of any grape that grows; neither is it the true Burgundy grape for which they got it." From hence it is easy to be gathered, if the fact was not well known, that these territories on the Ohio must be well adapted to vineyards; much more so than any maritime part of that continent; for near the sea the rains are almost incessant, whereas upon the Ohio the climate is very dry, and on the Mississippi it rarely rains. This is a circumstance extremely favourable to the vineyard culture, which never does well in a country where much rain falls: all the fine wines come from countries which enjoy upon the whole, a climate dry on comparison with others, and some remarkably so.

Wine is another commodity which will bear no long land carriage, since to become an object of exportation from America to Britain, it much be afforded at a low price; wines upon the par with the red

port

2

port of Portugal ought not to exceed 10 or
12 l. a pipe, prime coft, and perhaps not
fo much; this is 20 or 24 l. a ton; fo that
hemp is, in proportion of weight, as valuable a commodity. It will certainly be
found, that the Miffiffippi muft be the
conveyance of both tobacco, hemp, and
wine, to the fea; land-carriage will add
too much to the expences: a frefh reafon
for the navigation of the Miffiffippi being
immediately and accurately examined. If
fhips of only 100 tons could (as the proprietors affert *large* ones can) be built on
the Ohio, and fent at a certain feafon of
the year, laden to Britain with hemp, tobacco, and wine, the advantage would be
the moft profitable application of the timber in the world; as well as cafks for the
wine and tobacco.

S I L K.

All this territory abounds with mulberry trees, in an extraordinary manner;
and it is very well known, that people in
the new colony will foon be in plenty;
the furplus of population in Penfylvania,
New York, Jerfey, Virginia, and Maryland; a furplus which is great, as is well
known from various circumftances before
men-

mentioned, such as numerous petitions to settle in the northern parts of New England; repeated ones for lands on the Ohio; and 30,000 people already settled there, even without the advantage of a government being established; also the well known want of *fresh* lands for tobacco. If the accounts we have had from all parts of the central colonies be well confidered, there can be no doubt remain that 500,000 persons at least will, in a few years, be found in this colony, since it is that tract of country which has for so many years been the object of their ardent desires. Silk therefore certainly promises to become an article of no slight consequence, *in case the people will be persuaded to give due attention to it*; and in such cases I have often remarked, that the only sensible persuasions are examples and rewards. Every person might make a pound of silk, without interruption of their agriculture, which would be to themselves, as well as to Britain, an object of consequence; but if the business was well attended to by whole families, who understood the conduct of it, then much larger quantities might be produced: and in such case it would be found, for the time

time it required, one of the moſt valuable
ſtaples in the world.

COTTON.

This plant grows ſpontaneouſly from the
ſouthern parts of Penſylvania to Florida:
in Virginia they have ſome that is excellent, and in ſome reſpects ſuperior to that
of the Weſt Indies, particularly for mix-
ing with wool. Upon the Ohio, the ſoil,
after being exhauſted by tobacco, would
yield large crops of this for ever; the climate is better adapted to it, and the quantity gained would be greater. Cotton is
not an article of ſufficient value to be the
ſole product of a plantation; but as a ſe-
condary object it might be cultivated with
good profit. This part of huſbandry is not
ſufficiently attended to in our colonies;
the planters beſtow all their time and attention to their grand ſtaple, ſo as to overlook all inferior articles; but this a miſ-
taken conduct; they can have no crop in
this latitude that will employ them the
whole year; the ſenſible management would
be to have ſeveral, ſo as to employ their
ſlaves on them in ſucceſſion. Wheat may
be the moſt valuable product of a Britiſh
farm; but this does not prevent the farmer

mer from fowing barley, oats, peafe, and
beans; nor does corn in general prevent
his cultivating turneps, carrots, and potatoes, which again leave time for clover
and graffes: and it is to this various application of his land, that he is as much
obliged for his profit, as to any other circumftance. Sawing lumber does not equal
(except in the lands that muft be cleared
for the crops) the culture of any ftaple:
among thefe fecondary objeds, cotton will
here be found of no flight importance.

INDIGO.

The fineft indigo is that of Guatimala,
the climate exceeding hot; in St. Domingo the French raife large quantities that is
excellent; and in Carolina it is become a
ftaple of great confequence: the profit depends much on the heat of the climate, as
may be judged from its being cut five times
in St. Domingo in a feafon, three or four
in Carolina, and two or three in Virginia;
for there is fome indigo planted in that
province, notwithftanding its making no
figure in the exports. On the Ohio there
is great reafon to fuppofe it may be cultivated

vated to good advantage, the foil being admirably rich, and the climate fuperior to Virginia ; but a ftrong proof is its having long been an article of export from the Illionois fettlements, which are full as northerly as any part of the colony of the Ohio. In Carolina they plant it on their dry fands; but this is for want of fuch a rich, deep, black mould as is found through the new colony, where foil may make good amends for want of fo hot a fun ; a point which feems almoft proved by St. Domingo fo much exceeding Carolina, though the fummers (notwithftanding the difference of latitude) are hotter in Carolina than in that ifland; but in the latter it is planted on frefh woodlands to prepare them for fugar, and in the former on a poor fand. This article is perfectly well adapted to the Ohio in another refpect, which is that of its great value in proportion to its weight, which is fo high that the price of an expenfive carriage would be fcarcely felt. This is a product which might (as well as filk) be fent over the mountains to be fhipped in Virginia.

M A D-

MADDER,

An article of great importance in the manufactures in England, and bought of the Dutch in great quantities at the high price of from 80 l. to 90 l. a ton; from which we see it ranks among those that will very well pay the expence of carriage from the Ohio to Virginia. It is amazing that this article of cultivation has never been introduced in large in our colonies, though it is beyond doubt one which would agree as well with their climate as any thing they cultivate. In Europe the finest grows in Turkey, but the most in Holland, Flanders, and the Palatinate, from whence there can be no hesitation of its suiting the excellent climate of the Ohio. Madder requires a rich, deep, flexible mould; no degree of fertility is too great for it: of all soils I should suppose a new deep woodland would be the most proper for it; in this respect it would be a rival to tobacco, but then it would probably pay better for it, and in the value of the weight infinitely exceed it. In England there has been raised fifteen hundred per acre, and the expence *in labour* may be thus calculated from the totals mentioned in the account.

1767.

		l.	s.	d.
1767.	Four ploughings, -	0	4	8
	Ridging up, -	0	1	6
	Water-furrowing, -	0	1	6
1768.	Planting, - -	0	18	0
	Hand-weeding, -	0	12	0
	Horfe-hoeing, -	0	2	4
	Water-furrowing, -	0	1	0
1769.	Three hand-hoeings,	1	10	0
	Horfe-hoeing, -	0	3	0
	Water-furrowing, -	0	1	0
1770.	Two hand-hoeings	1	0	0
	Horfe-hoeing, -	0	1	6
	Taking up, -	3	0	0
	Drying, at 3s. -	2	5	0
	Total	10	1	6

Produce.

15 cwt. at 4l.   - · - £. 60 0 0

The drying, probably, at fo large an expence, is peculiar to the climate of England and Holland; but on the Ohio the
fun would be much fuperior to the ftove
drying, as it is for the wild madder of
Turkey. I fhewed, under the article of
Virginia, that the expence of an acre of

tobacco in England would in labour be 6 l. 1s. 8d. and the produce is only 5l. 6s. 8d. from whence it was plain, that it is an article of culture only fit for very cheap labour, such as that of negroes ; but on the contrary we find, that madder is far more valuable : 15 cwt. indeed was the greatest crop got by one gentleman with manuring, but then other persons in the same register got 20 cwt. and even 30 cwt. without manuring, only by planting on land of superior natural fertility : where is more fertile land to be met with than the fresh grounds on the Ohio ? Now the culture of tobacco without the produce being sufficient even to pay the expence of labour of whites, is extremely profitable by slaves ; the proportion would hold with madder, and it would be found far superior to tobacco; the expence on carriage and freight on a commodity worth 80 l. a ton would not be felt.

Rich, deep, black land, moist, but not wet, is the great article wanted for madder, or else such an immense plenty of dung, as will convert an indifferent loam into such a soil, which can be had only in three or four situations in a great kingdom : natural fertility is what we ought therefore

fore to feek ; the price of labour evidently
is of no weight—yet is this circumflance,
like all others in favour of America, for.
that the labour of flaves is as three to one
cheaper than that of Englifh labourers, was
fufficiently proved by the product of tobacco ; inftead of yielding a profit not an-
fwering the expence, but with negroes being advantageous enough to give fortunes
to the planters, did they know how to keep
the money they make.

This object of introducing madder as a
ftaple in the new colony, in order to fave
two or three hundred thoufand pounds a
year, which we at prefent pay to Holland
for the commodity, an abfolute neceffary
in our manufactures, ought to be well confidered. That it would thrive to admiration
there, cannot be doubted, fince the foil in
many tracts is equal to any in the world ;
and the climate very fimilar to that of Turkey, where it is a common fpontaneous
growth. No doubts therefore can be entertained of the produce ; as to labour, the
above account of 10 l. in England near
London would not be 4l. by means of negroes ; and if the product was no more
than 15 cwt. and the value 6ol. in London,
the account in general would ftand thus:

Labour,

	l.	s.	d.
Labour, - - - - -	4	0	0
Carriage from the Ohio to Alexandria, at 3l. 11s. 8d. per ton, - - -	2	13	9
Freight to London at 5l. 10s. per ton, -	4	2	6
Total	10	16	3

Thus would the Ohio planter land his madder at London at nearly the same expence that labour alone stands the Surry or Kentish planter in! If this is not an immense encouragement to them to enter deeply into the culture, nothing can; but they will in this, as in numerous other cases, want example, visible proof; which can only be given them by the proprietors establishing a plantation for experiments in large, which would presently ascertain this and other points of great importance.

There is one circumstance in this culture which would make it suit extremely the usual œconomy of a plantation in North America. It is three years in the ground, and might be left four or five with proportionable profit, during which time there is nothing to do to it in winter; all the operations it requires are over between March and October, and when taken up the drying is over in less than a month; thus would the negroes have the whole winter

to faw lumber, or to be employed in other
articles of culture, that required winter
operations : this a point much attended to
in America, and particularly by new fettlers; for coming to lands, great parts of
which are a foreft, it is of vaft confequence
to them to be able to convert the wood
into lumber, as faft as they clear the
ground, by which means they make that
preparatory work pay its own charges.
The great inducement to fuch numbers of
people to fettle in America, is the plenty
of land ; but if that land, as it generally
is, is covered with timber that can be converted to no ufe, the expence of clearing
would be too great to undertake; where
they now can take up an hundred acres,
they would not then be able to take up
ten. Here lies one of the great advantages of that noble navigation from the
Ohio down the Miffiffippi to the gulph of
Mexico, which the proprietors affure us is
a more ready and cheap conveyance, than
by fea from New York or Philadelphia.

Other ftaples might be mentioned for
this colony, which would fuit it in great
perfection, and which ought likewife to be
cultivated, but thefe are the material ones.
It is never advantageous to have the at-

ten-

tention of planters too much taken up
with one object, as has been the case long
in Virginia and Maryland; the consequence
of which is, that when land fails them for
their favourite staple, they have no suc-
cedaneum, but must turn mere farmers for
raising corn and provisions, which has actually been the case in those two colonies;
whereas by giving that attention to hemp,
flax, tobacco, vines, indigo, silk, cotton,
madder, &c. which English farmers give
to as great a variety of products, they
would be certain of some valuable staple
for ever; and also be able to apply every
part of their estates to some profitable purpose. Tobacco, indigo, or madder, hemp,
vines, silk, and cotton, might be in culture on the same plantation, and each on a
different soil. This would increase the profit of planting very much, and make the
produce of negroes much more than 20 l.
a-head, which is the calculation of those
employed on good land in tobacco.

Under the articles tobacco and Indian
corn, I have before remarked, that the
reason the planters in America did not, on
a given quantity of land, equal the profit
of the farmer's in Britain, was their exe-
cuting much work by hand labour, which
might

might as well and better be done by horfe work. In Virginia, a negroe pays about 16 l. in tobacco, and 4l. in fundry articles. It will admit of no doubt, that the fums will be higher on the Ohio; but at the fame time they ought by management to be carried as high as poffible; which can only be done by fubflituting the plough and horfe-hoes, inftead of the fpade and hand-hoe: the expence of horfes on the Ohio, or in Virginia, is not what it is here, for the price of the beaft is not more than a third or fourth, and his keeping not a tenth of what it is in Britain. If thefe ideas were adopted, their profit would rife greatly.

An Englifh farm of an hundred acres, 60 arable, and 40 grafs; or 70 and 30, or even 80 and 20, may be cultivated upon the moft improved methods in common crops, by three men and four horfes; and if the land is good the average produdt will be 4l. an acre, or 400l. a year; thus the working hands yield 133l. a piece, this is by the addition of four horfes, which indeed in Britain will, if well kept, coft full as much as four more men; but taking it in that light, and call the working hands feven, the annual produce per hand will be

X 4   57 l.

571. But this is quite different in America, for the four horses would not cost more that one man if a black; and if a white, 10 horses would not equal his expence: nor have I any doubt but by a proper and experienced use of horse work, every working hand might in the Ohio be made to produce 50l. or 60l. a-head at least: they would then have an assignment of many acres per head, instead of which two or three per slave is the common allowance; however, without supposing any such good management, it would be a very moderate supposition to calculate the produce per working hand, at 5 l. more than in Virginia, or Maryland, which the great superiority of fresh lands, so extraordinary for their fertility, may well allow; and with the advantage of so large a range as the planters will have here, and have not generally in the old tobacco colonies, a point of vast consequence, would justify an higher idea. If madder was undertaken, a much larger sum should be named; and yet how easy to introduce this upon a plantation, and extend the culture by degrees. Silk, madder, and indigo, of each but a small quantity, or only madder and silk, being so valuable, would pay the extra ex-

expence of carriage and freight on the other commodities; but I shall suppose, by adopting these articles in part, each working hand to pay 25 l. and the extra expence of carriage of some articles more than is felt in Virginia. Upon this footing I shall calculate the expences of establishing a capital plantation on the Ohio; previous to which it may not be amiss to point out to the first settlers some signs whereby they are to judge of the soil, not only here, but through all these central colonies, and also those to the southward.

The trees, which are the spontaneous product of the land, should in general be first attended to; if they abound with fine tall, red hiccories, white oaks, chesnut oaks, scarlet oaks, tulip trees, black walnuts, locusts, mulberry trees, &c. they may be pronounced good, and the value will usually be in proportion to the size and straitness of those trees; pines, live oaks, laurels, bays, liquid amber, and water oaks are, among others, signs of bad land; and in general that soil will be best which is free from under-wood: nor should the planter take a few trees of any sort as his guide, but a predominancy of them in whole woods. This rule of judging must be united with

that

that of the appearance of the soil when dug
into, particularly colour and depth; the
black mould on a bed of loam is best; that
on clay, good; but the light sandy tracts are
in general bad, unless they are of a dark
colour, and moist, with good trees growing
from them; in that case they may be excellent; for sands differ as much as loams;
the misfortune is, that in America the sands
are generally white and dry, and produce
little besides pines.

Besides tracts which may come under
this description, he is farther to examine
the meadows which are composed of similar soils, but without any trees, being covered with grass; these are to be judged by
the height, thickness, and luxuriance of
that grass. These tracts are common on
the Ohio, and prove how valuable the
country should be esteemed: they, like the
woodlands, should be examined with the
spade, in order to know the appearance of
the soil. Besides these there are marshes
or swamps, but not in great quantities, as
in the maritime parts of America: the value of these depend on two circumstances,
the richness of the soil, and the ease of
being drained: the former is seen by the
products; cedars are good signs, though

not

not very common ; cypreſſes generally are found in them, and the excellency of the land perceived from the tallneſs, ſize, and beauty of their ſtems : as to draining, it depends on the ſituation, and on examining the means of carrying off the water, as in all other countries. Theſe ſwamps and marſhes when drained, if the ſoil is ſtiff, are the proper lands for hemp, not that it will not thrive as well on fertile uplands ; but they may be applied to other crops. There are beſides theſe hilly tracts, and the ſides of mountains, generally of a gradual aſcent, but ſometimes ſharp and rocky ; on the latter vineyards may be planted, and alſo olives ; on the former indigo, tobacco, madder, if rich, if indifferent, cotton, &c.

Theſe are the ſoils and ſort of tracts which are to be met with in the new colony ; and I ſhould obſerve that every kind of land here is equal to any in the world for the growth of wheat, maize, barley, oats, peaſe, beans, &c. all ſorts of roots, and every kind of garden-ſtuff and fruit known in Europe. Of this no doubts can be entertained, when it is conſidered how well all theſe thrive in Maryland and Virginia, in the ſame latitude ; whereas the Ohio is more fertile in ſoil, and far more tempe-

temperate and regular in climate, being free
from exceſſive heats, and thoſe violent colds
which are found in the maritime parts of
the continent.

. In the diſpoſitſon of new plantations it is
of conſequence that the planters give ſome
attention to the ſituation of their houſe and
offices, a point which, in the hurry of the
firſt building, is ſeldom thought of enough,
not only as a matter of convenience and
agreeableneſs, but alſo of health. In this
continent the north-weſt wind brings the
ſevere weather, and the worſt ſeaſons; a
houſe ſhould be well ſheltered from it by
wood, but inſtead of having any idea of
ſhelter, planters in general attack all the
timber around their houſes with ſuch un-
diſtinguiſhing rage, as not to leave themſelves in a few years a tree within ſight.
For convenience, as well as health and plea-
ſure, the beſt ſituation would be in the
centre of a ſpace of wood in form of a creſ-
cent, open to the ſouth, and in front of the
navigation which is to convey the product
of the plantation, always chuſing an elevated
ſituation, yet not the top of a hill, leaving
as much aſcent of wood behind the building, as deſcent of lawn before it. At all
events a ſpot ſhould be choſen where the
ſhores

ſhores of the river are high and bold, becauſe nothing is more unwholeſome than to
live in the neighbourhood of a marſh or flat
land that is apt to be overflowed. This in
many of our colonies is not attended to, but
it is becauſe ſituations free from it are not
very common; and in the ſouthern ones,
the rice culture makes them ſeek for ſwamps,
the conſequence of which is the unhealthi-
neſs ſo much complained of.

Agriculture is followed in ſo imperfect
a manner in our old colonies, owing to
plenty of land, that one cannot expect to
ſee it well managed here, where land is ſo
much more plentiful; yet do I wiſh to ſee
ſome plantations laid out in a manner that
ſhall obviate the objections to the careleſs
huſbandry of the Americans. I here mean
particularly to hint at incloſures—not to
ſow or plant any piece of ground that is not
well and ſubſtantially encloſed with a ditch,
a bank, and live hedge; the expence would
bear no proportion to the numerous advantages of it; beſides that uncommon ſuperiority in point of neatneſs and beauty: and
in the diſpoſition of the fields, ſome ſhould
undoubtedly be left occupied with the timber that is upon them, as a future ſupply,
which will be a matter of great conſequence,

not

not only to the public good of the colony,
but alſo to the future private advantage of
the planter.

And here I ſhall once more obſerve, that
for gaining the requiſite knowledge of ſo
extenſive a tract of ſo noble a country, the
proprietors would act with a patriotic ſpirit
if they were to eſtabliſh a plantation in a
well choſen ſpot, including every variety of
ſoil for trying large experiments on the preceding liſt of ſtaples, and others that might
be named. The expence would not be
conſiderable ; under the direction of a ſenſible, intelligent overſeer, who was a man
of integrity ; the produce would be highly
ſufficient, after the firſt expences, to pay
the annual charge. In ſuch a plantation
might be introduced the culture of hemp
and flax on every ſort of ſoil, to ſee how far
it might become the colony ſtaple. Madder might be tried with the ſame deſign ;
vineyards ſhould be planted, both of foreign
and native grapes, for wines and raiſins; ſilk
ſhould be made in large quantities ; cotton
tried with equal attention ; and experiments
made on indigo, to ſee how far fertility of
ſoil in an excellent climate would make
amends for the want of greater heat. The
native

native hemp, flax, filk-grafs, and other
indigenous plants brought into culture,
that their qualities might be known; thefe
would be noble defigns, and could not fail
of proving of great advantage to the colony, and of doing great honour to the
proprietors.

I fhall now proceed with the defign of
calculating the expences and profit of fixing a capital plantation on the Ohio, fuppofing the perfon to move from Britain,
and to have money enough for all neceffary
(but not fuperfluous) expences.

	£.
Freight and expences of a family of fix per- fons from London to Alexandria, at 25l.	150
Freight of 10 tons, - -	55
One year's living or board at 20l. -	120
A fecond year's houfe-keeping, - -	100
Fees of 10,000 acres at 30l. per 1000 -	300
Building a houfe, - - -	200
———— offices, - - -	150
Furniture, - - - -	150
Carriage of neceffaries from Alexandria to the Ohio,	50
A canoe, - - - -	50
Boats, - - - -	15
Implements, - - -	200
Machine for rooting up trees, - -	80
A faw-mill, - - -	500
50 horfes, mares, and ftallions, - -	250
50 cows, - - - -	150
50 young cattle, - - - -	50
100 fwine, - - - -	25
500 fheep, - - -	125

Carried over £. 2720

Brought forward £. 2720

Poultry,	- - -	5
Repairs of implements,	- - -	50

Labour.

Attendance on cattle,	£.	30
Bailiff, (one year) -		40
Labour in clearing 20 acres of wheat, at 1l. - }		20
Ditto 40 oats, at 16s. -		32
70 turneps, at 1l. - -		70
5 potatoes at 5l. - -		25
On hay, mowing and making, &c. - arpent of natural meadows, }		30
On fencing,		50
Orchard and garden, -		20
Sundries, - -		30

*347

40 negroes at 50l. - - - -		2000
Annual expence of negroes per head, overfeer, 1l. }		40
Cloaths, 1l. - -		40
Sundry expences, - -		40

160

Seed.

20 acres of wheat at 8s. -		8
40 oats at 8s. - -		16

24

Carried over £. 5306

---

* All these articles are usually done by negroes for a third of this expence, but they are here reckoned at the rates of the labour of white servants, that the planter may not be supposed to have nothing but blacks about him.

8

	l.	s.	d.
Brought forward	5306	0	0
70 turneps, 1s. - 3 10 0			
5 potatoes, 8s. - - 2 0 0			
	5	10	0
Taxes, - - -	30	0	0
Two years interest on 5300l. -	530	0	0
£.	5871	10	0

Produce of second year.

40 negroes at 20l. - -	800	0	0
N. B. The first year of their labour reckoned 5l. a-head lower than when experienced more.			
	800	0	0

Third year.

Taxes, - - -	30	0	0
Buildings, - - -	10	0	0
House-keeping, - - -	100	0	0
Repairs and addition to implements -	50	0	0
Labour as before, - -	347	0	0
Seed ditto, - - -	29	10	0
Incidents, - - -	50	0	0
Interest of 5400l. - -	270	0	0
Allow towards carriage or freight of bulky products, - -	50	0	0
Expences on 40 negroes at 3l. -	120	0	0
Purchase of 20 at 50l. - -	1000	0	0
£.	2056	10	0

Produce.

40 negroes at 25l. - - -	1000	0	0
20 ditto at 20l. - - -	400	0	0
£.	1400	0	0

VOL. I.   Y   Fourth

Fourth year.

	l.	s.	d.
Taxes, - -	30	0	0
Buildings, - -	20	0	0
House-keeping, - - -	80	0	0
Implements, - - -	50	0	0
Labour, - - -	347	0	0
Seed, - - -	29	10	0
Incidents, - - -	40	0	0

Interest - -	2000	0	0
	800	0	0
	1200	0	0
At 5 per cent. -	60	0	0
Before - -	270	0	0

	330	0	0
Freight, - - -	60	0	0
Expences on 60 negroes at 3l. -	180	0	0
Purchase of 20 at 50l. - -	1000	0	0
£.	2166	10	0

Produce.

60 negroes at 25l. - -	1500	0	0
20 ditto at 20l. - - -	400	0	0
£.	1900	0	0

Fifth year.

Taxes, - -	30	0	0
Buildings, - -	20	0	0
House-keeping, - - -	80	0	0
Implements, - - -	50	0	0
Labour, - - -	347	0	0
Seed, - - -	29	10	0
Incidents, - - -	40	0	0
Carried over £.	596	10	0

	l.	s.	d.
Brought forward	596	10	0
Interest, - -	2166	10	0
	1400	0	0
	766	10	0
At 5 per cent. -	38	0	0
Before - -	330	0	0
	368	0	0
Freight, - - -	70	0	0
Expences on 80 negroes at 3l. -	240	0	0
20 at 50l. - - -	1000	0	0
£.	2283	10	0

Produce.

	l.	s.	d.
80 negroes at 25l. - -	2000	0	0
20 ditto at 20l. - - -	400	0	0
£.	2400	0	0

Sixth year.

	l.	s.	d.
Taxes, - - - -	30	0	0
Buildings, - - -	20	0	0
House-keeping, - - -	80	0	0
Implements, - - -	60	0	0
Labour, - - -	347	0	0
Seed, - - -	29	10	0
Incidents, - - -	40	0	0
Interest, - - 2283 10 0			
1900 0 0			
383 10 0			
At 5 per cent. - 19 3 0			
Before, - - 368 0 0			
	387	3	0
Carried over £.	993	13	0
Y 2			

		l.	s.	d.
	Brought forward	993	13	0
Freight, - - -		80	0	0
100 negroes at 3l. - - -		300	0	0
20 ditto at 50l. - - -		1000	0	0
	£.	2373	13	0

Produce.

		l.	s.	d.
100 negroes at 25l. - -		2500	0	0
20 ditto at 20l. - - -		400	0	0
	£.	2900	0	0

Here we find the receipt is more than equal to the annual expence, including the increafe of 20 negroes bought every year, confequently the whole fum wanting for fuch a plantation is to be afcertained.

				l.	s.	d.
Firft capital, - - -				5871	10	0
Expences of third year,	2056	10	0			
Produce of fecond,	800	0	0			
				1256	10	0
Expences of fourth year,	2166	10	0			
Produce of third, -	1400	0	0			
				766	10	0
Expences of fifth year,	2283	10	0			
Produce of fourth, -	1900	0	0			
				383	10	0
		Total		8278	0	0
Annual intereft, -				413	18	0

If

If no increase of negroes, the account,
would be :

	l.	s.	d.
Taxes, - - -	30	0	0
Buildings, - - - -	20	0	0
House keeping, - - -	80	0	0
Implements, - - -	50	0	0
Labour, - - - -	347	0	0
Seed, - - - -	29	10	0
Incidents, - - -	40	0	0
Interest, - - -	413	18	9
Freight, - - ' -	80	0	0
Expences on 120 negroes at 3l. -	360	0	0
£.	1450	8	0

Produce.

120 negroes at 25 l. - - -	3000	0	0
Expences, - - -	1450	8	0
Profit, - - - -	1549	12	0
House-keeping, - - - -	80	0	0
Interest, - - - -	413	18	0
Total receipt, - - -	2043	10	0

which from 8278l. is per cent. 24l.

During the preceding time, no produce
is supposed from cattle, that in so great a
space of country they might increase to
great herds and flocks ; but afterwards the
annual product would be very great, as the
numbers would be two or three thousand
head of cattle, five or six thousand sheep,
and two or three thousand hogs ; such

herds

herds have been known the property of
single people in North Carolina, where
they have not greater advantages, nor yet
so great, as on the Ohio: these would
yield annually near 1000l. a year in hides,
wool, and barrelled meat for the West
Indies, but I shall calculate only 300l.

	l.	s.	d.
Receipt above, - -	2043	10	0
Cattle, - -	300	0	0
£.	2343	10	0

which from 8278l. is per cent. 28l.

This profit is considerable, not so much
in itself, as in the circumstance of the
planters being able annually to incorporate
it into the old capital, and thereby yield a
compound interest at that proportion. I
am of opinion, that husbandry in England
will yield a greater profit than 24 l. per
cent. if so large a sum as 8000l. is expended in stocking a farm. Calculations have
been published of English husbandry,
which shew that so high as 33 per cent.
may be made in any part of the kingdom
by *good* and *improved* husbandry, and a-
bove 20 per cent. by the most common
crops. And I am clear, that if potatoes,

carrots,

carrots, madder, hops, &c. were calculated (which do not come into thofe calculations) the profit might be carried to
40 or perhaps 50 per cent. in certain fituations ; in this refpect I am confident, that
America cannot equal Britain, but in other
points the fuperiority is entirely with her :
that of the annual increafe of culture is a
very effential one.   What a vaft difference
between the Englifh farmer putting out
his favings at 4 per cent. and his brother
on the Ohio doing the fame at 24 compound intereft!   What a difference between the one living on another man's land,
with a leafe of twenty-one years, which
is a long one, fubjected to the caprice of a
landlord or a fteward, or fure of quitting
at the end of his term, and the other living on his own extenfive freehold of 10,000
acres! What a difference between 80 l. a
year fpent in all forts of neceffaries, even
bread, meat, malt, &c. by the farmer for
houfe-keeping ; and the fame fum by the
planter for tea, fugar, coffee, chocolate,
fpices, rum, and manufactures. Bread,
meat, venifon, fruit, fifh, fowl, game in
the utmoft plenty, befides tne corn, &c.
the expence of which is before reckoned,
but no produce !

In all thefe circumftances there can be no comparifon : at the fame time that the Ohio planter makes near as great intereft from his firft capital as the Englifh farmer ; at the fame time that he is able to throw his favings annually into bufinefs at 28 per cent. compound intereft ; he lives like a country gentleman in Britain who has an eftate of 2000 l. a year, and if the latter fpends half the year at London, much better ; while the farmer, it is very well known, muft fare very coarfely. I draw this comparifon with no defign to fend Britifh farmers to the Ohio. I am clear not one in the three kingdoms will go ; had I thought a book would be an inducement to them, I would not have drawn up this calculation : it is written for the ufe of thofe who will go to America, whether books are publifhed or not; and to them it is meant merely as advice, that they make a proper choice of the colony they fettle in : many go to Nova Scotia, to New England, to New York, &c. where they can raife nothing advantageous to the commerce of Britain, and where they muft live in a climate that is odious to a Britifh conftitution, at leaft during the feverity of winter. There is no object in the whole

range

range of American affairs of more importance than the directing new settlers, whether from Britain or foreign countries, to
those parts of our colonies, which from
their staple productions are really valuable
to the mother-country; yet this matter,
of as great consequence as it certainly is,
has not by any means been so much attended to as it ought; for government has paid
the freight of more men to Nova Scotia,
than it has too Virginia and Maryland;
though the former has no staple, and can
only rival Britain in her fishery, and the
latter one so valuable in every respect as
tobacco.

CHAP.

CHAP. XIX.

NORTH CAROLINA.

*Climate of North Carolina—Productions—
Soil—Common husbandry—Staples—Exports—Defects in their agriculture—Improvements proposed.*

THIS province lies between lat. 34¼
and 36¼ : it is hotter than Virginia,
but in other respects the climate of these
two provinces is very similar ; North Carolina being hotter as you advance southward, until the most southerly parts are as
hot as South Carolina. This gradation of
heat is such as may be supposed from the
variation of latitude ; but not to be compared with the same parallels in other quarters of the world, no more than the other
American territories. In winter they have
frosts here sometimes very sharp, though
not in general so cold as in Virginia ; and
a warm day often follows a very cold
night. The same distinction is also to be
made between the maritime and back parts
of the province that I mentioned before in
Vir-

Virginia ; the coaft, as far as it continues
a flat country, is exceffive hot and very unwholefome, like all the low fea-coafts in
thefe fouthern countries; but when the
country rifes, and begins to be hilly,which
is about one hundred or one hundred and
fifty miles from the fea, and continuing till
you come to the weftern mountains, in
this part the climate is pure, temperate,
and healthy.

The products of North Carolina are rice,
tobacco, indigo, cotton, wheat, peas,
beans, Indian corn, and all forts of roots,
efpecially potatoes. Rice is not fo much
cultivated here as in South Carolina: but
in the latter they raife no tobacco, whereas in North Carolina it is one of their
chief articles. It grows in the northerly
parts of the province, on the frontiers of
Virginia, from which colony it is exported. Indigo grows very well in the province, particularly in the fouthern parts,
and proves a moft profitable branch of culture. Cotton does very well, and the fort
is fo excellent, that it is much to be wifhed they had made a greater progrefs in it.
The greateft articles of their produce which
is exported are tar, pitch, turpentine, and

7   every

every species of lumber, in astonishing quantities.

The soil in the flat country is in general sandy, and great tracts of it but indifferent in fertility; but others are rich, and will produce cotton, indigo, and Indian corn freely. It is in this part of the country that the swamps are to be found, which when drained yield rice: this forms a distinction between North Carolina and Virginia; they have vast swamps on the coast of Virginia, but cultivate no rice, not because it would not grow, but from an idea that it requires, in order to yield large crops, a hotter sun. The swamps in North Carolina are some of them very rich, but remain undrained for want of people. In the back part of the country the soil is very fine, and in several tracts equal to the best of Virginia; and it improves as you advance towards the mountains. This is the case with all these colonies in the southern parts of America. In many of these backward tracts the land is a rich black mould, of a good depth, and highly fertile, especially the country on the river Pedee, &c.

It is extraordinary that more settlements should not have been made in this country,

try, notwithstanding the obstacles I have mentioned, considering the pleasantness of it, and extreme fertility of the soil ; these circumstances were also known many years ago, as appears by the travels through it of a Mr. *John Lawson*, surveyor-general of North Carolina in the year 1700, which were published in 1718 *. There are many curious particulars in it, and especially of the appearance of the back country, as will appear from the following extracts, which I make because the book is very scarce. " We went directly for Sapona Town : that day we passed through a delicious country (none that I ever saw exceeds it.) We saw fine bladed grass six feet high, along the banks of pleasant rivulets. Coming that day about thirty miles, we reached the fertile and pleasant banks of Sapona river, whereon stands the Indian town and fort. Nor could all Europe afford a pleasanter stream, *were it inhabited by christians*, and cultivated by ingenious hands. These Indians live in a clear field, about a mile square, which they would have sold me. This most pleasant river may be something broader than

---

* *The History of Carolina*, small quarto.

the

the Thames at Kingſton, keeping a continual pleaſant warbling noiſe with its re-
verberating on the bright marble rocks.
It is beautified with a numerous train of
ſwans and other water-fowl. One ſide of
the river is hemmed in with mountainy
ground, the other ſide proving as rich a
ſoil to the eye of a knowing perſon with
us, as any this weſtern world can afford:
it is as noble a river to plant a colony on as
any I have met withal. Next morning we
ſet forward; all the pines were vaniſhed,
for we had ſeen none for two days. We
paſſed through a delicate rich ſoil this day,
no great hills, but pretty riſings and levels,
which made a beautiful country; we paſſed
likewiſe over three rivers this day. We
were much taken with the fertility and
pleaſantneſs of the neck of land between
theſe two branches. It is called *Haw* river, from the *Siſſipabaw* Indians who dwell
upon this ſtream; there being rich land
enough to contain ſome thouſands of fami-
milies, for which reaſon I hope, in a ſhort
time, it will be planted. This river is
much ſuch another as Sapona, both ſeem-
ing to run a vaſt way up the country.
There is plenty of good timber, and eſpecially oak; and as there is ſtone enough in
both

both rivers, and the land is extraordinary rich, no man that will be content within the bounds of reafon can have any grounds to diflike it. Some Virginia-men we met, afking our opinion of the country we were then in, we told them it was a very pleafant one: they were all of the fame opinion, and affirmed that they had never feen twenty miles of fuch extraordinary rich land, lying all together like that betwixt *How* river and *Acbonedry* town." Long after this account was written (viz. near feventy years) Dr. Mitchel gives it in general the fame character. "There are five large rivers, fays he, which rife in the inland parts of North Carolina, the banks of which are rich and fertile, although the hills between them fill partake of the barrennefs of Carolina, as we are well informed by feveral whom we have recommended to fettle in the country. This feems to be the moft improveable part of all the Britifh dominions on this fide of the Miffiffippi. But they have no navigation nor ports to the more fruitful parts of the country, if it be not by the river *Pedee*, which runs through all this inland part of North Carolina, and falls into the fea at Wineau (or Winyaw) which now belongs

to

to South Carolina, and for that reafon it is neglected and never ufed by the other, which poffeffes the fruitful lands belonging to this port." From all which accounts it is extremely plain that thefe back parts of North Carolina are to be ranked among the fineft in our colonies.

Notwithftanding thefe great advantages, there are very few people in North Carolina ; this has been owing to feveral caufes : there were obftructions in fettling it, which occafioned fome to leave the country, and a general idea was fpread to its difadvantage; but the principal evil was the want of ports, of which there was not one good one in all North Carolina : the river Pedee falls into the fea at Winyaw, which is in South Carolina, and that has prevented an exportation of products from thence of the growth of North Carolina. And this want of good ports, and a trading town, has checked the culture of rice a good deal ; but it has had another effect, which may probably prove a great advantage ; it has driven the new fettlers back into the country, and thrown them very much into common hufbandry, on a foil and in a climate that will do for productions much more valuable than rice ; thefe, fuch as filk, indigo, and

cot-

cotton are coming in by degrees, and will in a few years change the face of this colony entirely, and enrich it prodigiously; it is this spreading about the country that makes the produce of the woods almost the staple at present of the colony.

It is this circumstance that has thrown them into common husbandry, as I observed before; and it is this common husbandry which deserves our attention particularly, since in many respects it is different from that of any other part of America.

The two great circumstances which give the farmers of North Carolina such a superiority over those of most other colonies, are, first, the plenty of land; and, secondly, the vast herds of cattle kept by the planters. The want of ports, as I said, kept numbers from settling here, and this made the land of less value, consequently every settler got large grants; and, falling to the business of breeding cattle, their herds became so great, that the profit from them alone is exceeding great. It is not an uncommon thing to see one man the master of from 300 to 1200, and even to 2000 cows, bulls, oxen, and young cattle; hogs also in prodigious numbers. Their ma-

nage-

nagement is to let them run loose in the woods all day, and to bring them up at night by the sound of a horn ; sometimes, particularly in winter, they keep them during the night in inclosures, giving them a little food, and letting the cows and sows to the calves and pigs ; this makes them come home the more regularly. Such herds of cattle and swine are to be found in no other colonies ; and when this is better settled, they will not be so common here ; for at present the woods are all in common, and people's property has no other boundary or distinction than marks cut in trees, so that the cattle have an unbounded range ; but when the country becomes more cultivated, estates will be surrounded by enclosures, and consequently the numbers of cattle kept by the planters will be proportioned to their own lands only.

It may easily be supposed that these vast stocks of cattle might be of surprising consequence in the raising manure, were the planters as attentive as they ought to be to this essential object : they might by this means cultivate indigo and tobacco to greater advantage than their neighbours ; some few make a good use of the advantage, but more of them are drawn from it by the

plenty

plenty of rich land, which they run over, as
in the northern colonies, till it is exhausted,
and then take fresh, relying on such a change,
instead of making the most of their manure,
which would add infinitely to their profit.

Their system is to depend (where they
have no navigation, and are at a considerable distance from it, which however is
not the case in many parts) on the hides of
their cattle, and on barrelled meat, with
some corn, roots, and pitch and tar, &c.
for the profit of their plantation ; but the
most bulky of these commodities yield but
little, unless near some river ; accordingly
there are not many plantations at any distance from water, since it is not an inland
navigation that is wanted in North-Caroli-
na, but ports at the mouths of the rivers
that will admit of large ships.

The mode of common husbandry here is to
break up a piece of wood land, a work very
easily done, from the trees standing at good
distances from each other ; this they sow with
Indian corn for several years successively,
till it will yield large crops no longer : they
get at first fourscore or an hundred bushel
an acre, but sixty or seventy are common :
when the land is pretty well exhausted they
sow it with pease or beans one year, of

which

which they will get thirty or forty bushels
per acre; and afterwards fow it with wheat
for two or three years: it will yield good
crops of this grain when it would bear Indian corn no longer, which fhews how excellent the land muft be. But let me remark that this culture of wheat to fuch advantage is only in the back part of the province, where the climate is far more temperate than on the coaft; upon the latter
it does not fucceed well, a circumftance
much deferving attention; for we may lay
it down as a univerfal rule, that where
wheat thrives well, *there* the climate is
healthy, and agreeable to the generality of
conftitutions: it does well neither in extreme cold, nor in great heat.

In this fyftem of crops they change the
land as faft as it wears out, clearing frefh
pieces of wood land, exhaufting them in
fucceffion; after which they leave them to
the fpontaneous growth. It is not here as
in the northern colonies, that weeds come
firft and then grafs; the climate is fo hot,
that, except on the rich moift lands, any
fort of grafs is fcarce; but the fallow in a
few years becomes a foreft, for no climate
feems more congenial to the production of
quick growing trees. If they planter does
not

not return to cultivate the land again, as may probably be the cafe, from the plenty of frefh, it prefently becomes fuch a wood as the reft of the country is; and woods are here the pafture of the cattle, which is excellent for hogs, becaufe they get quantities of maft and fruit; but for cattle is much inferior to paftures and meadows.

Befides thefe crops they cultivate all forts of roots, particularly potatoes, of which they get large crops; fome they fell into Virginia, and the reft are given to their hogs. Fruit in none of the colonies is in greater plenty, or finer flavour; they have every fort that has been hitherto mentioned in this work : peaches, as in the central colonies, are fo plentiful, that the major part of the crop goes to the hogs. In a word, all the neceffaries, and many of the luxuries of life abound in the back parts of this province, which, with the temperate climate, renders it one of the fineft countries in America; fo fine, that every body muft be aftonifhed at finding any fettlements made on the unhealthy fea coaft, which is nearly the reverfe.

Refpecting their ftaples, tobacco I have been fo particular in treating of under the article Virginia and Maryland, that little

remains

remains to be said here, as the management of it is the same; the climate for this plant is not better than that of Virginia; but as there are more lands that are fresh, the crops will for some time be larger: four hogsheads have been made for a share here on a small plantation (near the northern forks of the river Pedee) for several years; and five have been known for a season or two in the same plantation. Such crops, and even less, would well pay the expence of sloops taking the crop to the ships at sea which cannot come into port.

Rice is cultivated only in the maritime part of the province, in the swamps. As this article of husbandry is the grand staple of South Carolina, where infinitely greater quantities are made, I shall not enter into the process here : but observe, that the planters do not make so great a profit by this article as many do in South Carolina, which may be owing to the latter country being hotter, and perhaps the swamps are somewhat richer.

Pitch, tar, and turpentine are made throughout this province in vast quantities, which is a proof, among others, that the country is very far from being well settled

even

even yet. These commodities are the produce of that species of pine called the *pitch
pine*; they are all made by different preparations from the resin of this tree. Turpentine is this resin or gum as it flows from
the tree through holes cut for that purpose; the heat of the sun assists this extrac-
tion, and the operation is performed while
the tree is growing. It is well known that
oil of turpentine is a distillation of it.
From the holes cut to gain the turpentine,
little channels are made in the trees to conduct the resin down to the foot of them,
where boxes or bowls are placed to receive
it. After the oil is distilled from the turpentine, the residuum is the resin in a very
thick consistence, which is dried, and then
is in the lumps we have it in England.

Tar is the same gum, but gained in a
different manner; the method is as follows,
which I shall give in the words of an intelligent writer : " First, they prepare a cir-
cular floor of clay, declining a little towards
the centre, from which there is laid a pipe
of wood, extending, near horizontally, two
feet without the circumference, and so let
into the ground that its upper side is near
level with the floor : at the outer end of
this pipe they dig a hole large enough to
hold

hold the barrels for the *tar*, which when forced out of the wood naturally runs to the center of the floor as the lowest part, and from thence along the pipe into the barrels : thefe matters being firft prepared, they raife upon that clay floor a large pile of dry pine wood fplit in pieces, and inclofe the whole pile with a wall of earth, leaving only a little hole at the top, where the fire is to be kindled ; and when that is done, fo that the inclofed wood begins to burft, the whole is ftopped up with earth, to the end that there may not be any flame, but only heat fufficient to force the tar out of the wood, and make it run down to the floor : they temper the heat as they think proper, by thrufting a ftick through the earth, and letting the air in at as many places as they find neceffary. In order to gain pitch they boil the tar, and the folid part being feparated in that operation, is the pitch." It is found much more profitable to apply the timber they cut down to this ufe than to faw it, or export it in any kind of lumber ; and the tar &c. being far more valuable in proportion to bulk, is a circumftance of great importance in a country that does not abound with good ports.

To

To shew what the back part of this colony is capable of, I shall insert the account of the labour of ten negroes in one year upon the plantation on the Pedee above-mentioned, premising that it is not to be taken as an *annual* product, this being an extraordinary year; the account does not contain all the circumstances I could wish, but as it is put into my hands, so I insert it.

Products raised and made by ten negroes in one year in the plantation.

	l.	s.	d.
31 hogsheads of tobacco at 8l. 5s.	255	15	0
400 bushels of Indian corn and pease at 1s. 6d.	30	0	0
114 barrels of tar at 6s. 9d.	38	9	3
Skins	8	10	0
Shingles 4000 at 12s. a 1000	2	8	0
	£. 335	2	3

which is 33l. 10s. per head, besides making corn and other provisions for the family, cattle, poultry, &c. and keeping the buildings in repair.

Upon good fresh land this may often be equalled, but doubtless there are many tracts of country in which the negroes do not equal half this profit. But if the conduct of their husbandry was well looked into,

and

and their modes of culture minutely examined, the low products would be found
oftner the result of bad husbandry than the
fault of either soil or climate; it is so in
Britain, and doubtless in a much greater
degree in America. It is however of consequence to know what in good years and
on good land may be done in planting tobacco; we see here a product of 25l. per
head in that staple alone, besides the other
articles of the plantation. This is a point
at which emulation should strive to arrive;
and spirited endeavours have a wonderful
efficacy in gaining points; but planters, like
farmers, are too often content to move on
in the old line, without daring to think
that a deviation can be beneficial.

The following are the exports from this
province.

	£.
Rice, 2000 barrels at 40s. - -	4000
Tobacco, 2000 hogsheads at 8l. - -	16,000
Pitch, tar, and turpentine, 51,000 barrels at 7s.	17,850
Boards, staves, joists, shingles, masts, and lumber - - }	15,000
Indian corn, pease, and other grain, - -	7,000
Live stock of different kinds -- -	5000
Skins of different kinds - - -	5,500
Total *	70,350

---

* *American Traveller*, pag. 89.

But

But I muſt remark that this account does not at all agree with another which has been given on good authority; yet this account is drawn up for the years ſince the peace; and that which I am now going to inſert, for the year 1753. The former ought to be much the greateſt, inſtead of which it is the leaſt.

	l.	s.	d.
Pitch, tar, and turpentine, 84,012 barrels at 7s.	29,404	4	0
Staves 762.330 at 4l. 5s. 2 1000	3,230	0	0
Shingles, 2,500,000 at 11s. 5d. per 1000	1,427	1	0
Lumber, 2,000,647 feet at 5l. per 1000	10,000	0	0
Corn, 61,580 buſhels, ſuppoſe 2s.	6,158	0	0
Peaſe, 10,000 buſhels, 1s. 6d.	750	0	0
Pork and beef 3,300 barrels, 23s.	3,795	0	0
30,000 deer ſkins *	5,500	0	0
Rice omitted, therefore taken from the other account	4000	0	0
Tobacco (ditto)	16,000	0	0

Beſides wheat, bread, potatoes, bees-wax, tallow, candles, bacon, hogs-lard, ſome cotton, and a vaſt deal of ſquared walnut timber and cedar, and hoops and headings, alſo ſome indigo.

Total † 80,264 5 0

There can be little doubt, from the number of articles omitted, but the total muſt amount to 100,000l. and it is well

---

* The price by tale not known, the ſum is therefore taken from the firſt account.

† *Account of European Settlements*, vol. ii. p. 260.

known

known that this province is now making a
great progress in its cultivation and exports:
after being long neglected it was but little
known, but since the back country has
been settled, the planters have succeeded so
well as to draw great numbers after them,
so that there is scarcely a part of America
that is at present filling faster: the new
colony on the Ohio will give a check to
this; had not that been established, North
Carolina must have soon become as flourish-
ing as her want of ports would allow,
which must ever keep her comparatively
low. The country would thrive more if
their husbandry was better, but, like all
the American farmers, they are spoiled for
good husbandmen by plenty of land.

Among the defects of their agriculture,
I shall mention in the first place, their almost total neglect of inclosures; this they
carry to a degree that is not even found in
the provinces I have already described.
Even their corn fields are open to the depredations of their own and others cattle;
nor are the fences of their rice and tobacco
grounds made with that care and attention
which in England is bestowed on the least
valuable fields. This circumstance, where-
ever it is found, is a sign of extreme bad
hus-

hufbandry : it is owing to the planter being fparing of expence in every article that is not of immediate confequence ; the expence of fences in Carolina, where wood grows with fuch amazing luxuriance, would be trifling, and the advantages of good ones too great to need expatiating on.

The fyftem purfued here is as faulty as in moft other parts of America ; it confifts in cropping the land with tobacco as long as it will bear it ; then they will take two crops of maize, and after that throw in wheat, peas, &c. for feveral years longer ; after which they leave the land to become foreft again ; as faft as they want more, they take it from the old woodland, ferving it in the fame manner. It is owing to this wretched fyftem that many of their corn-fields are fo full of weeds, that in fome it is difficult to know what is the crop.

Even in the northern parts of the province, upon the frontiers of Virginia, where they give their principal attention to the little tobacco they cultivate, they do not manage it with any fpirit ; not being in feveral inftances fo good planters of that commodity as their neighbours. They do not
feem

feem fo attentive to keeping the hillocks
clean from weeds; this may be owing to
the general circumftance of the planters not
being fo rich, or having fuch large ftocks
of negroes; for in North Carolina it is but
of late years that men of property have fettled in it; and they obferve in America, as
well as in all other parts of the world, that
the richer the cultivator, the better will
the land be cultivated; whether the crop
be tobacco, rice, corn, fugar, indigo, or
whatever it may. In one refpect, however, they have made an improvement in
North Carolina in the tobacco culture,
which is the introduction of a machine between the rows of tobacco inftead of a
plough, being between a plough and a harrow, and fomething in the nature of horfe-
hoes ufed in England. It is not however
a common tool there, but from its ufe, it is
expected to become more general.

Another very great defect in their management, is the carelefs manner in which
they conduct their cattle: immenfe herds
are kept that yield a profit to the planters
more inconfiderable than can at firft be imagined; this is not for want of a market,
fince no commodity more readily yields its
price

price in North America, than beef and pork in barrels; and hides are every where a commodity easily to be turned into money; but it is owing to a want of attention—to keeping a proper proportion of them to the winter food—to not fatting them well, and many not at all, which is owing to a want of pasturage, and also to leaving them too much to themselves in the woods without a sufficiency of attendants to watch and take care of them. The mere multiplication of cattle is not the only object, though it sounds greatly; bringing them up in health and vigour, of a due size and fatness, are as essential; but the stunted diminutive size of all the cattle in North America, to the northward, as well as in the southern colonies, shews plainly the great want of pastures.: cattle will live and multiply in their woods, but they will never be cattle of any value; and yielding a profit as inconsiderable as their worth.

In raising manure they are, notwithstanding their numerous herds, no less negligent. This is owing also to plenty of land; while they can get good crops of any thing on fresh land without dung, they care little about raising any; but with the advantage of fresh and good land, aided

by

by their numbers of cattle, they might very well make three and a half or four hogsheads of tobacco a share, which would be 28 l. or 32 l. a head, and, with lumber, tar, corn, &c. would make their slaves on an average worth at least 30 l. a-piece to them, which would be a profit their neighbours very seldom reap.

As to the improvements which might be made in this colony, they are as great as in any other, if not more so, for it has been more neglected than most. What I should propose is, that the new settlers that came there should fix themselves in the very back part of all the country, upon the rivers that run among the Apalachian mountains, of which there are the Pedee with five considerable branches, Cape Fear river, and others: some of these are navigable for middling sized boats above two hundred and fifty miles from the sea coast; and it is in this country, at the foot of the mountains, where the soil ranks among the richest in America, and where the climate is perfectly temperate, healthy, and agreeable. I would not propose them to settle here to raise bulky commodities, because the navigation is not good enough to convey them away—and because there are other territories bet-

ter

ter fituated for them; but for indigo, filk, cotton, and fome other valuable commodities, no fituation in all America exceeds this: here the foil is fo fertile—fo deep—and of fuch an excellent nature, that the products of indigo, &c. would be far greater than what is known in South Carolina; and thefe commodities are all fo valuable, that very fmall boats would carry the amount of a great value. Indigo and cotton would here pay at leaft 25 l. a-head for all labouring hands, befides raifing neceffaries for the fupport of the plantation: this would prove of greater advantage to the fettlers than any thing they could do with other products. The navigation of Virginia and Maryland, and the Ohio will give them a fuperiority in tobacco; and the fame circumftance, with better fwamps, and a hotter fun, will render South Carolina fuperior in rice; but in the commodities I have mentioned, the lands in queftion would have a yet greater fuperiority. Nobody difputes the excellence of the foil in the back parts of North Carolina; it excels that of South Carolina; and the climate is known to be equal to any in the world, being as different from the mari-

time

time parts of the continent, as much as Hudson's Bay varies from Jamaica.

This is an improvement which would much advance the interests of Britain, for indigo, cotton, and silk are commodities which she buys of foreigners at a great price; and if she had more than supplied the confumption of her own manufactures, they are articles of ready fale all over Europe, fo that nothing more demands the attention of the mother country than fuch parts of her colonies as are fitted by nature to produce them. Silk can only be produced in proportion to the number of people in the country; but then it is of confequence that the inhabitants of our wide fpread plantations fhould all make as much as they can. It is a common obfervation on this point of producing filk in the colonies, that the country is not populous enough to make any progrefs in a bufinefs that requires fo many hands; but nothing can be more miftaken than fuch reafoning. The culture of filk is of that nature, that if there were only one folitary plantation in a whole province, the fame quantity of filk might be made on it, as proportionably in a whole country, though ever fo populous;

lous; it is a bufinefs that requires only a few weeks in a year, were it therefore otherwife, it could not anfwer to any one to meddle with it. Every perfon might make one or two pounds of filk annually with very little or no interruption of their ufual occupations. Hence we may affert that nothing can be more abfurd than the argument of the inutility of filk becaufe the country is not populous; when the country becomes populous the quantity will be an object of confequence; but if the work is not begun till then, it will probably never be begun at all: a few people in one colony, a few in another; fome thoufands here, fome thoufands there, feparately taken, the quantity of filk they could make might not be a national object; but when all thefe numbers were added together, and united with the people in all the colonies, who enjoy a climate that would do for the bufinefs, the affair is then no longer a trifle: this we may be convinced of by re-flecting on the numbers we have from Flo-rida to Jerfey inclufive; in all which tract filk might be produced in any quantities the population of the country would admit of: would but all the people in this line of country make each a pound per head, it

would

would fupply Britain with all fhe ufes, and
more, and be worth both to her and the
colonies, much above a million fterling per
annum.

It is upon this principle therefore that
it ought to be recommended particularly
to enter into the bufinefs of making filk,
however thin the population; and efpecially in fuch excellent climates as the back
parts of this province, at the foot of the
mountains: for more than an hundred
miles in breadth, quite among the mountains, the whole territory is covered with
mulberry-trees; nature points out what
might be done in this country, but if the
induftry of man will not co-operate, it is
in vain to fee thefe rich gifts on every
fide.

No part of America would be more
proper for the growth of wine than this;
but at prefent we know not of a navigation that would be fufficient for the cheap
conveyance of it. Yet I fhould remark
that the rivers in this country are not fufficiently known. Nothing is of more importance in the management of our American concerns than to know accurately
how far the waters in that continent are
navigable, and for what boats; furveys
fhould

should be made of them with the greatest
care possible: tracts of country may be neglected under a notion of the rivers not
being navigable, while the fact may be
quite otherwise. In the back and hilly
parts of this province are numerous situations which would do admirably well for
vineyards, the soil and climate equally pro-
mising success, and the wild vines every
where found in immense quantities. Nothing is supposed to be wanting but a navigation, which ought to be well enquired
into.

Every reason of effect conspires to shew
the propriety of settling the back parts of
this province in preference to the maritime ones; in the latter rice must be the
staple, which is not wanted, since it is the
grand staple of South Carolina, where
there are swamps sufficient to raise more
than they will ever be able to sell. Indigo
they may cultivate, but the crop will be
far inferior to those on the rich, deep, black
land in the back country; and as to tobacco, the soil on the coast is not comparable to that on the Ohio, where the
planters will rival them entirely, not to
speak of the want of ports. At the same
time that these points give such a great

supe-

superiority, there is an equal one in the articles of health and pleasure. A temperate and healthy climate is, for profit as well as pleasure, of the greatest importance; the life of a negroe employed on indigo in the back parts of the province, would be worth ten years purchase more than one employed on rice in the maritime part: and the same difference must necessarily be found in the population of whites. The destructive swamps in which rice is cultivated must never be expected to breed people; whereas the high, dry, and healthy regions of the western parts are so liberally blessed with every circumstance of climate, soil, and productions, that the people would increase prodigiously, as in fact they are found to do in all the back settlements of the southern colonies.

In the next place let me recommend to the planters of North Carolina, whether living in the eastern or western part of the province, to pursue a better conduct relative to their cattle. Instead of keeping such vast herds of half-starved, stunted beasts, let them provide good pastures, and keep fewer beasts; the consequence of which will be, that five head will pay them better than twenty. In the very

back-

backward parts of the colony they have good meadows and pastures, but these are where the settlements are most scattered; and in all the rest of the country all the pastures the cattle have are the woods: this ought on every account to be remedied, so as to draw a greater profit from the stocks, and at the same time make them contribute largely to manuring the plantations, which at present they are far enough from doing. This good effect is only to be brought about by providing them pastures, as I said; in order to which the system of crops which I have so often condemned must be changed, and the land, when corn, &c. is no longer sown on it, must be left in sufficient order, and sown with grass seed, that good pastures may come in succession, instead of the land becoming forest again. There are sorts of grasses indigenous in the country, which might be brought into culture, that would answer this purpose; but the readiest way to effect it would be to sow lucerne, which I before recommended to other colonies: the hotter the climate, the greater the necessity of employing this grass, or some one similar to it in the great length of the root, which penetrates so deeply in the ground

A a 4

as

as to secure the plant from all damage by
the heat of the sun beams; most grasses,
from having fibrous roots, which spread
near the surface, are in these climates burnt
up, but lucerne will bear the hottest sun,
and thrive in it.   By means of the culture
of this plant they would be able to provide
well for their cattle, both horned cattle,
sheep, and swine, to all whom it is equally
grateful; a few acres cropped with it
would go as far as a great number of woodland : the cattle would thrive, their size
and breed be improved ; and, instead of
yielding little or no profit, they would become one of the best branches of the
planter's business.

In England it has been found necessary to
plant lucerne in rows, in order to keep it
free from the natural grass, which otherwise soon choaks and destroys it ; but in
such climates as Carolina, the heat of the
sun is such an enemy to the vegetation of
grass, that none is to be found in the flat
country but in rice swamps : this precaution therefore would be unnecessary, and
it might be sown broad-cast with the last
crop of corn, in the same manner as clover
in England.   This would (if properly introduced in the system) prove of wonderful
utility

utility to the cattle, and be of more confequence to the planter than almost any
other improvement. But I am aware that
a North Carolina man would be apt to fow
lucerne with the last crop of fuch a fystem
as this:

1. Tobacco.
2. Tobacco.
3. Tobacco.
4. Tobacco.
5. Indian corn.
6. Indian corn.
7. Wheat.
8. Peafe.
9. Wheat.
10. Wheat.

In which cafe he muft not expect it to
prove the valuable plant I have mentioned :
for fuch a fystem leaves the land a caput
mortuum for fome time, until the growth
fpontaneous to the country appears, which
is wood of feveral kinds; and it is not to
be expected that a crop of any value fhould
grow after fuch treatment. But lucerne
being to planters, circumftanced as the
North Carolina ones, of great value, it
would well deferve better treatment. Suppofe the fystem begins with frefh woodland; it fhould be fown with the laft crop
of

of some such system as this, in which I
have partly allowed the planters to be bad
husbandmen, as they all will be, till the
luxuriance of the fresh land is a little
tamed.

1. Tobacco.
2. Tobacco.
3. Indigo.
4. Cotton.
5. Wheat.
6. Cotton.
7. Indian corn.
8. Potatoes.
9. Cotton.
10. Potatoes.
11. Oats, or Pease, and with it, Lucerne. In case cotton is not planted, some
crop should be taken instead of it, that is
not a great exhauster of the land. There
are other roots which thrive well in the
climate, as turneps, carrots, and several
sorts of cabbages. These should certainly
be introduced in the field culture, to yield
food for the cattle in winter, which is as
necessary as lucerne for the summer; since
hay is to be had only in rice swamps cleared, or in the natural meadows near the
mountains.

It

It is only in the introduction of such plants in their systems of crops that they can be able to keep their lands in tolerable heart, or vary their present bad husbandry: no land, however good, will bear such exhausting crops for ever, as tobacco, indigo, and corn; it must be exhausted, vary them how you will; but by introducing potatoes (which is a native plant to the Carolinas) turneps, carrots, cabbages, or other plants, for the winter food of cattle, the land would be kept fertile twice as long, and be in good heart when laid down to lucerne.

The present general management of the cattle I should adhere to, that is, to let them wander about the woods all day, and and keep them at home in the night, with only this variation, they should in the pens and folds be *well* fed both winter and summer, which at present is far enough from being the case. In summer lucerne should be mown and given green in racks; and in winter they should have roots or cabbages, or the hay of lucerne: and the hogs also well fed with roots or cabbages, and such offal as the plantation yields: the advantages of this conduct would be great, not only in the superior growth of the cattle, and

and the larger quantity of produce yielded by them, but also in that article essential to all husbandry, *dung*: thus managed they would make much more dung, and of a quality far superior to that which the planters gain at present; for every farmer knows the difference between the dung of cattle well fed and that of cattle half starved: this would be a new assistant to them in keeping their fields in good heart, and would vastly increase the profit of their plantations.

This conduct would soon make a great change in the appearance of the country, and in its value; now almost as much returns to forest as is broken up, by the strange management they have of roaming from piece to piece, and touching none without ruining and exhausting it. What a great difference would it make, if when they took in a fresh piece of land, the old one was kept in value under lucerne, or some grass that would suit the climate. We should then see extensive and wide-spreading pastures of excellent herbage, instead of those numerous spots, which, having been under culture, and exhausted, lie absolutely barren for some years,

years, and then are covered gradually with weeds, bushes, and rubbish, among which forest-trees at last shoot up. This great change would make cattle as profitable to them as their staples, instead of keeping monstrous herds, which yield little or no produce. The planters should remember that in proportion as the country settles, the woodlands diminish, and the number of their cattle must necessarily fall off; then they would find the advantage strongly of keeping the land under good grass which they had had in culture: without this precaution, they will by and by, instead of boasting of a thousand or fifteen hundred head of cattle, with difficulty be able to keep a fourth of the number; and they will then be forced to the very culture of grass and other food for cattle as a necessary; it will then be a difficult and expensive business to get good grass on land so ruined and exhausted as their old plantations will be found.

In carrying such ideas into execution, supposing it ever done, fences should be much more attended to than they are at present in North Carolina: it ought to be an universal rule, never departed from, to
bring

bring into culture no piece of ground without previously fencing it in a secure and lasting manner by a live hedge. bank, and ditch. There is no part of the world in which this can be done better than in Carolina, from the quick growth of wood in land not exhausted by planting. And these fences should not only be kept up while the land yields a crop, but afterwards when it is under grass or lucerne, that the fences may be secure enough to keep all cattle out, in order for mowing the crop to feed with at night. When the lucerne began to fail from age, or the planter wanted the land again for corn, &c. then he would find the fences prove of great utility. It is observable that under grass or lucerne the land, if well laid down, and in heart, would continually improve in fertility until in some years it would prove highly profitable for a fresh system of crops.

There is no greater defect in the husbandry of this province than the foulness of the crops with weeds, &c. the improvement in this case would follow of course from adopting a different system of crops, as recommended above.

CHAP.

C H A P. XX.

SOUTH CAROLINA.

Climate of South Carolina—Productions—Soil.

THE province of South Carolina lies between lat. 31° and 35° N. but no idea is to be formed of the climate from that parallel, which in all other countries is found to be the finest on the globe; whereas this province experiences degrees of heat and cold rarely felt in other countries. This will appear from the following authentic account, said to be written by governor Glen. "Our climate is various and uncertain, to such an extraordinary degree, that I fear not to affirm there are no people upon earth who I think can suffer greater extremes of heat and cold; it is happy for us they are not of long duration. No idea of either one or the other can be formed from our latitude, which on other continents is found to be very desirable; nor dare I to trace by any physical reasoning the causes of these extremes, lest I should

8

I should amuse with vain conjectures those
to whom I would not write any thing but
truth; I shall therefore content myself
with setting down what we are sure of by
experiments. In summer the thermometer hath been known to rise to 98 degrees,
and in winter to fall to 10 degrees. The
weather perhaps is no where more variable,
with respect to heat and cold, than in Carolina; the changes are frequent, sudden,
and great; but the decreases of heat are always greater and more sudden than its increases. On the 10th of January, 1745,
at two o'clock in the afternoon, the thermometer was at 70 degrees, but the next
morning it was at only 15 degrees, which
was the greatest and most sudden change
that I have seen.

In summer the heat of the shaded air at
two or three o'clock in the afternoon is frequently between 90 and 95 degrees; but
such extremes of heat, being soon produc-
tive of thunder showers, are not of long
duration. On the 14th, 15th, and 16th
of June, 1738, at three o'clock in the afternoon, the thermometer was at 98 degrees,
a heat equal to the greatest heat of the human body in health! I then applied a thermometer to my arm-pits, and it sunk one
degree;

degree; but in my mouth and hands it
continued at 98 degrees. Sixty-five degrees
and a half may be called the temperate heat
in Carolina, which exceeds 48 degrees, the
temperate heat in England, more than that
exceeds, 32 degrees, the freezing point.
The mean heat of the shaded air, taken
from the mean nocturnal heat, and from
the mean heat at two or three o'clock in
the afternoon, during the four seasons of
the year, is as followeth: in spring 61
degrees, in summer 78, in autumn 71, and
in winter 52. The mean heat of the
shaded air, at two or three o'clock in the
afternoon, is 65 degrees in the spring, 82
in the summer, 75 in autumn, and 55 in
winter. The mean nocturnal heat in those
seasons is 57 degrees in the spring, 74 in
the summer, 68 in autumn, and 49 in
winter. Therefore our winter's mean nocturnal heat exceeds the temperate heat in
England.

 " As the weather here is generally very
serene, the sun's rays exert more constantly their full force; and therefore when we
are abroad, and exposed to the sun, we are
acted upon by a much greater degree of
heat than that of the shaded air; for the
thermometer, when suspended five feet

from the ground, and expofed to the fun
and to reflected rays from our fandy ftreets,
hath frequently rifen in a few minutes
from 15 to 26 degrees above what were
at thofe times the degrees of heat in the
fhaded air. But I have never yet made
that experiment when the heat of the
fhaded air was above 88 degrees; when
therefore we are in the ftreets in a ferene
day in the fummer, the air we walk in and
infpire is many degrees hotter than human
blood; for fuppofing the heat of the fhaded
air be 88 degrees when the thermometer
would rife 26 degrees higher if fufpended
and expofed to the fun, &c. as before
mentioned; or fuppofe that the heat of
the fhaded air be 98 degrees when the
thermometer would rife 26 degrees higher
by fuch fufpenfion and expofure: in the
firft of thofe two cafes, the heat of the air
in the ftreets would exceed 98, the natural
heat of the human blood, by 16 degrees;
and in the laft cafe it would exceed fuch
heat by 26 degrees.

" The firft inftance of intenfe cold that
I fhall mention, relates to a healthy young
perfon of my family, who at the time was
two or three and twenty years of age, and
ufually flept in a room without a fire: that
perfon

perfon carried two quart bottles of hot water to bed, which was of down, and covered with Englifh blankets; the bottles were between the fheets, but in the morning they were both fplit to pieces, and the water folid lumps of ice. In the kitchen, where there was a fire, the water in a jar, in which was a large live eel, was frozen to the bottom; and I found feveral fmall birds frozen to death near my houfe; they could not have died for want of food, the froft having been but of one day's conti-nuance. But an effect much to be regret-ted is, that it deftroyed almoft all the orange trees in the country; I loft above three hundred bearing trees; and an olive tree of fuch a prodigious fize, that I thought it proof againft all weathers; it was near a foot and a half diameter in the trunk, and bore many bufhels of excellent olives every year. This froft happened on the 7th of February, 1747."

Another account, written alfo by a per-fon who refided long in Carolina, gives fome other particulars deferving notice. " The air is more clear and pure here than in Britain, being feldom darkened with fogs; the dews however are great, ef-pecially in the end of the fummer, and be-

B b 2　　　ginning

ginning of the fall. The rains are heavy, but commonly short, and observe no particular season or time of the year.

" The winds are generally changeable and erratic, blowing from different points of the compass without any regularity; about the vernal and autumnal equinoxes they are commonly very boisterous; at other seasons are moderate.—The northerly winds are cold, dry, and healthy—they disperse fogs and mists, giving a clear sky— the north-west is the coldest we have; it comes to us over an immense tract of land, and from the snow-capped Apalachian mountains; whenever it blows the air is cool, and in the winter it generally brings us frost, and often snow : it is vulgarly and deservedly called the great physician of the country, as by its force it clears the air of the putrid autumnal effluvia; and by its coldness shuts up the pores of the earth, and of the trees, keeping in their vapours, the principal sources of the epidemics of the warm season. This refreshing, invigorating, and bracing wind is anxiously expected about the month of October by all, but by those particularly who have the misfortune to be afflicted with the more obstinate intermittents, to whom it generally

rally affords relief : the easterly winds are always cool ; from them we have our most refreshing summer showers ; when they blow for any continuance they occasion coughs and catarrhal fevers. The south and south-west winds are warmest and most unhealthy ; in whatever season they blow the air is foggy, and affects the breathing : in summer they are sultry and suffocating ; an excessive dejection of spirits and debility of body are then an universal complaint ; if this constitution lasts any considerable time, hysterics, hypo, intermitting and remitting, putrid, slow, or nervous fevers are produced. This province is subject to frequent and dreadful tempests of thunder and lightning in May, June, July, and August."

From this account of the weather in South Carolina is to be drawn several important conclusions ; that the maritime part of the country is in one of the most unhealthy climates in the world cannot be doubted. The heat rises to an extreme which is felt in very few, if any places on the globe, of which accounts have been given : at the same time the changes to intense cold are so violent and sudden, that instances are to be met with no where but

B b 3 in

in America, and not in that quarter to fuch
a degree as in South Carolina. Now of
all other circumftances of weather, there
are none that are found fo infalubrious to
the human conftitution as fuch fudden
changes, nor any which demands fo much
caution in drefs and living. Another point
to be obferved is, this immoderate and exceffive heat of climate is in a country, the
major part of which is fpread with ftag-
nated waters of no depth, for fuch are the
marfhes, fwamps, and all the rice grounds;
from the mud of thefe ftinking finks and
fewers the heat exhales fuch putrid effluvia,
as muft neceffarily poifon the air, and render it more fimilar to the Campania of
Rome than any thing elfe an European can
compare it to.

But at the fame time that this character is perfectly juft to the marfhy fea
coaft, and generally to all the flat country, we muft obferve that it holds no
further : this flat country reaches from
eighty to a hundred miles from the fea coaft,
but then the foil begins to rife into little
hills and beautiful inequalities, which continue increafing in height and variation till
you reach the Apalachian mountains, at
three hundred and three hundred and fifty
miles

miles from the sea. In all this range of
country the climate is nearly the reverse;
they have neither those extremes of heat,
nor the excess of cold that is felt on the
coast. On the contrary, they have a
charming, pleasant, and temperate climate,
which in health and agreeableness yields to
none in the world. This is to be attributed to the difference in the surface of the
two countries; in one it is high, dry, and
hilly; and wherever a country is of that
sort, or rocky, let it be in whatever latitude it may, it is sure to be healthy; but
the other is a flat, marshy tract, full every
where of stagnant water; and this is
throughout the world a never failing sign
of an unhealthy air.

Hence therefore a distinction is to be
made in every article that depends on climate between the eastern and western parts
of this province: an inhabitant of Carolina
may assert that country to be one of the
most healthy and pleasant in the world,
and nothing can be more true: an inhabitant of Carolina may assert that country to
be in unhealthiness the sink of the earth;
nothing more true: but let them explain;
one will be found to live in the east of it,
the other in the west; countries as different

almost

almoſt as Iceland and Bengal. If it is aſked, how it comes that any people will live in the flat country when the back parts are ſo ſuperior; it muſt be attributed to two cauſes, the one is the contiguity to the ports and trade; the other, the neceſſity of ſwamps for cultivating their grand ſtaple, rice; were it not for theſe it is to be ſuppoſed that all the inhabitants would flock backwards.

Relative to the products of South Carolina, it will be neceſſary to know them with tolerable preciſion, as they will mark the nature of the country better than any other circumſtance. I ſhall begin with timber: the uncultivated parts of the province are one continued foreſt, with not much underwood. Among the trees are found oaks of ſeveral ſorts, viz. the *cheſnut oak*, which is the largeſt in the province; ſome are three or four feet in diameter, and ſixty feet high to the firſt bough: they grow chiefly in low land that is ſtiff and rich. *Scarlet oak*, uſed, as well as the former, in ſhip-building; it grows on dry land. *Red oak* grows ſometimes very large and lofty, but is porous, and not durable; uſed for rails, ſtaves, &c. *Spaniſh oak*, more durable, is uſed ſometimes

in

in fhip-building, and rives well into clapboards. *Baftard Spanifh oak*, ufed for rails
and clapboards. *Black oak* is durable under water, ufed alfo for building. *White
iron oak*, very durable, is reckoned the
beft of all for fhip-building ; grows on dry
lean land. *Live oak*, the moft durable of
all, but unfortunately affords not long
plank clear of boughs. The weight and
firmnefs of this wood is extraordinary ; the
particles have fuch an adhefion, that when
a nail is once driven in, it is almoft impoffible to draw it out again, it grows in
frefh water ponds and fwamps. *Willow
oak*, fo called from the near refemblance of
the leaf to that of a willow : thefe are not
all the forts of oak found in this province,
there are feveral other varieties, but thefe
are the principal diftinctions : I muft remark that all of them yield acorns, generally in plenty, and fome of them in immenfe quantities, that fcarcely ever fail ;
and feveral of them that are as good for
fwine as chefnuts, having a ftrong refemblance of that fruit ; and they are in general much better food for hogs than our
Englifh acorns ; and fuch as will not only
keep hogs, but fat them admirably, without any expence to the planter. This is a
great

great object to the Carolina people; for there is not a farmer or planter in the country who has not great flocks of hogs kept in the woods, and even fattened there.

Ash is a common tree here, but differing somewhat from that of England. Elm they have of two forts; one grows on the high lands, which resembles that of Britain; the other fort grows in low lands. Tulip trees grow to an immense size; some of them have been found one and twenty feet in circumference, and some even ten feet in diameter; they have also a story current in Carolina, that a new settler, not having a better habitation, took his abode for some time in a decayed tulip-tree, in which he had his bed and other furniture; yet this man, poor as he may seem from hence, lived to become a considerable and wealthy planter. The use the wood of this tree is put to, is generally that of shingles, wainscot, planks for buildings, and lasts longer under ground.

Beech is often met with, and grows to a large size; it is very like that of Europe; the only use it is applied to in Carolina is for firing; it yields plenty of mast for swine. Hornbeam is common here. Saffafras is one of the articles of their exportation;

tion ; it comes fometimes to a large fize,
even to two feet diameter ; they ufe it for
turners ware, houfe-building, pofts, and
does well for all ground work. Dogwood
is very plentiful, and generally found on
light lands that are rich ; they ufe it in
building, where it is not expofed to the air.
Laurel comes here to a great fize; fo that
planks are fawn out of it, but it is not durable when expofed to the air : both bay and
laurel grow principally in low fwampy
ground. The red cedar grows chiefly on
fwamps or fand banks ; it is much valued
for durability, and ufed for building floops,
boats, &c. as well as by the joiners ; nor
will the worm touch it for many years, and
the floops built of it are efteemed for good
failers. White cedar is no lefs efteemed
for other ufes, particularly top mafts, yards,
booms, bowfprits, &c. and the beft fhin-
ples are made of it.

The cyprus grows to an immenfe fize,
perhaps larger than any other tree in Carolina, both in refpect of height and thicknefs ; fome have been found of thirty-fix
feet in circumference. The Indians make
their canoes of fingle cyprus-trees fcooped
out, and fome of them have been thus made
large enough to carry thirty barrels ; and
others

others that are split down the bottom, and a piece added thereto, will carry eighty or an hundred.

The locust-tree is very durable, and will bear being exposed to the weather; it is never found in swamps or low places, being a general sign of dry, healthy, good land. They have four sorts of pines here; the pitch pine grows to a great size: I before mentioned this tree yielding tar, pitch, &c. The white pine they saw in various species of lumber; it makes also masts, yards, &c. the almond pine does also for masts. The dwarf pine is of no great account. The hiccory is a kind of walnut, the timber not all durable. The common walnut is called the *black* walnut, to distinguish it from the hiccory: it affects good land, and grows therein to a vast size: it is hard and durable. The maple is common here. The chinkapin is a sort of chesnut, and durable in the weather; it is used in building boats, shallops, &c. Birch grows on the banks of the rivers, high up the country, but seldom found on the coast. Willows, sycamores, and hollies, are found here. Three sorts of mulberry-trees abound in Carolina, wherever the land

land is light ; and rich fhumac and hazel wood are alfo common.

In the next place we are to attend to the fruit-trees of this country, which are very numerous.

Among thefe we find the wild fig, which grows only on the mountains or their neighbourhood. The wild plums are of feveral forts ; they are of quick growth, bearing in five years from the ftone. They have a kind of currants, the bufhes of which grow feven or eight feet high. Apples of various forts, and in great plenty. Three or four forts of pears. Three forts of quinces, the fruit of which is very large, and much beyond thofe of England. The leaft flip of this tree planted will bear in three years; a furprifing vegetation. Peaches are the moft common fruit in the country, and no wonder, for every ftone that falls becomes a bearing tree in three years ; all are ftandards ; the quantity of this fruit is fo great, that the hogs have much the larger fhare of it : they are generally fuch great bearers, that the branches of the trees are broken down with the weight of the fruit; they grow to the fize of common appletrees.

The

The apricot grows to a very great fize, exceeding moft apple-trees : they are raifed from the ftone. Red and black cherries are found very plentifully. Goofeberries do not agree well with the climate, but common currants do well. Rafpberries are plentiful. Strawberries thrive greatly, and bear amply. Native vines are met with all over the province ; but the fineft are in the back parts upon the dry hills, where they are five times as large as on the coaft. From the native black grape, which does not ripen till October, wine has been made, of an excellent quality, and very ftrong ; but the vineyards which have been tried of European grapes, have all failed from their ripening in Auguft.

Befides thefe fruits, South Carolina produces others more valuable and fought after, as oranges, fweet and four, lemons, citrons, limes, olives, pomegranates, all forts of melons, water-melons, &c. Oranges and lemons are an article of exportation, great numbers being fent abroad annually. Olives are not cultivated in common, which is a neglect ; though none of thefe fruits can be depended on, as in a country where no frofts are felt ; whereas in Carolina, as before

fore remarked, they are fometimes fo fevere, as to kill all tender trees to the
root.

In the kitchen garden are found every
fort of ufeful plant that is commonly cultivated in the gardens in England. Potatoes
no where thrive better, and they have them
of feveral forts; many forts of peas and
beans, with cabbages, broccoli, cauliflow-
ers, &c. Some of thefe are in a perfection
which is unknown to us in Britain, owing
to the fuperior heat of the climate; yet in
general we fhould remark, that garden-
ftuff, which will grow at all in the cli-
climate (fruits excepted) is preferable more
to the north, in Maryland, Virginia, and
the fouthern part of Penfylvania; but in
the back parts of Carolina, near the mountains, all thefe articles are yielded in a perfection that cannot be exceeded.

The products which refpect hufbandry
in particular are Indian corn, which thrives
very well here; wheat, which does well in
the backward parts, but very badly in the
maritime fide of the province; barley the
fame; both thefe grain, as well as oats,
are very little cultivated, nor can they be
till the fettlements reach further back;
beans and peas of feveral forts, particularly

7 the

the Indian kinds, thrive well all over the
province. As to the staples of rice, indigo, &c. I shall speak more particularly of
them in another place.

The soil of Carolina must, like the climate, be divided before one can speak of
it with any precision, into the eastern and
western parts of the province ; that is, the
maritime part, and the back country ; the
former reaches above an hundred miles
from the coast : this tract contains several
kinds of land, which the planters distinguish by calling them pine land, oak land,
swamps, and marshes.

Pine land is much the most general, containing perhaps four-fifths of the country ;
the soil is a dry white sand, covered with
pines : if there is any underwood it is very
poor, only the whortleberry and chinkapin,
which Dr. Mitchel calls the *beath* of America.   This land is very poor, and will
bear scarcely any thing but its spontaneous
growth ; in spots it contains a little grass,
but of so bad and sour a nature, that cattle
will not touch it unless half starved. The
writer I just now mentioned has an observation on this pine land, which deserves
attention.   " These pines with which all
our southern colonies are covered for one

hun-

hundred or one hundred and fifty miles
from the fea-coaft, and in fome all over
them, are the moft pernicious of all weeds;
they not only deftroy every thing upon the
face of the earth, but the very land they
grow upon; infomuch that nothing will
grow among them, and hardly any thing
after them.   It is a general obfervation,
that the lands are not only barren on which
they grow naturally, but if they happen to
come up on other lands, they fpoil them,
and render them more or lefs barren.
Having often examined what this could be
owing to, I could not attribute it altoge-
ther to their large fpreading roots, which
fpread all over the furface of the earth like
a mat, and exhauft its fubftance, but chiefly to the ftrong acid juice of their leaves,
which diftills from them in the fpring of
the year like oil of turpentine, and poifons
both the earth and every thing upon it; as
it is well known that all acids are a poifon
to vegetables, and all alcalies a rich manure.   But whatever may be the caufe, the
matter of faƈt is certain, that nothing will
grow among pines in America; and M. du
Hamel makes the fame obfervation in
France.   The whole furface of the earth is
covered with their acid leaves; they over-

top and deſtroy every thing ; and if a little
graſs ſhould happen to come up among
them where they grow thin, it is ſo ſcarce,
yellow, and ſour, that to ſee any beaſt feed
upon it, is a certain ſign of the miſerable
poverty of a country, where they are re-
duced to the laſt extremity.   Yet theſe are
the only paſtures they have in many of our
colonies : what is worſe, theſe pernicious
weeds are not to be extirpated ; they have
a wing to their ſeed, which diſperſes it every
where with the winds, like thiſtles, and in
two or three years forms a *pine thicket*,
which nothing can paſs through or live in.
Thus the land becomes a perfect deſart inſtead of a profitable paſture, in a few years
after it is cleared.   Corn upon ſuch land
looks as yellow as the turpentine with
which it is fed, and graſs will not grow."
There is a great deal of truth and good ſenſe
in this paſſage ; but at the ſame time it is
not ſtrictly true, that nothing will grow
after theſe pines, for it is well known that
the planters get Indian corn and peas from
theſe lands after they are cleared ; and when
they lie low enough to be flooded, rice.
But the principal uſe they are put to is for
indigo, in which they anſwer tolerably ;
but this is only becauſe they have no bet-

ter

ter that is dry; for indigo delights in dry, rich, deep, black mould. When you abuse their pine barrens, a Carolina planter will answer you by saying, that they do for their richest crop, indigo; which is very true, as I just observed; but they do for it only as poor sands in England do for the culture of wheat: the farmers sow it because they have no better, and get half crops, which is just the case with indigo on pine barrens.

Oak land is another sort; it is a black, rich sand, and produces oaks, walnut, hiccory, and black mulberry-trees, and is to all intents excellent land; but the misfortune is, that the quantity of it is very small; it is found only in narrow stripes between the swamps and pine barrens, and between the latter and creeks or rivers. This is the only land they have that will produce good crops of corn and indigo.

Swamps are of several sorts, and they judge of them by their produce; the best are the white oak swamps, which have generally a clayey foundation; but these are rare in South Carolina, or else being on the large rivers are too deep to clear and drain. Others bear canes, and are therefore called cane swamps: these are generally rich and good; but the most general are cyprus

C c 2 ones,

ones, which is the spontaneous growth of all, where the soil surrounding them is a poor land. However, it is to be noted, that all these swamps, when drained, produce the grand staple of the country, rice, yielding crops of it, as in other cases of a goodness proportioned to their fertility. The face of the country in general is that either of a swamp or a pine barren. Marshes they divide into the salt and fresh water marshes; when the water is low enough they pasture them with horses and cattle; and if they bestow the labour of draining on them they make tolerable good meadows.

There can be no doubt but that all this maritime part of America has been covered with the sea, it has every sign of it; upon digging you find no clay, stones, rocks, nor minerals, it is all sand, or beds of shells; and the flatness of the country, with the gradual shallowness of the sea, shew it sufficiently.

The varieties of land just given include all the maritime part of the province; but the back country, which reaches to the Apalachian mountains, is very different; swamps and marshes are there unknown, or at least but rarely met with, from
whence

whence proceeds the healthiness of it. The face of the country is hilly, and either covered with tall stately trees, or spread into extensive meadows of dry, rich, deep land ; which is the general nature of the soil, except where rocks abound, which is on the broken parts of some of the mountains, and on the banks of some of the rivers.   Pines are in this part of the province seldom met with ; on the contrary, the timber is oak, elm, hiccory, walnut, and mulberry : no lands in the southern part of North America have an appearance of being more fertile ; and the most retired of our plantations, which are seated only where this fine country begins, find that one acre will yield as much produce of any kind as three in the maritime part of the province.   The fresh wood lands here are deep, and *black* for two feet deep ; such is the right land for indigo, tobacco, corn of all sorts, and, in a word, for every thing that is sown upon it.   This extraordinary fertility of the soil is united with a climate as mild, temperate, healthy, and agreeable, as that of the eastern part of Carolina is the reverse.   It is the rice swamps that alone keep the inhabitants near the coast ; the planters are accustomed to that culture,

C c 3   and

and will not change it for a different one: no rice is to be cultivated here, which is the circumstance that is the glory of the country: from this country it is that silk and wine must come, if ever they are had from Carolina.

It is the peculiar blessing of these back tracts of country, that they have every product that is valuable, which is known in the maritime part of the province, except rice; and at the same time they are exempted from those of little or no use, or that are pernicious, such as the pine; a character we may fairly give it (notwithstanding its yielding tar, pitch, &c.) whenever it grows on land that could be applied to any other use.

This is the part of Carolina to which all new settlers should be recommended; here they will increase their numbers greatly from the healthiness of the country, which is not the case with the swamps and marshes on the coast. They may raise much better and more valuable staples than rice.

CHAP.

CHAP. XXI.

Staple productions—Rice—Culture of it—
Management of the plantations—Profit—
Indigo—Culture—Profit—Observations
—Other staples—Remarks.

RICE is yet the grand staple production of South Carolina, and that for
which the planters neglect the healthy,
pleasant back country in order to live in the
Dismals on the coast, for so the Americans
justly call the swamps: rice can only be
cultivated in land which lies so low as to
admit of floating at pleasure, and all such
lands in Carolina are necessarily swamps.
The first business is to drain the swamp, in
which work they have no particular methods deserving notice, or which are unknown in England. The moment they
have got the water off they attack the trees,
which in some swamps are very numerous;
these they cut down at the root, leaving
the stumps in the earth, and, oftentimes
even the trunks and branches of the trees
are left about the ground : some planters
pile them up in heaps, and leave them to
rot ;

rot; others, more provident, cut them into lengths, and convert them into fome fort of lumber. However they do not wait for the ground being cleared of them, but proceed to plant their rice among the ftumps. In March, April, and May they plant; the negroes draw furrows eighteen inches afunder, and about three inches deep, in which the feeds are fown; a peck is fufficient for an acre of land: as foon as planted they let in the water to a certain depth, which is, during the feafon of its growth, repeated, and drawn off feveral rimes; but moft of the growth is while the water is eight, nine, or ten inches deep on the land. The great object of the culture is to keep the land clean from weeds, which is abfolutely neceffary, and the worft weed is grafs: if they would fay a man is a bad manager, they do not obferve fuch a perfon's plantation is not clean, or is weedy, but *fuch a man is in the grafs*; intimating that he has not negroes enough to keep his rice free from grafs. This is the only object till it is reaped, which is ufually about the latter end of Auguft or beginning of September. Like wheat in England, they prefer cutting it while the ftraw is a little green, leaving it on the ftubble to dry and wither two or
three

three days in cafe the weather is favourable:
after which they lay it up in barns or ftacks,
in the fame manner as corn in Europe.

The next operation, as in other forts of
corn, is the threfhing of it, after which it
is winnowed, which was formerly a very
tedious operation, but now much accelerated
by the ufe of a wind-fan. When winnowed
it is ground, to free the rice from the hufk;
this is done in wooden mills of about two
feet diameter: it is then winnowed again,
and put into a mortar large enough to hold
half a bufhel, in which it is beat with a
peflle by negroes, to free it from its thick
fkin; this is a very laborious work. In
order to free it from the flour and duft
made by this pounding, it is fifted; and
again through another fieve, called a market fieve, which feparates the broken and
fmall rice, after which it is put up in barrels, and is ready for market.

The reader muft obferve upon this account that the cultivation of it is dreadful:
for if a work could be imagined peculiarly
unwholefome, and even fatal to health, it
muft be that of ftanding, like the negrofs,
ancle, and even mid-leg deep in water,
which floats an ouzy mud; and expofed all
the while to a burning fun, which makes
the

the very air they breathe hotter than the
human blood; these poor wretches are
then in a furnace of stinking putrid effluvia: a more horrible employment can hardly be imagined, not far short of digging in
Potosi. We are told indeed that South Carolina breeds more negroes than she destroys, which is certainly a fact, as appears
by the annual exportation of a few; but
then let it not be imagined that it is in
these properly denominated *dismals* : we are
to remember that the proportion between
the domestic and other negroes and planting ones, is as 30,000 to 40,000, when
the total is 70,000 ; and we are further to
remember, that many are employed on indigo where there are no rice swamps, and
also in other branches of culture; all these
with the 30,000, may certainly increase
greatly; but it does not from hence follow
that those employed on rice do not decrease
considerably, which is a certain fact, and
it would be miraculous were it otherwise.
It will therefore be no impropriety to determine that there must be a considerable
expence in recruiting those negroes that
are employed on rice, and more considerable far than what attends others employed

ed on tobacco, indigo, or indeed any plant not cultivated in a fwamp.

As to the product of rice, it varies much, which is in proportion to the goodnefs of the fwamp, and to the culture that is beftowed on it ; the land it likes is the ftiff, deep, miry mud on clay ; the worft is the fwamp with only a fandy bottom. Governor Glen obferves that thirty flaves are a proper number for a plantation, and to be attended by one overfeer. The common computation throughout the province is, communibus annis, that each working hand employed in a rice plantation, makes four barrels and a half of rice, each barrel weighing four or five hundred pounds weight neat; befides a fufficient quantity of provifions of all kinds for the flaves, horfes, cattle, and poultry of the plantation for the year enfuing ; the price 6s. 5d. per 100lb. or from 1 l. 5 s. to 1 l. 12 s. per barrel ; but fince this gentleman wrote, the price has rifen to 2 l. and 4 l. per barrel. We are told in an account written in 1710, that the product was from 30 to 60 bufhels; fuppofe 40, and that a bufhel weighed 65lb. at 450lb. a barrel this would be $5\frac{1}{4}$ to the acre ; and at 2 l. the amount would be 10 l. 15 s.

The

The firſt account of 4½ barrels at 2l. is 9l. per working hand, at the price rice is at preſent. A late account of Carolina, publiſhed in 1770, makes the labour of the ſlaves 10l. each ; theſe agree therefore very well. But Dr. Stork makes the profit per head 20l. by this culture, and ſays that where the ſoil and climate are proper for rice, there is no grain in the world yields ſo much profit to the planter ; this is evidently a miſtake, and a great one. If we allow 10l. a head upon the former, and better authority, we cannot be far from the truth. I before calculated the annual expence of negroes as follows :

	l.	s.	d.
Overſeer - - -	1	0	0
Cloaths - - -	0	10	0
Sundries - - -	1	10	0
	3	0	0

But the decline of value muſt be in all reaſon reckoned in rice work ; if 2l. the expences will be 7l. and the produce but 10l. ſo the planter's profit per head will be only 3l. from which muſt be farther deducted the intereſt of his coſt, or 50l. which at 5 per cent. (not reckoning the rate per cent.

of

of the colonies) come to 2l. 10s. and leaves
neat from the flave 9l. 10s. But as this
would by no means pay the planter for his
other expences and his time, he makes a
fhift to fave fomething in the articles of
overfeer and cloathing; but ftill the product from rice alone would be infufficient:
the method in which they make it up is
partly by lumber, as the flave will have time
in the winter to threfh and drefs more rice
than he can plant in the fummer; and
confequently can fpare it for fawing lumber. But yet rice would not anfwer were
it not for other affiftance; this is chiefly
indigo. I before remarked that between
the pine barrens and fwamps are dry flips
of oak land, which is rich and good; on
this they plant indigo, and to good profit,
with this further advantage, that indigo
requiring no winter work, the flaves may
affift in manufacturing rice, and fawing
lumber, &c. Upon this plan indigo is extremely profitable, but for want of enough
of it, they plant it likewife on the pine barren, where it is but little better than rice.
It is this fecondary object of the rice
planters which makes their bufinefs advantageous enough to fupport them; but upon

8   this

this circumftance I muft make a few obfervations.

What can induce them to have any thing
to do with an article of culture, which,
taken fingly, would not even pay charges ?
That this is the fact is not to be difputed,
for we have the produce per working hand
from the beft authority, the governor of
the province, who refided in it many years ;
and let any perfon judge if a negroe can
ftand in lefs than 7l. or 8l. a year in fo pernicious an employment as that of making
rice. And it is alfo clear enough that the
wear of tools, buildings, charges, inci-
dents, intereft of other money, &c. &c.
muft likewife come to fomething confiderable.

What therefore I fay can induce the
planters to engage in fuch a bufinefs ?

Poffibly it is owing to habit, and being
accuftomed to confider rice as their grand
dependance, which it was to their fathers
before indigo, filk, cotton, &c. were known
here ; and having been ufed to this idea,
they find it difficult, like all cultivators of
the foil, to change old cuftoms. If it is
not owing to this, it is difficult to fay to
what it can be owing. In the back country of the province the land is of infinitely
greater

greater fertility, and would produce much more valuable ftaples, at the fame time that the healthinefs of the climate would both to the planter and his family, as well as his flaves, be invaluable : their being fo much addicted therefore to rice, is founded on no good and fubftantial reafons.

There is another circumftance which fhould make the government attentive to encouraging every ftaple, but particularly indigo, tobacco, filk, wine, &c. more than rice, which is its being a rival to one of the moft valuable articles of our trade, that of corn ; for all the rice fold to Spain and Portugal is but enabling them to do without fo much of our wheat; and that is partly the cafe with Germany : not that I would infinuate that reftrictions on rice fhould be laid, for obvious reafons, and particularly, the not knowing whether we can fupply thofe markets with corn, fuppofing they would take it of us—and alfo the value of the rice being all laid out in Britifh commodities. But indigo, tobacco, &c. have all the fame advantages without *any* difadvantages, nor even the appearance of any.

INDI-

INDIGO.

There are three forts of indigo cultivated in South Carolina—the *Hifpaniola*, the *Babama*, which is a falfe Guatimala, and the *native*; the two firft are the moft valuable, but the laft is much better adapted to the climate. The former is an annual plant, but the wild fort, which is common in the country, is perennial; its ftalk dies every year, but it fhoots up again next fpring; the indigo made from it is of as good a quality as the other, the fuperiority of that being owing to the fuperior fertility of the Weft Indies, and a better climate for it. Dr. Mitchel reckons Carolina to have a great inferiority to the Weft Indies in this article: his words are, "Indigo thrives very indifferently either in the foil or the climate. Indigo is one of thofe rank weeds like tobacco, which not only exhauft the fubftance of the earth, but require the very beft and richeft lands, and fuch as have a natural moifture in them; whereas the lands in Carolina are extremely poor and fandy, and have a barren drynefs in them, which renders them very unfit to produce fuch a crop as this to any manner of advantage. This

is

is planted by the French on the fresh woodlands of St. Domingo, which are too rich
and moist even for sugar, and is intended
to exhaust their luxuriant fertility, as we
do with tobacco, in order to render them
fit for that and other crops. They likewise
cut it every six weeks, or eight times a year,
and for two years together ; whereas in Carolina it is cut but thrice ; and as the land
has not substance and moisture to make it
shoot after cutting, and the summers are
too short, the third cutting is but of little
value, as even the second is in Virginia.
Neither does the soil or climate seem to be
fit to yield that rich juice which makes this
dye in any plenty or perfection. The French
and Spaniards make great quantities worth
eight and ten shillings a pound, when the
little we make in Carolina is not upon an
average worth above two shillings, and a
great deal has been sold for a shilling and
less."

The proper soil for indigo is a rich, light,
black mould, such as is commonly found
in the back country ; but in the maritime
part they chuse oak land for it, not having
the other ; and as this is but in small quantity, they are forced to cultivate their poor

white fands for indigo, which will not yield
near the produce which all cultivators of
this commodity ought to be defirous of,
and indeed which will always be gained
when proper land is employed for it. The
deficiency of common products appears
from governor Glen's account, who afferts,
that 30 lb. an acre is all that is to be expected in common, though good land will
produce 80.

Refpecting this point of produce, our
accounts differ greatly, and none yet in
print are fully to be depended on ; Mr.
Glen's account is, that one acre of *good
land* will produce 80 lb. and one flave may
manage two acres and upwards, and raife
provifions befides, and have all the winter
months to faw lumber, and be otherwife
employed : 80 lb. at 3 s. the prefent
price, is 12 l. per acre ; and 2½ acres at
that rate amount to 30 l. per flave, befides lumber, which is very confiderable :
but I fhould obferve, that there is much
indigo brought now from Carolina, which
fells in London for from 5 s. to 8 s. a
pound, and fome even higher, though the
chief part of the crop may not yield more
than 3s. or 4s. this will alter the average
price ;

price; but how much, is almoſt impoſſible to aſcertain, as it depends on many unknown circumſtances.

Before I quit this ſubject, I ſhall, in order to give the reader all the ſatisfaction poſſible, tranſcribe part of an account of the indigo culture, written in 1755, before the province had got ſo largely into the management of it as it has done ſince. "Whoever plants indigo muſt be careful to have a good command of water in his reſervoirs, which if in the center of his field, the better, to ſave time in bringing the plant when cut to the vats. We plant two kinds of land in Carolina, viz. high land and low land. The firſt is of the richeſt kind, overgrown with oak or hiccory, in which the plant will ſtrike its roots very ſtrait and deep. The ſecond is either our river or inland ſwamps, where we plant rice, which lands are generally covered with huge oaks and cypreſſes; ſo that to gain a field of twenty acres in this country, as many noble trees muſt be felled and burnt, as in England would bring many thouſands ſterling.

" This low land is banked, ditched, trenched, and drained; but the soil must lie on a clay bottom, otherwise indigo will not thrive in it. In those lands the indigo roots spread horizontally, as in the high lands perpendicularly."—This idea of our author seems contradictory to the best accounts I have received, which confine the culture of indigo to hiccory land and pine barren, as it requires a dry soil, though as fertile as possible, and consequently a swamp must be well *drained* indeed to be rendered proper for it: but what he says himself shews that the high land is the best for it, since all plants that strike a perpendicular root ought to be planted in a soil that will admit such roots shooting: a perpendicular root spreading horizontally, proves clearly that the soil is improper; it meets with the wet retained by the clay, which prevents its running deeper. His situation, within forty miles of Charles Town, prevented him, I suppose, from mentioning the deep black loams of the back country, which are the only ones that will yield *great* crops of indigo. But to return,

" If

" If the planter prefer the quality before the quantity of his indigo, he will be very careful to let his plants but juſt bloſſom before he cuts; for the more young and tender the plant, the more beautiful will be the colour of the indigo, though it will not yield perhaps ſo much as if cut a week or two later; but what he loſes one way he will gain another. On the contrary, if he lets his plants be overgrown, and ſtand too long, he never can expect bright indigo. Indigo has a very diſagreeable ſmell, while making and curing; and the *fæces*, when taken out of the ſteeper, if not immediately buried in the ground (for which it is excellent manure) breeds incredible ſwarms of flies.

" The quality of indigo, when made, may be known by its brightneſs, cloſeneſs, and fine violet blue, inclining to copper. It is better by being kept ſome time, and ought to be light enough to ſwim on the water; the quicker and more it ſinks, the worſe its property. The very beſt and fineſt is of a fine lively blue, inclining to the violet; brilliant, of a fine ſhining colour when broke, and more beautiful within than without. A buſhel of good indigo

D d 3   weighs

weighs about 50 or 55 pounds. The methods for trial of its goodnefs, is firft to throw a cake into a glafs of water, where it will foon diffolve entirely, if pure and well made ; but if mixed with any foreign matter, the heterogeneous parts will fink, Secondly, another method is to burn it : good indigo entirely confumes away ; but if adulterated, it will be difcovered by the falfe mixtures remaining after the true indigo is confumed.

" Our indigo making ceafes with the fummer. As foon as cold weather fets in, little or no fermentation can be excited. Double beating and labour is required ; and in drying the indigo the cakes will break into powder. The firft frofty night concludes our feafon.

Expence of purchafing a plantation in Carolina within 40 miles of Charles Town.

	l.	s.	d.
To 1000 acres of land (one third of which ought to be good fwamp, the reft oak and hiccory, with fome pine barren, at 11s. 5d. - - - -	575	0	0
To a dwelling houfe, barn, ftable, overfeer's houfe, negro huts, &c. - -	142	15	0
To two valuable negroes, (a cooper and a carpenter) at 71l. 7s. 6d. - -	142	15	0
To 26 other negroes, (two thirds men and one third women) at 35l. 10s. -	927	10	0
To two ordinary old negroes to look after the poultry, kine, hogs, &c. -	57	0	0
To a waiting boy, - - -	28	10	0
To a houfe-wench, - -	40	15	0
To 20 head of oxen, cows, &c. at 1l. 8s.	28	0	0
To 2 ftallions and 4 breeding mares, at 5l. 14s.	11	8	0
To hogs, fheep, and poultry, - -	21	8	0
To plantation tools, a cart, plough, &c.	21	8	0
To 2 riding horfes for yourfelf, family, over-feer, bridles, faddles, &c. - -	28	0	0
To cloaths, provifions, &c. for negroes, feed, vats, &c. for the firft year,	35	15	0
To contingencies, nails, oil, &c. -	15	15	0
	£. 2075	19	0

The plantation per ann. after the firft year.
N. B. This calculation is for good years, and exclufive of accidents.

To the overfeer's wages, and allowance for rum, &c. - - -	35	15	0
To 32 pair of fhoes for negroes, at 2s. 6d.	3	0	0
To 160 yards of white plains (5 yards each negro) at 1s. 5d. - - -	11	6	8
Carried over £. 50	50	1	8

D d 4

	l.	s.	d.
Brought forward	50	1	8
To thread, buttons, &c. - -	0	14	3
To one third of 32 blankets given every } third year, - - -	3	17	0
To physic for each negro, as per agreement } with the doctor, - - -	4	14	6
To Osnabrug, lime, oil, nails, and iron ware,	8	13	6
To freight and cooperage of 50 barrels of } rice, at 2s. 10d. - -	7	1	8
To ditto of 6 of indigo, at 3s. 2d. -	0	19	0
To tax and quit-rent of 1000 acres of land,	2	2	6
To tax of 32 slaves, about - -	4	4	0
To purchase of two slaves annually, to keep } up the original flock, which it is judged } this and their increase may do, -	71	5	0
To wear and tear, - - -	14	10	0
£.	168	3	1

By the produce of 60 acres of indigo at } 50 lb. per acre, at 2s. 10d. per lb. or } 7l. 1s. 8d. per acre, - -	425	0	0
By 50 barrels of rice, on 25 acres, each bar- } rel 500 lb. net, at 6s. per cwt. -	66	18	0
By 50 barrels, - - -	3	13	6
Total,	495	11	6
Expences, - - - -	168	3	1
Balance, planter's profit, - -	327	8	5

N. B. It is here supposed, that the family resides on the spot, and that the surplus of hogs, poultry, &c. raised above their own consumption, will be sufficient to find the family in butchers meat, and other necessaries, save cloathing.

" This

" This computation is made of two acres of indigo and one of rice to each hand ; they raife their own provifions befides.

" If rice is not planted, fome of the hands may be employed in the winter feafon in making naval ftores, cutting of lumber, fhingles, &c." *.

There are fome valuable particulars in this account ; but in others it is either erroneous, or does not hold good at prefent, when they reckon that the flaves, well appointed and taken proper care of, keep up their own numbers with any new purchafe, which indeed appears from Carolina genenerally exporting a few. As to the rice, if 66l. in 500l. with a lofs of lumber, is all the recompence for fixing in the low fwampy country, it fhews at once how juft my former obfervations were, that the back country is not only in point of health and agreeablenefs infinitely fuperior to any thing within forty miles of Charles Town, but alfo by far the moft profitable to the planter. The foil is there greatly fuperior for every production except rice ; this fuperiority would alone more than equal the

___

* *Gent. Mag.* Vol. xxv. p. 258.

amount

amount of 66l. befides the product of lumber. All the accounts we have had of this country only confirm the truth of the general obfervation, that the back country is that to fettle.

Befides rice and indigo, there are fome other ftaples cultivated in Carolina, which though not of any great importance, yet demand a little attention. Cotton thrives well in the foil and climate, and though it is applied at prefent only to the home confumption of the province, yet it might certainly be extended fo as to become a confiderable article of exportation. Indigo and rice at prefent engrofs all their attention, not becaufe they cannot raife other ftaples, but becaufe thefe, while the demand is great, are more profitable. Cotton will hereafter be a valuable ftaple. Wine, filk, oil, hemp, and flax, are other products, which in the back country may be cultivated in the greateft plenty; but this is not to be expected, till the value of that healthy and fertile part of our fouthern colonies is better known and peopled.

It is an obfervation that demands much national attention, that this very important colony fhould cultivate more ftaples than rice and indigo; it is of confequence

that

that our colonies fhould not depend on one or two ftaples which are not of a permanent nature: indigo is the only article that ranks among the ftaples of South Carolina, which is fecure of a future fale, proportioned to the future increafe of culture: I do not think that this is the cafe with rice, the fale of which depends very minutely on the plenty of corn in Germany, the North, Spain, and Portugal; . for in thofe countries is its principal fale; and the immenfe growth of the rice plantations in Carolina has of late years been much owing to a great failure in the corn crops of Europe, a failure which has been and is at prefent likely to prove of no flight advantage to this colony.

But filk, wine, oil, hemp, flax, &c. not forgetting tobacco, would, if well attended to in the back country, fecure to this province thofe advantages which can only flow from the poffeffion of various ftaples in common demand throughout the world; by which means, their profit would be greater than at prefent, and under the fecurity of a much longer duration than will ever be found attendant on the exportation of rice.

Be-

Befides thefe articles, which are at prefent cultivated in large or fmall quantities,
(it is to be obferved that every one of the
products here mentioned are planted for
private ufe, and in fome in fmall quantities
for fale) there are others which deferve
mention ; among thefe we find an exportation of the fame fruits which are fent from
Spain and Portugal, oranges, lemons, citrons,
&c. pitch, tar, turpentine, rofin, naval timber, pot-afh, faffafras, lumber, tallow, wax,
leather, fkins, &c. Thefe are articles which
demand attention, and for which all endeavours fhould be tried to increafe, fince it is a
number of ftaples upon which a flourifhing
colony depends for any permanency of profperity : and this is the more neceffary, as in
proportion as the fettlements extend, in
fuch proportion does the benefit of lumber
fall off; fince the clearing the woods pays
the expence in lumber only in the maritime part of the province: now in plantations which are deprived of the advantage
of lumber, there muft accrue a certain
lofs, if a variety of ftaples be not introduced. Indigo and tobacco employ only the
negroes the fummer half of the year, and
leave time fufficient for filk in the fpring,

I   an

an harvest in summer, and a vintage in autumn, besides the winter for other purposes, and completing the labour of other staples.

This object deserves the more attention, from the circumstance of the eagerness of the Carolina planters in the culture of their grand staples, rice and indigo, which is carried on to such a degree, as to render them little solicitous about other objects. Herein they consult what we are to look for from all mankind, great attention to what they think their present interests, and very little idea of futurity; this disposition which is so general among all people, does very well for the present time, and for present interests, but it will rarely, if ever, bring in those improvements, which, in the introduction of new staples, become, in future, objects of the greatest importance. It is in such points as these that the attention of government is wanted, which can alone effect such material improvements, by bringing people to an attention to other objects, besides their immediate interests, by rewards and other encouragement.

The administration of our government has in these instances shewn too great an inattention to such important objects; our
colonies

colonies have increased greatly in population and product, which has satisfied us, although the benefits received might have been greatly increased, and been of such a nature, as to promise a much longer and more secure duration than what they enjoy at present.

CHAP. XXII.

Account of the means, expence, and profit of forming a plantation in South Carolina—Explanations—Remarks.

SOUTH Carolina has of late years increased in a most prodigious degree, both in people and the exportation of valuable staples, which has been owing to several causes I shall mention hereafter ; and this great increase, with the fortunes made by planting in this part of the continent, have induced very great numbers to settle in this province, and it is much to the advantage of Great Britain that this is so ; for in all these provinces to the south, valuable staples are produced, which enable the inhabitants to purchase the manufactures of Britain, a case not to be met with in the

the northern settlements : for this reason it is highly expedient, that the profit accruing from agriculture in this province be well understood, that all those persons who are in doubt which part of America they should go to, may be induced to make choice of those colonies which produce staples for Britain ; among which South Carolina fi-figures greatly.

A calculation drawn from actual experience of the expences, produce, and profit of a considerable plantation in this province.

	l.	s.	d.
Freight and expences of six persons in one family, from London to Charles Town, at 25l.	150	0	0
Freight of 10 tons, at 40s.	20	0	0
A couple of riding horses,	40	0	0
Expences in searching for a plantation,	40	0	0
Patent fees of 10,000 acres,	62	10	0
Building a house,	200	0	0
———— offices, rice barns, &c.	700	0	0
———— tobacco-house,	20	0	0
———— saw mill,	500	0	0
Furniture,	150	0	0
A canoe,	50	0	0
Boats,	30	0	0
Year's house keeping,	120	0	0
Implements of culture,	200	0	0
20 horses at 5l.	100	0	0
100 cows at 30s.	150	0	0
Swine,	20	0	0
Poultry,	5	0	0

Carried over 2557 10 0

l.   s.   d.

Brought forward, 2557 10 0

Wear and tear of implements,   -   -   20 0·0

Sundry labour exclusive of negroes.

On cattle, - -	15 0 0	
100 acres of wheat at 20s.	100 0 0	
40 acres of oats at 16s.	32 0 0	
10 potatoes at 40s. -	20 0 0	
Making hay, - -	20 0 0	
Orchard and garden,	15 0 0	
Sundries, - -	30 0 0	
		232 0 0
40 negroes at 50l. - - -		2000 0 0

Expences on ditto.

Overseer, - - -	1 0 0	
Cloaths, - -	1 0 0	
Sundry expences, - -	0 10 0	
Province tax, - -	0 3 0	
	2 13 0	——86 0 0

Seed.

100 acres of wheat, at 8s.	40 0 0	
40 oats 8s. - -	16 0 0	
10 potatoes 8s. - -	4 0 0	
		60 0 0
Taxes ; a quit-rent of 2s. per 100 acres,		10 0 0
		4965 10 0
Two year's interest at 5 per cent. -		496 10 0
		5462 10 0
Interest, - - - -		273 10 0

Pro-

Produce of fecond year.

	l.	s.	d.
100 acres of wheat, 20 bufhels an acre, at 3s.	300	0	0
40 negroes at 15l. - -	600	0	0
	900	0	0

Third year.

Expences.

Taxes as before, - -	10	0	0
Repairs of buildings, - -	50	0	0
Houfe-keeping, - - -	100	0	0
Implements - - - -	40	0	0
Labour, - - -	200	0	0
Incidents, - - -	50	0	0
Intereft, - - -	273	1	0
Freight of products to fhipping, -	80	0	0
Expences on 40 negroes at 2l. 13s. -	86	0	0
£.	889	1	0

Produce of third Year.

Wheat, - - - -	300	0	0
40 negroes at 25l. - - -	1000	0	0
A faw-mill of 7 faws will cut 5000 feet of boards per week, at 6s. per 100 feet, 15l. per week, which is per annum, - -	780	0	0
Deduct labour, repairs, freight and fundries, - -	280	0	0
Remains - - -	500	0	0
But fay - - - -	0	0	0
£.	1300	0	0

.Fourth

Fourth year.

Expences.

	l.	s.	d.
Taxes, - - -	10	0	0
Repairs of buildings, - -	50	0	0
House-keeping, - - -	100	0	0
Implements, - - -	40	0	0
Labour, - - -	200	0	0
Incidents, - - -	50	0	0
Interest - - -	273	1	0
Freight, - - -	80	0	0
15 negroes at 50l. - -	750	0	0
Expences on 55 ditto at 2l. 13s. -	145	15	0
£.	1698	16	0

Produce.

	l.	s.	d.
Wheat, - - -	300	0	0
40 negroes at 25l. - -	1000	0	0
15 ditto at 20l. - -	300	0	0
£.	1600	0	0

Fifth year.

Expences.

	l.	s.	d.
Taxes, - - -	10	0	0
Buildings, - -	50	0	0
House-keeping, - -	100	0	0
Implements, - - -	40	0	0
Labour, - - -	200	0	0
Incidents, - - -	53	0	0
Interest, - - -	273	1	0
Freight, - - -	110	0	0
10 negroes, - - -	500	0	0
65 ditto at 2l. 13s. - -	172	5	0
£.	1508	6	0

Produce.

			l.	s.	d.
Wheat,	- - - -	-	300	0	0
55 negroes at 25l.	-	-	1375	0	0
10 at 20l.	- -	-	200	0	0
Saved last year,	-	-	300	0	0
		£.	2175	0	0

Sixth year.

Expences.

			l.	s.	d.
Taxes,	- - -	-	10	0	0
Buildings,	-	-	50	0	0
House-keeping,	-	-	100	0	0
Implements,	- -	-	40	0	0
Labour,	- -	-	200	0	0
Incidents,	- -	-	53	0	0
Interest,	- -	-	273	1	0
Freight,	- -	-	140	0	0
25 negroes at 50l.	-	-	1250	0	0
90 ditto at 2l. 13s.	-	-	238	10	0
		£.	2354	11	0

Produce.

			l.	s.	d.
Wheat,	- - -	-	300	0	0
Cattle (supposed by this time to bring in a regular profit,	-	-	100	0	0
65 negroes at 25l.	-	-	1625	0	0
25 ditto at 20l.	-	-	500	0	0
		£.	2525	0	0

Seventh year.

Expences.

			l.	s.	d.
Taxes,	- -	-	10	0	0
Buildings,	-	-	50	0	0

E e 2   Carried over £. 60 0 0

	l.	s.	d.
Brought forward	60	0	0
House-keeping,	100	0	0
Implements,	40	0	0
Labour,	200	0	0
Incidents,	53	0	0
Interest,	273	1	0
Freight,	140	0	0
30 negroes at 50l.	1500	0	0
120 ditto at 2l. 13s.	318	0	0
£.	2684	1	0

Produce.

	l.	s.	d.
Wheat,	300	0	0
Cattle,	100	0	0
90 negroes at 25l.	2250	0	0
30 ditto at 20l.	600	0	0
£.	3250	0	0

Eighth year.
Expences.

	l.	s.	d.
Taxes,	10	0	0
Buildings,	50	0	0
House-keeping,	100	0	0
Implements,	40	0	0
Labour,	200	0	0
Incidents,	53	0	0
Interest,	273	1	0
Freight,	180	0	0
36 negroes at 50l.	1800	0	0
156 ditto at 2l. 13s.	413	8	0
£.	3119	9	0

Produce.

	l.	s.	d.
Wheat,	300	0	0
Cattle,	100	0	0
Carried over £.	400	0	0

		l.	s.	d.
Brought forward	400	0	0
120 negroes at 25l.	3000	0	0
36 ditto at 20l.	720	0	0
	£. 4120	0	0

Ninth year.
Expences.

Taxes,	10	0	0
Buildings,	50	0	0
House-keeping,	100	0	0
Implements,	40	0	0
Labour,	200	0	0
Incidents,	53	0	0
Interest,	273	1	0
Freight,	180	0	0
60 negroes at 50l.	3000	0	0
216 ditto at 2l. 13s.	572	8	0
	£. 4478	9	0

Produce.

Wheat,	300	0	0
Cattle,	100	0	0
156 negroes at 25l.	3900	0	0
60 ditto at 20l.	1200	0	0
	£. 5500	0	0

Tenth year.
Expences.

Taxes,	10	0	0
Buildings,	60	0	0
House-keeping,	150	0	0
Implements,	80	0	0
Carried over	300	0	0

				l.	s.	d.
Brought forward,				300	0	0
Labour,	-	-	-	200	0	0
Incidents,	-	-	-	53	0	0
Interest,	-	-	-	273	1	0
Freight,	-	-	-	200	0	0
80 negroes at 5ol.	-	-	-	4000	0	0
296 ditto at 2l. 13s.	-	-	-	784	8	0
			£.	5810	9	0

Produce.

Wheat,	-	-	-	300	0	0
Cattle,	-	-	-	100	0	0
216 negroes at 25l.	-	-	5400	0	0
80 ditto at 20l.	-	-	1600	0	0
		£.	7400	0	0

Eleventh year.

Expences.

Taxes,	-	-	-	-	10	0	0
Buildings,	-	-	-	60	0	0
House-keeping,	-	-	-	150	0	0
Implements,	-	-	-	80	0	0
Labour,	-	-	-	200	0	0
Incidents,	-	-	-	53	0	0
Interest,	-	-	-	273	1	0
Freight,	-	-	-	200	0	0
110 negroes at 5ol.	-	-	5500	0	0
406 ditto at 2ol.	-	-	1075	18	0
		£.	7601	19	0

Produce.

Wheat,	-	-	-	300	0	0
Cattle,	-	-	-	100	0	0
Carried over,			400	0	0

	l.	s.	d.
Brought forward,	400	0	0
296 negroes at 25l.	7400	0	0
110 ditto at 20l.	2200	0	0
£.	10,000	0	0

Twelfth year.

Expences.

	l.	s.	d.
Taxes,	10	0	0
Buildings,	60	0	0
House-keeping,	150	0	0
Implements,	80	0	0
Labour,	200	0	0
Incidents,	53	0	0
Interest,	273	1	0
Freight,	200	0	0
150 negroes at 50l.	7500	0	0
556 ditto at 2l. 13s.	1473	8	0
£.	9999	9	0

Produce.

	l.	s.	d.
Wheat,	300	0	0
Cattle,	100	0	0
406 negroes at 25l.	10,150	0	0
150 ditto at 20l.	3,000	0	0
£.	13,550	0	0

And now having arrived at the greatest number of negroes met with on any plantation in Carolina, (above 500, which are found on two or three) it will be proper

to

to clofe the account with the next year, by fuppofing no new ones bought.

Thirteenth year.

Expences.

	l.	s.	d.
Taxes,	10	0	0
Buildings,	70	0	0
Houfe-keeping,	150	0	0
Implements,	80	0	0
Labour,	200	0	0
Incidents,	53	0	0
Intereft,	273	1	0
Freight,	200	0	0
556 negroes at 2l. 13s.	1473	8	0
	£. 2509	9	0

Produce.

Wheat,	300	0	0
Cattle,	100	0	0
556 negroes at 25l.	13,900	0	0
	13,900	0	0
Expences,	2,509	9	0
Profit,	11,390	11	0
Houfekeeping,	150	0	0
Intereft,	273	1	0
Total receipt,	11,813	12	0

This profit is immenfe, and yet upon revifion there do not feem any articles that are

are calculated too low. I am fenfible that there are not any planters in South Carolina that lay up, or make an income of 12,000l. a year; but calculations of what may be done can take no cognizance of private conduct. There are fome planters in this province who have more than 500 flaves; but very many caufes may confpire to reduce their profit to a trifle, compared with what we fee here : of 556 negroes only 40 were here fuppofed to be originally bought; all the reft were purchafed annually by favings out of the preceding years products ; but if inftead of this the planter fpends his income, and borrows money to increafe his ftock of flaves, the profit at the end of the term will turn out very differently. The great profit here ftated, is entirely owing to an accumulation of profits for twelve years, the planter living upon 100l. or 150l. a year; but the event would prove very different if he takes at firft a larger fum for his houfe-keeping ; and if, inftead of waiting the firft twelve years patiently, in order afterwards to live more at his eafe, and in almoft any degree of affluence he pleafes ; if, inftead of this, he frequents the taverns and concerts of CharlesTown more than his plantation, any

man

man may, without much ſagacity, account
for calculation turning out differently from
real life. The only means of coming at
uſeful truth in ſuch caſes as this, is to calculate what may be done—what ſuch a buſineſs, under given circumſtances, can produce: as to the caprices of individuals,
they are beyond the power of calculation ;
but the profit here ſuppoſed will admit of
great deductions in ſeveral articles which
ſeem the loweſt ſet in expence, and yet the
remainder will turn out ſo conſiderable, as
to prove that planting in this country may
be made the way to immenſe fortunes.

Now it muſt be apparent, at firſt ſight,
that no huſbandry in Europe can equal this
of Carolina ; we have no agriculture in
England, where larger fortunes are made
by it than in any other country, that will
pay any thing like this, owing to ſeveral circumſtances which deſerve attention. Firſt,
land is ſo plentiful in America, that the
purchaſe of a very large eſtate coſts but a
trifle, and all the annual taxes paid afterwards for ten thouſand acres, do not a-
mount to what the window duty in England comes to on a moderate houſe ; no
land-tax, no poor's rate, no tythe. This
plenty

plenty of land, which is at the same time
so excellent, enables the planter to proportion his culture every year, to the saving of
the preceding, which is the grand circumstance in the increase of his fortune; since
it is this which converts simple interest at
5 per cent. with an English farmer, to
compound interest at 100 per cent. with
an American planter. Were the waste
lands of Britain in the same situation as
those of America, to be granted to whoever would settle and engage to cultivate
them, this would be the case with them;
but the profit from the inferiority of the
land, and the dearness of labour, would not
equal that above stated. As these wastes
are private property, and cannot be gained
by other people, there is no comparison remains between them; and as to common
agriculture, the profit of 20 or 30 per cent.
without any ability of increasing the business annually, it cannot be named with this
of America. Secondly, the price of labour is incomparably cheaper in Carolina
than in Britain : a negro costs 2l. 13s. per
annum, to which if we had 2l. 10s. the
interest of his prime cost, the total is only
5l. 3s. and as the common calculation is,
that one English labourer does as much
work

work as two negroes, a labourer to the planter costs 10l. 6s. a year, whereas to an English farmer he costs from from 20l. to 25l. The difference is 125 per cent. this article therefore is very decisive in favour of the planter. Thirdly, we are to remember the peculiar circumstance of the prices of the planter's products and consumptions : his crops, whether of indigo, tobacco, &c. are of a constant high value, the price rising, as it has done indeed for these fifty years ; but his consumption of corn, meat, fruit, fowls, game, fish, &c. being chiefly the produce of his own plantation, stand him in little or nothing for his family. The common idea of the article game and fish is, that one Indian, or dextrous negro, will, with his gun and nets, get as much game and fish as five families can eat ; and the slaves support themselves in provisions, besides raising the staples mentioned above ; but in Britain the servants kept in the house cost the farmers 12l. or 15l. a-head in board, besides his own house-keeping being in the same articles as those he sells from his farm ; so that he cannot in his sale have the advantage of high prices, without being proportionally taxed in his consumption. This point in a large family

mily is of great importance, and would,
if calculated for a courfe of years, be found
to amount to a very confiderable fum. Befides this great fuperiority in refpect of profit, the pleafing circumftance of being a
confiderable freeholder, and living in a
moft plentiful, and even luxurious manner,
is a point that has nothing among Britifh
farmers for oppofition to it.

Thefe three grand articles, plenty of good
land free from taxes—cheapnefs of labour
—and dearnefs of product fold, with cheapnefs of that confumed, are, united, fufficient to explain the caufes of a Carolina
planter having fuch vaftly fuperior opportunities of making a fortune than a Britifh
farmer can poffibly enjoy.

Confidered in a national light, no bad
confequences can refult from making known
the great profit which may be made by
planting in Carolina ; for all the inhabitants of this province are well employed
for Britain, and hufbandry is too profitable
an employment for them to fuffer any one
to think of manufactures ; all their cloathing, furniture, tools, and a variety of other
articles, come from Britain, befides the exportation and importation employing many
fhips and feamen for the mother-country.

Nor

Nor are we ever to forget the great importance of taking every meafure to induce
new fettlers in our colonies, emigrants
from Europe, to fix in thofe fettlements,
which from climate, foil, and ftaples, are
of fuch importance to Britain, as the Weft
Indies, Carolina, and the tobacco colonies
are found to be.

If the ftate of Europe at prefent be confidered, which is that of a military ftate, from
one end to the other, infomuch that in fome
parts of this quarter of the world the military out-number the reft of the men ; if
this be confidered, furely all mankind muft
think, with peculiar pleafure, of a country which holds forth an afylum to protect
them from the cruelties of the military government, and the horrible oppreffions of
the defpotic fway in all other matters :
thefe are fuch curfes on human nature, that
it is aftonifhing any men of fmall fortunes,
or to the amount of from one to five or fix
thoufand pounds, fhould remain in fuch
countries, that deny them moft of the comforts, enjoyments and fecurity of life. On
the contrary, thefe fouthern colonies of the
Britifh dominions in America hold forth
the very contraft to the unhappinefs they
experience in Europe. They may have
what-

I

whatever land they pleafe, at a price next to nothing; that land as rich, if chofen with judgment, as in any country in the world; in a climate that produces the richeft commodities, and at the fame time abounds with all the neceffaries of life, in a plenty not to be equalled throughout any other countries on the globe; and at the fame time that both foil and climate, and plenty of land, join to yield fuch advantageous offers: the government is the moft mild in being; liberty reigns in perfection; taxes are too inconfiderable to be mentioned; no military fervice; no oppreffions to enflave the planter, and rob him of the fruits of his induftry. When all thefe great and manifeft advantages are confidered, I think it muft appear furprifing, that more emigrants from different parts of Europe are not conftantly moving from thence to America: nothing but that love for the native country, univerfal thro' mankind, could prevent whole crowds of people from flying from mifery and oppreffion, to wealth and freedom.

The calculation here inferted is that only of a confiderable plantation; but it is a circumftance peculiarly fortunate, in the hufbandry of thofe parts of America where

negroes

negroes are used, that a small, and even the smallest plantation is proportionally as profitable as the largest. There is no necessity of employing an overseer for the negroes; if the number is small, the planter himself takes that office on him. Men establish even such small plantations, as employ only two or three negroes, and make by them a sum proportioned to what their more considerable neighbour enjoys from as many hundreds: indigo is of that nature in the culture, that even a single negro may be employed on it; since the apparatus for it does not even, for three or four slaves, cost above ten or a dozen pounds. Husbandry in England on so small a scale is carried on with scarce any advantage; for no profit, public or private, accrues from the smallest scale of farms; since our best writers on the subject of husbandry agree, that the occupiers of such farms live much harder and fare worse than our day-labourers. But nothing can be more different than this from Carolina, where the little planter, whose freehold amounts only to one or two hundred acres, with his two or three negroes, makes not only a most comfortable living for himself, but also such an annual profit, that if he is at all saving

and

and diligent, he may fpeedily increafe his negroes and his plantation, and in no long term of years become a man of handfome fortune.

And here let me once more obferve, that the calculations which have been given are particularly deduced from the circumftances of the back country, and not from the culture of rice in the deftructive and unwholefome fwamps en the coaft; fo that this large degree of profit is to be gained in a country whofe climate is equal to the foil, being healthy and pleafant to as great a degree as any country in a hot climate that is to be found in the world; and to the generality of conftitutions, taking the world through, perhaps more wholefome than many parts of Europe. Was fuch a profit only to be made by cultivating rice fwamps, I fhould be far enough from dwelling upon the advantages of it; but as they flow not from rice, but indigo, tobacco, corn, hemp, flax, &c. which admit of culture better in the back country than on the coaft, all the benefits I have dwelt on are reaped without any fuch attendant inconveniencies as are met with in the rice plantations; a circumftance of infinite im-

portance to the mother-country as well as
to the colony.

CHAP. XXIII.

*Exports of South Carolina at different peri-
ods—Rapid progress of the trade of this
province—Present state—Remarks.*

THE great increase of the population
of the northern colonies is not near
of such advantage to Great Britain as that
of the southern ones, which in proportion
to the increase of population has a corre-
sponding increase in the production of true
staple commodities, the circumstance on
which the interest of Britain depends ;
those colonies which have not staples, we
have found from long experience, can afford to purchase but a small part of their
manufactures and other necessaries from the
mother-country ; common agriculture will
not effect it ; accordingly we see, that in the
northern settlements, that is, the settlements
to the north of Maryland, they are forced
to make up their deficiency of staples by
fisheries and commerce, in both of which
articles

articles they interfere confiderably with Britain; fo that their import of manufactures is by no means of the value of that of the fouthern fettlements, as they get the money to make their purchafes, by rivalling the fifheries and commerce of Britain. Hence therefore appears the conftant expediency of watching anxioufly the increafe of population in the fouthern parts of America, and taking every meafure to increafe it. Nor can any conduct in the adminiftration of our government be of fuch great importance, as inducing the people fettled in the northern colonies to quit them in favour of the fouthern ones. The truth and propriety of thefe fentiments will appear from the following tables of the exports of South Carolina.

Exports from Charles Town from Nov. 1747, to Nov. 1748.

COMMODITIES.	Quantity.	Rates.		Amount Sterling.
Corn and Grain.				£. 88,600
Rice,	55,000 bushels	0 6 5	per 100 lb.	88,600
Indian corn,	39,308 bushels	0 1 5	per bushel	2,789
Barley,	15 casks	0 14 3	per cask	10
Roots and fruit.				
Oranges,	296,000 in number	0 17 1	per 1000	251
Pease,	6,107 bushels	0 1 5	bushel	432
Potatoes,	700 bushels	0 0 8	bushel	23
Onions,	10 casks	0 14 3	cask	7
	200 ropes	0 0 4	rope	3
Cattle, Beef, &c.				
Live stock { Bullocks,	28	1 11 5	bullock	44
{ Hogs,	158	0 8 6	hog	63
{ Sundries,				357
Beef,	1764 barrels	0 18 6	barrel	1631
Pork,	3114 barrels	1 8 6	barrel	4436
Bacon, about	2200 lb.	0 0 4	lb.	36
Butter,	130 casks	1 2 10	cask	148
Naval Stores.				
Pitch,	5521 barrels	0 16 5	barrel	1771

		£	s	d		
Tar { Common,	2784 barrels	0	5	0	ditto	696
Green,	291 ditto	0	7	1	ditto	103
Turpentine,	2397 ditto	0	7	1	ditto	847
Rosin,	97 ditto	0	7	1	ditto	34
Masts,	9 in number	2	2	10	each	19
Bowsprits,	8 in number	0	17	1	each	7
Booms,	6 in number	1	8	6	each	8
Oars,	50 pair	0	2	10	pair	5
Vegetable produce of other sorts.						
Indigo,	134,118 lb.	0	2	6	per lb.	16,764
Pot ashes,	3 barrels	2	17	8	barrel	8
Oil of turpentine, {	9 jars	1	8	6	jar	13
	7 barrels	2	2	10	barrel	15
Cotton wool,	7 bags	3	11	5	bag	25
Saffras,	22 tons	2	2	10	ton	67
Lumber.						
Boards,	61,148 feet	5	14	3	per 1000 feet,	349
Cedar boards,	8,189 ditto	0	17	1	per 100	70

F f 3

Carried over, £ 119,631

Lumber.	Quantities.	Rates.	Amount Ster. lig.
		Brought over, £.	119,631
Cedar plank,	1,331 feet	0 1 5 a foot	92
—— posts,	52 ditto	0 1 5 ditto	3
Cypress boards,	21,000 ditto	5 14 3 per 1000	111
Ditto,	979 boards	0 1 9 each	84
Heading,	13,975 ditto	5 14 3 per 1000	79
Ditto,	127,652 feet	4 5 8 ditto	546
Ditto pine,	148,143 ditto	5 14 3 ditto	849
Ditto,	1,293 boards	0 2 1 each	53
Ditto plank,	22 in number	0 2 1 ditto	2
Baywood plank	98 ditto	0 8 6 ditto	41
Scantling,	2,000 feet	0 10 0 per 1000	10
Shingles,	635,170 in number	0 11 5 ditto	364
Staves,	132,567 ditto	4 5 8 ditto	567
Timber,	4,000 feet	0 14 8 per 100	28
Ditto,	9 pieces	0 5 8 each	2
Walnut,	739 feet	1 14 3 per 100	13
Ditto,	66 pieces	0 2 10 each	10
Hogsheads,	80 in number	0 8 6 ditto	34
Tierces,	43 ditto	0 7 1 ditto	16
Hoops,	3,000 ditto	1 14 3 per 1000	5

	Quantity	£	s	8 per 100	£. 2	3
Canes,	800 in number					
Pumps,	1 fet					
Animal produce of other forts.						
Skins, { Beaver,	200 lb.	0	4	3 per lb.		42
Calf,	141 in number	0	5	8 each		40
Deer,	720 hhds,	50	0	0 ditto		36,000
Tallow,	81 barrels	1	8	6 per barrel		115
Hogs lard,	25 jars	0	17	1 jar		20
Raw filk,	26 cafks	2	0	0 cafk		52
Wax { Bees,	8 boxes	28	11	5 box		229
Myrtle,	1000 lb.	0	0	8 lb.		33
	700 lb.	0	0	8 lb		22
Manufactures.						
Leather tanned	10,356 lb.	0	0	0 lb.		2,589
Soap,	7 boxes	1	8	6 box		10
Candles,	34 ditto	2	2	10 each		73
Bricks,	7000 in number	0	14	3 per 1000		5

£. 161,361

Sundry articles exported from Charles Town in 1754.

	Quantities.	Rates.				Amount Sterling.
						£
Rice,	104,682 barrels	1	15	0	per barrel	183,193
Indigo,	216,924 lb.	0	2	6	lb.	27,115
Deer-skins,	460 hhds.	50	0	0	each	23,000
Pitch,	5,869 barrels	0	6	5	per barrel	1,881
Tar,	2,945 ditto	0	5	0	ditto	736
Turpentine,	759 ditto	0	7	4	ditto	266
Beef,	416 ditto	0	18	6	ditto	384
Pork,	1,560 ditto	1	8	6	ditto	2,223
Indian corn,	16,428 bushels	0	2	0	per bushel	1,642
Pease,	9,162 ditto	0	1	5	ditto	648
Shingles,	1,114,000 in number	0	11	5	per 1000	631
Staves,	260,000 ditto	4	5	8	ditto	880
Total of these articles,						£ 242,579

These

These articles not containing the whole export, the total does not shew the full increase; but rice and indigo being the two grand staples of the province, their increase shews how quick the cultivation of South Carolina had advanced in those years.

Exported in ten months, 1761, from Charles Town.

	Quantities.	Rates.	Amount Sterling.
Rice,	100,000 barrels	1 15 0 per barrel	£ 175,000
Pitch,	6,376 ditto	0 6 5 ditto	2,043
Tar,	931 ditto	0 5 0 ditto	232
Turpentine,	4,808 ditto	0 7 1 ditto	1,702
Oranges,	161,000 in number	0 17 1 per 1000	137
Ditto,	141 barrels		
Pork and beef,	1,149 ditto	1 13 0 per barrel	1,894
Bacon,	13 barrels		
Indigo,	399,366 lb.	0 2 6 per lb.	49,920
Deer-skins,	422 hhds.	50 0 0 each	21,100
	331 bundles		
	390 loose		

Carried over, £ 252,028

	Quantities.	Rates.		Amount Sterling.
		Brought forward		£. 252,018
Tanned leather,	5,869 sides	0 1 5 per bushel	- -	784
Pease and corn,	11,128 bushels	0 0 8 lb.	- -	224
Bees wax,	6,721 lb.	4 5 8 1000	- -	1,014
Staves,	236,850 in number	5 14 0 1000	-	2,657
Boards, &c.	466,186 feet	1 14 3 1000	- -	50
Hoops,	29,600 in number			
				£. 256,767

This

Besides many other articles.

This incomplete table shews another confiderable increase of export, and the following will continue the progreffion.

Exported from South Carolina upon an average of three years fucceeding the peace of 1762.

	l.	s.	d.
Rice 110,002 barrels at 40s. -	220,000	0	0
Pitch, tar, and turpentine, 8000 barrels, at 6s. 8d. - -	2,666	13	4
Pickled pork and beef, - -	25,000	0	0
Deer and other fkins, - -	45,000	0	0
Indigo 500,000 lb. at 2s.	50,000	0	0
Boards, mafts, ftaves, joifts, &c.	20,000	0	0
Indian corn, peafe, beans, and calavanches, 12,000	0	0
Live ftock and fundries, -	15,000	0	0
Ships built for fale, 10 at 600l. -	6,000	0	0
Total, £.	395,666	13	4

And fince this account I have been favoured with another for the year 1771, which is as follows:

	l.	s.	d.
140,000 barrels of rice, at 3l. 10s.	490,000	0	0
Pitch, tar, and turpentine, 10,000 barrels, at 10s. - -	5,000	0	0
Pork and beef, - -	30,000	0	0
Corn and other provifions, -	13,500	0	0
Deer-fkins, &c. - -	50,000	0	0
Lumber, - - -	32,000	0	0
Live ftock, - - -	17,000	0	0
Ten fhips, - -	6,000	0	0
Indigo, 750,000 lb. at 3s. -	112,500	0	0
Total, £.	756,000	0	0

This

This acount shews in how extraordinary
a manner the improvement of South Carolina has been carried on ; and it has been
a peculiar felicity to this province, that
the prices of its staples have rifen confiderably at the fame time that the quantity
raifed has increafed immenfely. This circumftance, which is of fuch uncommon value, has advanced the interefts of the country prodigioufly, and now renders it one of
the moft flourifhing colonies we poffefs in
America ; at the fame time that the quantity of land which yet remains to be cultivated, is beyond comparifon greater than
what is yet improved. It is alfo to be re-
membered, that the parts unfettled being more rich, fertile, and healthy, than the
coaft which yields the commodities hitherto exported, and is in particular far more
luxuriant in the production of indigo : now
it is to be obferved, that the grand ftaple
of this province, rice, has not fo good a
probability of future increafe as indigo ; the
latter is fo valuable a drug, and produced
in fo few countries, that Carolina may look
forwards to almoft any quantity, even till
the whole confumption of Europe, America, and parts of Africa and Afia, are fa-
tisfied, before a ftop will be put to her market

ket for this commodity; for there is little doubt of her being able to underfell both French and Spaniards. But with rice, the cafe may be different; for being an article of food, it is rivalled by other articles: good harvefts of wheat in Europe and Africa would fink the price; for it has rifen from 15s. and 20s. a barrel to 3l. 10s. and 4l. from the high price of wheat in Europe; if grain fhould fall much, the price of rice muft fall with it: indeed it is at prefent fo dear, that the rate may fall greatly, and yet leave the planter fufficient inducement to increafe the culture of it.

The exports of this province will not be many years in rifing to a million fterling; it will gain this point of equality with Virginia and Maryland put together, before it has a fifth of the inhabitants found in thofe provinces, which fhews how valuable the climate is to produce fo largely in exportable ftaples. I do not compare the ftaples, for certainly tobacco is far more valuable to Britain than rice, and perhaps than indigo; but tobacco is produced in the back part of South Carolina, and of a quality fuperior to that of Virginia; the quantity however is but fmall yet: a navigation for large canoes that will carry from five to

ten

ten ton, is wanting, when you get far back, which navigation in the culture of tobacco is very neceffary.

CHAP. XXIV.

Improvements propofed in the culture of this province.

HOWEVER wealthy the produ&ion of ftaples may make a country, it is common hufbandry alone on which firft depends the intereft of any people; and it ever behoves them much to carry this to as high a degree as poffible. All our A-merican colonifts are very bad farmers; this is a remark I have had occafion to make when treating of every one of them: it is almoft uniformly owing to the great plenty of land, which enables every body to gain the neceffaries of life with fo much eafe, that an accurate and induftrious cultivation appears ufelefs.

The produ&ions of common hufbandry in Carolina, by which I mean corn and provifions of all forts, have rifen of late years to fo high a price, that I have been affured by feveral confiderable planters and

.mer-

1

merchants in this province, that the farmers who have employed their negroes on
these objects alone have in several years
made a larger profit than has been gained
from rice and indigo ; and that on an a-
verage, there has been an equality. This
is a circumstance of prodigious consequence,
since the common husbandry is exercised in
the healthy and agreeable back country,
while rice only is to be had in the swamps
in the flat, maritime, and unhealthy part.

The articles cultivated are wheat (which
grain will not thrive in the flat country) Indian corn, Indian pease, barley, buck-wheat,
tatoes, and other roots, fruit, &c. The
hilly part of the province is wonderfully
fertile in these products, yielding, in very
bad modes of culture, crops equal to what
good husbandry will produce on many
tracts of land in Britain. But this excellence of soil and climate is very badly seconded by the skill of the farmer. Indian
corn is the principal grain they raise, which
is managed in the manner I have described
before ; they are very defective in the article of keeping the plantations of it clean
from weeds : the culture the intervals receive is only that of an insufficient hand-
hoeing or two; but, instead of this, the
horse-

horfe-hoeing hufbandry fhould be applied :
the fpaces between the rows fhould both
ways be horfe-hoed, for the double purpofe of keeping them free from weeds, and
in a loofe pulverized flate; and likewife for
earthing up the plants, which might be
performed with a plough much more effectually than'with hand-hoes, and for a tenth
of the expence : the latter never cut deep
enough, only fkimming the furface, whereas horfe-hoeings and hoe-ploughs loofen it
to any depth, giving the roots of the
plants the power of penetrating into frefh
earth, inftead of confining them to their
hillocks. This fingle improvement in the
management of Indian corn would vaftly
increafe the profit of that culture.

It is the cuftom in all the fouthern colonies to fow Indian peafe with Indian corn,
for the fake of their twining up the ftalks
of the latter ; this renders the culture the
more beneficial, as the product of peafe is as
valuable, and fometimes more fo, than that
of the corn itfelf. I would by no means
condemn a cuftom which has an appearance
of reafon for it ; but as fuch practices in
moft other branches of hufbandry are found
very difadvantageous, it is at leaft worth
fome accurate experiments to decide whether

ther as much is not loft in the Indian corn
as is gained in the peafe by this method,
which may poffibly be the cafe; the product of fuch large and vigorous plants as
Maize, ufually is proportioned to the nourifhment the roots meet with, and certainly the peafe cannot grow out of the fame
hillock without robbing them of much
nourifhment. A good hop-planter would
think it very bad management to fet a cabbage or a pea in a hop-hillock; bad ones
plant the intervals, but good hop farmers
decline even this practice; not becaufe
crops fo gained would not be valuable, but
becaufe more would be loft in hops than
gained in the other plants.

As to the preparation of the land for
maize, wheat, barley, &c. it is nearly fimilar; they take a piece of frefh land, and
plant it perhaps with indigo, which it
yields as long as any heart remains fufficient in the foil for that exhaufting crop;
then they plant it with wheat or Indian
corn, and afterwards with barley; and
when it will yield nothing any longer, they
leave it to itfelf, and treat other pieces in
fucceffion in the fame manner. This is
the fyftem of all the provinces from New
England to Florida; and it is a fyftem

from which they will all by-and-bye feel
the moſt monſtrous inconvenience. When
indigo is not planted, the firſt crop is Indian corn, which they follow by a ſecond
and perhaps a third of the ſame grain;
then wheat or barley as long as the land
will allow.

To this miſerable huſbandry it is owing,
that the province wants paſture, which is
only to be found in the woods or in drained rice ſwamps; though the planters all
know the importance of cattle to them,
they never think of ſowing any graſſes, but
exhauſt and ruin the land by corn, &c. and
leave it, not a paſture, but a deſart: the
heat of the climate is ſo great that there
is a want of good meadow in ſummer,
and this makes the woods the natural paſture of the country in its unimproved
ſtate. But this evil might be remedied by
ſowing graſſes, provided the land was laid
to them while it was in ſome heart. The
graſs, when properly conducted, would be
as profitable as the corn, and it might be
gained without any decreaſe in the quantity of corn, in a country where land is ſo
plentiful: this obſervation is particularly
applicable to Carolina, where the land is
cleared with ſo much eaſe; a given quantity

tity of acres in this province is cleared of all the timber with infinitely more eafe than one tenth of the land would be In Europe, with the advantage alfo of the timber paying the expence ; and if oak or pine, more than the expence.

Suppofe a planter has negroes fufficient to have every year 500 acres of corn, 250 acres Indian corn, 150 wheat, 100 barley, buckwheat, &c. If his fyftem of crops is

1. Indian corn.
2. Ditto.
3. Ditto.
4. Wheat.
5. Wheat.
6. Barley.
7. Barley.

He then is able to fupport the fyftem, by taking in a feventh of the 500 acres for frefh land every year, that is, 71 acres; and he has always 500 acres in culture, with no other profit from the reft of his eftate than what the woods yield him; he leaves 71 acres barren and ufelefs every year, which will foon run through a large grant; for fome years the land is abfolutely nought, then fhrubs come, and by degrees foreft wood rifes, and it is an age before it can

G g 2   yield

yield any profit. Now on the contrary,
let us suppose his system

   1. Indian corn.

   2. Ditto.

   3. Potatoes, pease, beans, legumes,&c.

   4. Wheat.

   5. Barley, and with it clovers, sain-
foine, or lucerne. In this system he must
take in 100 acres every year, and he every
year lays down 100 acres to grass. The
second year of pursuing such a plan he has
200 acres grass; the third year 300;
the fourth year 400; and so on. By which
means his whole estate will be in a profitable condition, and he will every year have
a greater plenty of food for his cattle; the
consequence of which will be his stocks of
cattle will be larger, and better fed; he
will raise much greater quantities of manure, and two acres of his corn must ine-
vitably produce more grain than three in
the other system.

   Relative to the grass, which should upon these principles be cultivated, the heat
of the climate will make it necessary to
have recourse to such plants as have a long
tap root, because by rooting deep they will
be more out of the power of the sun: sain-
foine and lucerne I should suppose would
                be

be found of fingular utility, efpecially the latter; both thefe plants have been brought into the colder parts of Europe from very hot countries. Lucerne is indigenous in Media and Afia Minor, and fainfoine in Calabria and Barbary; there can be no doubt therefore of their fucceeding admirably on the dry tracts of. land in the back parts of Carolina, and alfo in all the fandy hilly parts of the province. The culture would be attended with none of thofe inconveniencies which have been found in England, from the moifture of the climate · choaking the plantations with natural grafs and weeds: the heat of climate would entirely prevent thefe evils upon land well prepared; nor can any doubt be made but the crops would be very confiderable upon the fertile black loams of the interior country, and yield fuch plenty of food, both green and in hay, as to enable the planters to increafe their ftocks of cattle prodigioufly.

It is much to be doubted whether the clovers would fucceed in the maritime parts of the province; but no hefitation can be made about it in the interior country; and in this I ground my opinion upon the cafe of wheat, which thrives admirably two

G g 3

hun-

hundred or two hundred and fifty miles from the coaft, but will come to nothing in the flat country: there can be no doubt but it would be the fame with clover, which has been found profitable in all countries where wheat is cultivated. It fhould be made the general preparation for wheat in every fyftem, as it is equally (in this refpect) adapted to all climates in which it will grow, and to almoft every fort of land. In fuch climates as South Carolina there is likewife a circumftance in it, as a preparation for wheat, that much exceeds any other; a fallow or a tillage crop leaves the foil in fo loofe and hollow a ftate, that the roots of wheat, or any other fibrous-rooted plant, are too much expofed to the fun's rays; whereas, if it is fown in a clover lay, the particles of the foil are kept in a ftate of adhefion by the roots and fibres of the clover, which is an effect that in fuch a climate muft be attended with excellent confequences. With a view to this, the clover hufbandry, common in Britain of leaving it only one year upon the land, might not be fo advifeable in Carolina; it might be better to let the clover be two, or perhaps three years old before it is ploughed for wheat, in order

the

the more completely to bind the foil together, especially in fandy land. The crops
of this grafs would, like fainfoine or lu-
serne, prove of great ufe to the planter,
either in green food, or mown for hay, and
maintain him twenty times the flock that
the fame land would do if under wood.

In the fyftem above propofed, as an improvement of that of the Carolina farmers,
there are feveral corn crops in fucceffion,
under the fuppofition that they would not
at once come into an entire change, but
the true principles of good hufbandry are
the fame in Carolina as every where elfe;
fucceffive *exhaufting* crops ought never to
be found : between every two of that nature, one fhould intervene which is of a
meliorating nature, or at leaft which does
not exhauft. It has been found in all the
countries where the clovers have been cultivated, that the land improves under them.
The fame obfervation has been made upon potatoes, carrots, and other roots. Turneps and cabbages yielding crops before
they perfect their feed, have the fame quality. The grand principle of modern hufbandry, is to ufe thefe plants as fallows, or
preparations for exhaufting crops : and the
principle is equally good, whether the exhaufting

haufting crop be fugar, wheat, indigo, or
barley. The only diftinction to be made,
is for the planter to chufe fuch of them as
will pay beft in his country: fortunately,
all of them are food for cattle, and there
is no part of the world in which cattle are
not valuable, or in the cultivated parts of
it, where good hufbandry does not greatly
depend on cattle. In South Carolina nothing pays better, and the near neighbourhood of the Weft Indies affords an excellent market for as much meat and live
ftock as can poffibly be raifed: but the
importance of having plenty of cultivated
food for cattle, increafes every day in this
province; in proportion as the country is
cultivated, the foreft which was fpread over
the whole of it decreafes, and confequently will maintain the lefs; this is fo much
felt in fome diftricts, that many planters,
who formerly kept immenfe herds of cattle, can now have but very moderate ones:
it therefore much behoves them to cultivate grafs and winter food for cattle, as
well as corn. Potatoes in this province
yield as good a price, both for home confumption and the Weft Indies, as in many
parts of Britain; for of late years they have
.fold

fold at 1s. and 1s. 3d. a bufhel, confequently no crop can be more profitable.

Upon thefe principles, might not fuch
a fyftem as the following be rationally recommended to the farmers of South Carolina ?

1. Indian corn.
2. Potatoes.
3. Indian corn.
4. Peafe or beans.
5. Barley.
6. Clover.
7. Wheat.

In this fyftem no two exhaufting crops
come together ; peafe or beans, and in general the plants which bear a leguminous
flower, being of a different nature from
corn in this refpect. Or to fuit particular
purpofes, variations might be made.

1. Indian corn.
2. Potatoes.
3. Barley.
4. Clover.
5. Wheat.
6. Turneps or cabbages.
7. Indian corn.
8. Peafe or beans.
9. Wheat.
10. Potatoes.

11. Bar-

11. Barley.

12. Clover.

13. Wheat.

14. Cabbages, &c.

15. Wheat.

16. Lucerne, or other graffes, to remain. In fuch a fyftem of crops, the land would always be rich and clean ; the planter would be able to keep vaft flocks of cattle ; in fifteen years he would fell nine crops of corn and two of potatoes, and at the end of it he would have a much more fertile pafture than he found at the beginning.

Partial trials of new recommended practices may turn out very unfuccefsful without proving any thing againft them. Suppofe a Carolina farmer, ftruck with the idea of clover, fainfoine, or lucerne, was to throw it in among the fecond or third crop of wheat or barley, which followed two or three of maize; in fuch a mode of conduct, chance perhaps might give him a poor crop, inftead of none at all, which he would have reafon to expect ; he might neglect thofe graffes in future from fuch an experiment, but furely with very little reafon ; for fuch a conduct would be like expecting a great crop of rice on a mountain-top; or fields of pine apples in the

snows

fnows of Lapland. For this reason, such recommended practices had better not be tried at all, than to be partially or incompletely tried; since conclusions, however abfurd, are fure to be drawn from all experiments, and people will not be fo ready to difcriminate and enquire into the caufes of a failure, as to look at the fingle point; *such a thing was tried,* AND IT FAILED. A comprehenfive way of judging and talking, which faves the trouble of underftanding and refleǎion.

Befides reǎifying the very erroneous fyftems purfued in this province, it will be neceffary to remark, that the farmers are not attentive even to making the moft of the fpontaneous growths, of which the natural meadows, are a proof; in many plantations they have favannah land, which in the back parts of the province is very good meadow; but the planters let their cattle run over the whole in fummer, without ever thinking of mowing hay, notwithstanding the crops would often be confiderable, and notwithftanding their cattle are fometimes half ftarved for want of it: it is not fufficient to fay that a climate admits the cattle to be unhoufed all winter; their being in the woods or paftures is of

little

little confequence, if they can get nothing
to eat: the beft planters find the neceffity of baiting their herds well every night
when they come home from the woods in
winter; for though the climate is at
times amazingly hot, yet, as I have elfewhere fhewn, the frofts in winter are fe-
verer than thofe of England.

This part of their ill conduct is owing
in a good meafure to another branch of it,
which is their neglect of fences : it would
not be true to fay that they had none, but
the fact is, that they are confined too much
to the care of their rice, indigo, or other
valuable crop, and are apt to attend to a
field no longer than while it is fo occupied :
none of them would think (unlefs it were
a few fenfible, and at the fame time wealthy
men) that a meadow or pafture was worth
fencing : this is through that neglect which
arifes from their great plenty of land.

It would be in vain to adopt an advantageous fyftem of crops, if at the fame
time the planter was not attentive to have
all his fences equally good ; fince in good
hufbandry, that field which is at prefent
under a crop of fmall value, will in a few
years be occupied by one of the greateft ;
the neceffity therefore of this attention
muft

muſt be ſtriking. In the management too common, one part of an eſtate is under corn, and all the reſt is foreſt ; but in the propoſed improvement; every part once cultivated is always to be of value ; cattle will be grazing in clover or lucerne in the midſt of fields of Indian corn or wheat, and conſequently all the fences under an equal neceſſity of being good.

In the culture of roots, &c. for the winter food of cattle, they are very deficient. Where there is a very great ability of keeping any ſtocks in ſummer, but a confined opportunity in winter, it is much to be queſtioned whether thoſe crops which may be uſed as winter food, will not pay better in ſuch an application, than when ſold ; and this particularly with potatoes : there are many advantages in uſing ſuch crops upon the plantation ; freight and carriage are ſaved, which are articles of importance; but the great point is the ability which the planter reaps from it of keeping ſo many more cattle, and raiſing ſo much the more dung, which they all agree is of the firſt conſequence in making the moſt profit of their plantations : the effect we ſee in every part of Britain is ſimilar to this ; for the good farmers make it a rule never to ſell
thoſe

thofe articles of their produce which are
food for cattle, unlefs they bear a very great
price, being fenfible that it anfwers better
to confume them at home.

In the culture of indigo, the Carolina
planters are not fo attentive as they might
be : they err in their ideas of the foil which
they chufe for it ; becaufe it will grow in
a poor white pine barren, it has been very
abfurdly thought that this is the proper foil
for it : indigo requires, if great crops would
be gained, a rich, black, deep mould, fuch
as is no where to be found near the fea, or
at leaft only in fmall narrow flips adjoining
the fwamps, and even in them not comparable in fertility to large tracts in the interior country. Thofe planters who would
wifh to cultivate this drug to great profit,
fhould fix in the back parts of the province, where the land is not only plentiful, but excellent ; here they would raife
treble the products they are able to do upon the coaft, and the dye of a finer colour.
In the culture of the plant, they are alfo too
inattentive ; the hand-hoeings given by the
negroes are very infufficient, and not comparable to the ufe of feveral horfe-hoes,
which for other purpofes are ufed in England. Hand-hoes in all operations between
the

the rows of any crop fhould give place to horfe-work, which is deeper, more regular, and in every refpect more effective ; at the fame time that the expence of it does not near approach to that of hand-work.

There is another improvement which deferves mention here ; it is the culture of that fpecies of rice which fucceeds on dry ground, and even on hills and mountains. This fort is known in feveral parts of the Eaft Indies, and would, in the back country of South Carolina, be of ufe as a new dependence for the planters there fixed ; and it would be much more advantageous to have this grain from a healthy country, than from the unwholefome fwamps in the maritime part. It would be no difficult tafk to get fome feed of it from India, and would at leaft be worth the trial.

The culture of vines has been attempted in the back part of South Carolina, and with fuccefs ; but the hufbandry has not been profecuted with that vigor and attention which fo important an object well deferves. The moment any individuals fhewed a defire of undertaking this branch—as foon as there was the leaft reafon for thinking the plan feafible—their wifhes ought to have been prevented—their wants

fupsupplied—and every difficulty that arose, smoothed with the minutest attention. But instead of such a conduct being pursued, specimens of excellent wine have been sent home, and tasted by Lords of Trade, with application for encouragement in the undertakings made, and all without success. Were our governors bribed by the owners of the vineyards of Champaigne and Burgundy, a more impolitic conduct could not have been pursued : had a due attention been paid to those ingenious and industrious foreigners who have settled in these southern colonies, and entered upon the vineyard culture, by this time American wine would have been common in the London vaults; and the importance of this nation's buying her wines by the sale of her manufactures, is too obvious to need expatiating on. Such an undertaking as that, of planting vineyards in these provinces, should be taken in hand by government, at least in giving every assistance that could reasonably be required by those undertakers, who seemed to be well acquainted with what they were about; but unfortunately, a very different conduct has been pursued. Knowledge in this branch of agriculture was some years ago much wanting; but that is no no longer the cafe, there are many fettlers that have arrived within a few years in South Carolina, perfectly acquainted with the bufinefs, but whofe mean circumftances have proved the only obftacles they have met with : it is fuch men to whom public affiftance fhould be given, for the public is more interefted in their fuccefs than even themfelves.

This is an object which ought not to be left to itfelf; the import of wine into this kingdom carries out of it an immenfe balance in cafh, which throws a dead weight into very confiderable branches of our commerce. North America confumes large quantities of Madeira, which confumption will in part be varied to that of their own wines before they can be expected to be brought in any quantities into this kingdom : hence the neceffity of acting with fome vigour, if we expect to fee any beneficial confequences of many years.

Silk is another object which fhould be attended to with great ferioufnefs; the back parts of this province are full of mulberry-trees, and the climate is of that due temperature which is requifite for fuccefs in this culture : as fine filk has been brought from Carolina as ever came from China, infomuch that at fome of our mills it is preferred to any we receive either from the Eaſt Indies or Italy. The common objection of a want of people, I have before ſhewn is weakly founded in any caſe, ſince a few people, nay a ſingle family, may make as large aproportion of it, as if the whole country was employed about nothing elſe: it is ſo much a-head that may be made in a ſeaſon, perhaps a pound and a half, or two pounds; ſo that if a family conſiſts of twenty perſons, they may make thirty or forty pounds annually; if it conſiſts of two hundred perſons, the proportion will be the ſame; but if it is only two or three, it is equally ſo: the population of the country therefore has perhaps leſs to do with it than in any other article of culture. The objeſt wanting, is to induce the people to undertake it—to give them inſtructions how to feed the worms, and to manage the cocoons; but this is eaſily learned, and might become general through the province if proper meaſures were taken for it; which might be executed at an inconſiderable expence. It would be a very fine thing for this nation if all the inhabitants of our colonies, poſſeſſing a proper climate, were to make each, only a pound of raw ſilk;

filk ; it would be as valuable an acquifition as this nation could make : to acquire a Martinico or a Guadalupe would probably coft thirty or forty millions fterling ; but fuch a matter of mere internal management would be far more valuable, and might be had for one quarter of as many thoufands. In every inftance that can be named, domeftic improvement is of more confequence, and eafier of attainment, than military acquifition ; yet is mankind ever panting after one, and neglecting the other.

No trials have yet been made of madder in Carolina, though there are tracts of a rich, deep, black, and reddifh loams in the back parts of the province which would undoubtedly produce great crops of it, and the climate would probably fuit it better than that of England ; for it is not the madder of Zealand that is the moft extraordinary ; that of Turkey, Afia Minor, and Cyprus is of a vaftly greater fize and better quality without any culture at all; no doubt can therefore be entertained of the climate fuiting it. There is no crop upon which they can go that would pay them better ; madder is worth from 80l. to 90l. a ton ; in England the deduction of 6l. or 6l. 10s. for freight would be but a fmall proportion.

An

An acre of good land, well chosen and properly cultivated, would, in the climate of the back part of South Carolina, yield from a ton to a ton and a half; and one negroe would manage above an acre very well, and have the winter months to be employed on fences and lumber besides: there are no crops in America that would answer much better than this, since it would be above 40l. per slave per annum. The value of the commodity would also make it peculiarly adapted to those tracts of country that had not a good water-carriage for bulky commodities; a small canoe, which would run up any little branches of the rivers, would carry a ton of it, which would be more valuable than a ton of many other commodities: for the same reason indigo and silk should be particularly encouraged in those districts where water-carriage is indifferent or at some distance.

Hemp in this respect is not of the same importance, but for their lower grounds on a strong clay foundation in these back parts, where the low grounds are far more fertile than in the maritime part of the province, hemp would be a very valuable article of culture, if near a good navigation. Such tracts are numerous, and would, if well culti-

cultivated under hemp, save us no slight proportion of those immense sums which we annually pay to the Baltic for this commodity. Improvements in our colonies in this article ought every where to be most assiduously promoted; not in one settlement, by making it an only staple in the nature of the rice, indigo, or tobacco; it will not admit of this, because it is nice in soil, but all the spots suitable to it in all our colonies, from Nova Scotia to Florida, should be thus appropriated; no planter, unless he was particularly situated, need have hemp for his principal dependence; but all should have some of it that had but a small field of right soil : America would then much more than supply all our demand and her own too ; and as the colonies increased in cultivation, Europe would be a constant market for all they could produce. It is a fortunate circumstance that hemp grows best in a soil that is not suitable to any of the other staples of America, so that it could not rival them : it delights in a moist, low, rich loam, on a clay bottom, and never thrives to good advantage in a dry or light soil, however rich, but will not do in a swamp, unless very rich and perfectly drained. Indigo and tobacco require

the

the black dry loam, regardless of the stratum under it, provided it be not wet; and rice can only be had in a swamp under water: it is upon this account that hemp would not rival their present staples, in the soil it requires, which is a matter of consequence; for in many plantations the land suitable to these productions is not so plentiful as to make it a matter of indifference how the planter disposes of it, especially in the maritime part of the province.

Those who think the success met with in South Carolina in the culture of indigo and rice a reason sufficient for excluding or neglecting other articles of produce, are much mistaken in that idea. It is in all countries of vast importance that the profit of agriculture should not depend on one or two productions; since in that case a failure in one is of fatal consequence, or a falling off in the sale of it may prove the ruin of a country. But when the husbandry of a people is employed about many objects, they have the beneficial chance, that if one fails others will succeed, and thereby prevent any great evils following: it is also of consequence, that the labour attending the products of a plantation be so divided, that as many hands be employed at one season

as

as at another ; for if the flaves are only
employed in fummer, or only in fpring and
autumn, the planter cannot make fuch profit by his bufinefs as if they were employed
regularly the year through.   The planters
of Carolina and our other colonies have not
yet felt the neceffity of this doctrine, from
the circumftance of fawing lumber, for the
Weft Indies finding them employment at
all leifure times; but this branch of their bufinefs is confined to the amount of the Weft
India market ; befides there are numerous
tracts of country in which the timber has
been long ago deftroyed, but which are
full of plantations, and it is very plain that
in them lumber can be no dependence.

Winter fowing of feveral crops, threfhing, clearing, carrying, and felling others,
building fences, manuring, and other
works, fhould keep all the flaves of a plantation in regular employment through the
winter feafon, without a dependence for it
on lumber.   Spring fowings, and the vernal attendance on crops, with making filk,
would fill up that feafon.   The fummer
culture and cleaning which moft plants
require, with the harveft, are always fufficient to fil up feveral months ; then fhould
fucceed the vintage, and making crops of
madder,

madder, hemp, &c. In such a difpofition of the lands and bufinefs of a plantation, the planter would find much greater profit than what he now makes by the affiftance of two or three months of the flaves at lumber. And this is reafon fufficient were others wanting, which however is far enough from being the cafe, for inducing the Carolina planters to divide their attention more in imitation of the beft hufband-men in Europe.

END OF THE FIRST VOLUME.

www.ingramcontent.com/pod-product-compliance
Lightning Source LLC
Chambersburg PA
CBHW031817270326
41932CB00008B/453

* 9 7 8 3 7 4 2 8 3 2 4 6 7 *